W9-AUR-415

A Study of German Political–Cultural Periodicals from the Years of Allied Occupation, 1945-1949

A Study of German Political–Cultural Periodicals from the Years of Allied Occupation, 1945-1949

Clare Flanagan

Studies in German Thought and History
Volume 19

The Edwin Mellen Press
Lewiston•Queenston•Lampeter

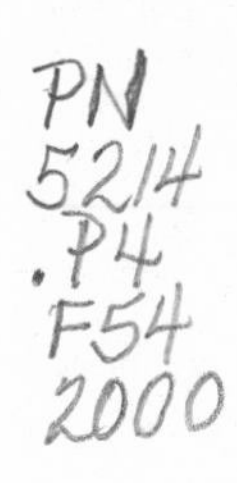

Library of Congress Cataloging-in-Publication Data

Flanagan, Clare.
A study of German political-cultural periodicals from the years of Allied occupation, 1945-1949 / Clare Flanagan.
p. cm. -- (Studies in German thought and history ; v. 19)
Based on the author's thesis (doctoral)--Gonville and Caius College, University of Cambridge.
ISBN 0-7734-7781-0
1. German periodicals--History--20th century. 2. Germany--Politics and government--1945-1990. I. Title. II. Series.

PN5214.P4 F59 2000
053'.1'09045--dc21

99-462037

This is volume 19 in the continuing series
Studies in German Thought and History
Volume 19 ISBN 0-7734-7781-0
SGTH ISBN 0-88946-351-4

A CIP catalog record for this book is available from the British Library.

The Edwin Mellen Press
Box 450
Lewiston, New York
USA 14092-0450

The Edwin Mellen Press
Box 67
Queenston, Ontario
CANADA L0S 1L0

The Edwin Mellen Press, Ltd.
Lampeter, Ceredigion, Wales
UNITED KINGDOM SA48 8LT

Printed in the United States of America

to my parents

CONTENTS

PREFACE

The study of periodicals can reveal much about the social and historical situation at the time. This usually takes place after they have ceased to exist, or have changed their character, or are only relevant as historical documents. The extraordinary wealth of them at the start of the twentieth century in German-speaking countries, especially the mainly short-lived expressionist examples, provides insights into the manipulation of the reading public and a forum for revolt against Wilhelmine society, its aggressive capitalism and the First World War. More recently, in the 1980s, clandestine publications in the former German Democratic Republic bear witness to growing dissatisfaction with the ruling regime and a focus for artists, writers and musicians who longed for the change that came in 1989.

As a further example of this, Dr. Flanagan's study is an important reminder of the role played in the early years after the Second World War by some of the major periodicals that were first set up under the occupying forces. At a time when the formation of public opinion with new values was one essential ingredient in the control and development of a country physically and morally shattered, the first newspapers appeared within weeks of the end of hostilities (*Tägliche Rundschau*, *Berliner Zeitung*, *Deutsche Volkszeitung*, *Das Volk*, *Neue Zeit*, *Der Morgen* and *Allgemeine Zeitung*). These were followed very quickly by periodicals edited by the occupying powers, and within months of the setting-up of the occupation zones, by the first new publications edited by survivors of the Nazi regime.

Dr. Flanagan examines five of the most important examples in detail, surveys the major articles and other features of each number, and draws independent conclusions. By concentrating on these five (*Aufbau*, *Ost und West*, *Der Monat*, *Der Ruf* and *Frankfurter Hefte*) she presents an effective cross-section, allowing for a balanced assessment of their particular significance and that of journals in general in Germany at the time. Her study thus becomes of essential interest for historians in several fields, such as German literature, politics and social studies. Several leading figures as editors are profiled (Johannes R. Becher, Klaus Gysi, Alfred Kantorowicz, Melvin J. Lasky, Alfred Andersch, Hans Werner Richter, Eugen Kogon, Walter Dirks), and a claim is made to consider them with their publications as a 'republic of letters'. Most of them were politically left of centre; however, as Dr. Flanagan points out, they each wrote to encourage a peaceful Germany, and their journals shared much in common. These were also a meeting-place for ideas expressed by famous writers who had either returned from exile, or who realized the political fragility of the post-war situation, and by the younger generation whose hopes for the future needed expression and form.

In her conclusions on the first journal, Dr. Flanagan highlights the manifesto of the Kulturbund, published in the first issue of *Aufbau* as that journal's programme. The anti-fascist slant, and its greater independence of action than expected are both noted, which Dr. Flanagan suggests means it should not be categorized solely as a communist publication. She later shows how Alfred Kantorowicz's *Ost und West* became a solely German publication, a protagonist of the 'Third Way' that was squeezed out of existence on the establishment of the German Democratic Republic. *Der Monat*, which lived on until 1971, known as a capitalist publication under the editorship of Melvin J. Lasky, is shown as a voice of the Cold War, international, anti-totalitarian and neither fully German, nor American in spirit. *Der Ruf* is described as heroic in its opposition to foreign occupation, representing German aspirations within a democratic system. Its setting-up and suppression by American authorities within two years are seen as a sign of its political reliability, and Dr. Flanagan outlines the reasons why it was attacked on all sides. Its radical rejection of collective guilt, of the re-education programme and denazification procedures meant that it spoke for a younger generation, and it is this that seems to have ensured its demise. The Christian backgrounds of the editors of *Frankfurter Hefte*, according to Dr. Flanagan, turned the journal into a humanist and centrist publication that foresaw the building of Europe on a new partnership between France and Germany. Such conclusions go beyond traditional definitions of these journals and suggest a common ground, despite their individual characteristics.

What makes this study important is its refusal to accept politically inspired and at times slanted interpretations of their aims, but also its pointing out of where each one in its separate way was vulnerable or partial. Its relevance for today perhaps lies in the emphasis Dr. Flanagan sees in the editors' definition and support of a 'Third Way', in allegiance to neither Western or Eastern ideologies, but supporters of idealism. She rightly points to the limitations of such idealism and to the varied definitions of solutions , according to the readers' perspective. There is much here too that provides historical and independent views on democracy, Europe and the concept of nationhood. Above all, these journals registered the arguments of articulate Germans of the immediate post-war era, separate from the ideologies under which they were obliged to live, and providing in Dr. Flanagan's terms 'a second tier to the Cold War debate'. Furthermore, it reminds the reader of the importance of the 'Kulturbund zur demokratischen Erneuerung Deutschlands' set up in July 1945 in Berlin, and it shows the role these journals played as a background to the foundation of the Gruppe 47 in September 1947. It is this political and literary context, and the resurgence of the problems discussed, that make Dr. Flanagan's study, fifty years on, an important contribution to understanding Germany both as it then was and today.

BRIAN KEITH-SMITH

ACKNOWLEDGEMENTS

I would like to express my gratitude to Dr Joachim Whaley, Gonville and Caius College, Cambridge, who supervised the thesis on which this book is based and whose continued criticism I have greatly valued. I am grateful to Professor Brian Keith-Smith for his advice on the preparation of this book for publication and to Dr John Hibberd for his most useful comments on the manuscript.

I am indebted to Melvin Lasky and Günter Caspar for their insight into times outwith my experience and to Professor Ingrid Kantorowicz for kindly allowing me access to her late husband's bequest. Professors Bernd Sösemann, Barbara Baerns and Gesine Schwan of the Freie Universität Berlin, Dr Norbert Frei, Ingrid Laurien and Doris Brelie-Lewien all helped with specific questions, and the staff at the Kulturbund archive, the former SED archive, the former East German Akademie der Künste, the Institut für Publizistik at the Freie Universität Berlin, and the Institut für Zeitgeschichte were most helpful.

The costs of this research were defrayed in part by a generous scholarship from the Scottish Education Department. Trinity Hall, Cambridge, contributed towards the costs of producing the thesis, and the Arts Faculty of the University of Bristol has helped with publication costs. To all these I express my thanks.

Finally, my very personal thanks go to Frank Vogel, Christine Schlie, Karin Rath and their families for their generous and continuing hospitality.

Bristol, 1999 Clare Flanagan

ABBREVIATIONS USED IN TEXT AND NOTES

ACC	Allied Control Council
AKN	Alfred-Kantorowicz-Nachlaß
BMG	British Military Government
CCF	Congress for Cultural Freedom
CDU	Christlich-Demokratische Union
CIC	Counter Intelligence Corps
CSU	Christlich-Soziale Union
EAC	European Advisory Council
EKD	Evangelische Kirche in Deutschland
FDGB	Freier Deutscher Gewerkschaftsbund
FDJ	Freie Deutsche Jugend
FDP	Freie Demokratische Partei
FRG	Federal Republic of Germany
GDR	German Democratic Republic
GLL	*German Life and Letters*
GQ	*German Quarterly*
HICOG	(Office of the U.S.) High Commissioner for Germany
ICD	Information Control Division (OMGUS)
IfZ	Institut für Zeitgeschichte, Munich
ISD	Information Services Division (British Zone)
JCS	Joint Chiefs of Staff
KA	Kulturbund-Archiv
KPD	Kommunistische Partei Deutschlands
OMGUS	Office of the Military Government for Germany, United States
AdK (East/West)	Akademie der Künste (East/West Berlin)
PWD	Psychological Warfare Division (part of SHAEF)
RIAS	Radio in the American Sector
SBZ	Sowjetische Besatzungszone
SED	Sozialistische Einheitspartei Deutschlands
SHAEF	Supreme Headquarters of the Allied Expeditionary Forces
SMAD	Soviet Military Administration
SPD	Sozialdemokratische Partei Deutschlands
VfZ	*Vierteljahreshefte für Zeitgeschichte*
VVN	Vereinigung der Verfolgten des Naziregimes
ZfK	*Zeitschrift für Kulturaustausch*
ZPA	Zentrales Partei-Archiv (SED) Berlin

INTRODUCTION

Historical Understandings

This study fits into the ongoing reexamination of this German past. In presenting a spectrum of opinion, it counters narrow teleological analyses and revises the picture of intellectual debate in the late forties. The end of the Cold War and the transformation of Eastern Europe since 1989 have precipitated renewed debate on questions of totalitarianism, historical continuity and the nation-state. Those events have been dramatically described as the failure of communism, the 'end of history', and, in the case of Germany, the 'national turn'.[1] All such attempts to capture the distinct historical moment demand certain assumptions; even to view it as 'das Ende der Nachkriegsordnung' is to assume a definition of forty-five years of German history that is clearly far too rigid.[2] The classification of 1945-1990 as a finite post-war order, evident in many recent analyses, denies the perspective of continuity and reduces the years 1945-1949 to merely a prologue.[3] Accordingly, the importance of these years has too often been overlooked.

Cold War interests have of course largely dominated research in the field of post-war history, with traditionalist and revisionist approaches keeping the Cold War interest central. Accordingly, research into the 1945-1949 period has often been characterized by ideological bias. East German analyses have tended to depict these years as those of the foundation of the communist GDR state, while Western analyses have focused on the emergent patterns of the Federal Republic. Although this allows scrutiny of the means by which the two separate states were

---

[1] See, for example, Stefan Berger, *The Search for Normality: National Identity and Historical Consciousness in Germany since 1800* (Providence, Oxford: Berghahn, 1997), p.2.

[2] Wilfried Loth, 'Das Ende der Nachkriegsordnung', *Aus Politik und Zeitgeschichte*, 18/91, (26 April 1991), 3-10.

[3] See, for example, *Nachkriegsdeutschland 1945-1949*, ed. by Peter Bucher (Darmstadt: Wissenschaftliche Buchgesellschaft, 1990).

established, these approaches cannot be regarded as complete, as they portray progress towards division as a simple process. They also in themselves reflect division and demand comparative reconsideration. That the occupation years provide explanations for subsequent events is self-evident, but to regard them as merely a prelude to the history of one or other part of divided Germany is to oversimplify. Such an approach may also give the erroneous impression that German involvement amounted to either total acquiescence or intellectual enslavement. There was, on the contrary, active participation by at least some of the population in their own division, and even more importantly, there was opposition to it. Misconceptions about these matters are likely to be modified given changed attitudes and readier access to archival material in the East.

Particularly in West Germany, the mid-1980s brought increased interest in the history and pre-history of the Federal Republic and as part of this, there developed theories of developmental phases.[4] One analyst, Klaus Doderer, identified three periods: 1945 until the *Währungsreform*; 1948 until the mid-1950s; and 1955 until 1960.[5] Recent large-scale studies of German history have already refined analysis of the period 1945-1949.[6] More recent contributions on specific areas of inquiry, such as the Soviet Zone and the intellectual anti-communist campaign, make valuable additions to the advancing debate.[7]

---

[4] Klaus Doderer, 'Über Zielsetzungen, Methoden und Ergebnisse', in *Zwischen Trümmern und Wohlstand: Literatur der Jugend 1945-1960*, ed. by Klaus Doderer (Weinheim: Beltz, 1988), pp.1-15 (p.5).

[5] ibid.; see also *Zäsuren nach 1945: Essays zur Periodisierung der deutschen Nachkriegsgeschichte*, ed. by Martin Broszat, Schriftenreihe der Vierteljahreshefte für Zeitgeschichte, 61 (München: Oldenbourg, 1990).

[6] See Mary Fulbrook, *Germany 1918-1990: The Divided Nation* (Oxford: OUP, 1992); Dennis L. Bark and David R. Gress, *A History of West Germany* (Oxford: Blackwell, 1989), I: *From Shadow to Substance 1945-1963*; Harold James, *A German Identity 1770-1990* (London: Weidenfeld and Nicolson, 1989); and *Die Gründung der Bundesrepublik Deutschland: Jahre der Entscheidung 1945-1949: Texte und Dokumente*, ed. by Manfred Overesch (Hannover: Niedersächsische Landeszentrale für Politische Bildung, 1989).

[7] For the Soviet Zone, see in particular *SBZ-Handbuch: Staatliche Verwaltungen, Parteien, gesellschaftliche Organisationen und ihre Führungskräfte in der Sowjetischen Besatzungszone*

Sources and Scholarship

By mid-1949, the two separate political systems were in place, the result not only of structural planning, but of active cultural division. Cultural activity in the immediate post-war years had been shaped by two often opposing forces — those of the German cultural community itself, and Allied political control. Research in this field, therefore, has had to contend with attitudes towards the occupation itself. This is particularly noticeable in work on the press, where the assumption frequently made is one of a simple progression from one or other zonal press to the corresponding East or West German press. The result has been that, in studies of the media in the years after 1949, the immediate post-war years are frequently mentioned solely to illustrate a point.[8] Research in the GDR aimed to demonstrate that a democratic press was the result of benevolent Soviet policies.[9] In the West's more open debate, there have been not only challenges to the nature and achievement of the occupation press (as part of revisionist questioning of Allied historiography), but also counter-challenges, which dismiss these as 'Marxist' criticisms.[10]

What is obscured by these biased attitudes is the breadth and the variety of journalistic endeavour, which vividly reflect this most chaotic of periods. This was

---

Deutschlands 1945-1949 (Im Auftrag des Arbeitsbereiches Geschichte und Politik der DDR an der Universität Mannheim und des Instituts für Zeitgeschichte), ed. by Martin Broszat and Hermann Weber (München: Oldenbourg, 1990), and David Pike, *The Politics of Culture in Soviet-occupied Germany, 1945-1949* (Stanford: Stanford University Press, 1992); and for the anti-communist campaign see Peter Coleman, *The Liberal Conspiracy: The Congress for Cultural Freedom and the Struggle for the Mind of Postwar Europe* (New York: Macmillan, 1989).

[8] See *Das Fischer Lexikon: Publizistik: Massenkommunikation*, ed. by E. Noelle-Neumann, Winfried Schulze, and Jürgen Wilke (Frankfurt a. M.: Fischer, 1989), p.267.

[9] See Reinhart Greuner, *Lizenzpresse: Auftrag und Ende: Der Einfluß der anglo-amerikanischen Besatzungspolitik auf die Wiedererrichtung eines imperialistischen Pressewesens in Westdeutschland* (Berlin: Rütten & Loening,1962), and Günter Raue, *Im Dienste der Wahrheit: Ein Beitrag zur Pressepolitik der Sowjetischen Besatzungsmacht 1945-1949* (Leipzig: Karl-Marx-Universität, 1966).

[10] Peter J. Humphreys, *Media and Media Policy in West Germany: The Press and Broadcasting since 1945* (New York: Berg, 1990), p.3.

most striking in the flood of new periodicals appearing in print and particularly in political-cultural journals. These provided a forum for political discussion and addressed the need for cultural and literary education in Germany. In articulating the ideas of an otherwise mostly silent population, they charted the breakdown in Allied unanimity and the effect this had on political and cultural debate in Germany.

The sudden rush of new titles after 1945 represented an unprecedented watershed in periodical production. The number and urgency of these publications convey an immediacy absent in subsequent historiography. They reflect a break with the traditional division between literature and politics in Germany and show the deepening crisis of the late forties. As literary culture was almost wholly dependent on them, these journals provide unique coverage of the forms and chronology of literary response and foreshadow literary developments of the next four decades. The journals made two particular contributions to literary life. Firstly, they acquainted the German public with new and previously banned German and foreign literature. Secondly, by virtue of the political commitment of their contributors, they drew their readership into political discussion. They demonstrate committed campaigning for an independent, neutral Germany. They also reveal the process of division and the breadth of opposition it engendered. They thereby expose the tragedy of division not just as the culmination of a period of occupation, but as a defeat of preferred and often reasonable alternatives.

The journals phenomenon has attracted scholarly interest since the sixties, and has been the focus of several study groups. In the 1980s a group of Göttingen academics began a research project on post-war journals, and in April 1992 researchers at Munich's Institut für Zeitgeschichte organized a debate involving former editors of some of the journals.[11] The choice of post-war journals as a

---

[11] Ingrid Laurien, *Politisch-kulturelle Zeitschriften in den Westzonen 1945-1949: Ein Beitrag zur politischen Kultur der Nachkriegszeit* (Frankfurt: Lang, 1991), p.383.

recent, post-'Wende', research topic at the Humboldt University in East Berlin underlines the value of this material in any reassessment of the history of the period.

Publications on the journals include studies of individual publications, such as *Der Ruf*, *Ost und West* and the early *Frankfurter Hefte*, and bibliographical reference works on *Aufbau* and *Ost und West*.[12] Some scholars have subjected Catholic journals and journals of the western zones to comparative analyses.[13] Wider investigations of the periodical industry have illuminated the scale and importance of the journals market.[14] Yet no attempt has been made to compare journals from East and West in more than a cursory study of general trends. Moreover, some significant journals have simply been overlooked. This study aims to address these imbalances. The journals selected reflect the range of political opinions at the time. The synchronicity of their comment affords insight into the climate of political tension and into both Allied and German cultural politics.

Obstacles exist, however, to exploring this field. Original documentation is rare; paper was in short supply, it was of poor quality and it was reused. Keeping records was not a priority, especially in the worst days of the paper shortage, and,

---

[12] See Hans-Gerd Ewald, *Die gescheiterte Republik: Idee und Programm einer "Zweiten Republik" in den Frankfurter Heften (1946-1950)*, Europäische Hochschulschriften, 31 (Frankfurt a. M.: Lang, 1988); *Aufbau: Berlin 1945-1958: Bibliographie einer Zeitschrift*, ed. by Dieter Noll (Berlin: Aufbau-Verlag, 1978); Ewald Birr, *Ost und West: Berlin 1947-1949. Bibliographie einer Zeitschrift* (München: Saur, 1993); Jérôme Vaillant, *Der Ruf: Unabhängige Blätter der jungen Generation (1945-1949): Eine Zeitschrift zwischen Illusion und Anpassung* (München: Saur, 1978); and Barbara Baerns, *Ost und West: Eine Zeitschrift zwischen den Fronten*, Studien zur Publizistik, Bremer Reihe, 10 (Münster: 1968) respectively.

[13] See Doris von der Brelie-Lewien, *Katholische Zeitschriften in den Westzonen 1945-1949: Ein Beitrag zur politischen Kultur der Nachkriegszeit* (Göttingen: Muster-Schmidt, 1986); and Laurien, *Politisch-kulturelle Zeitschriften in den Westzonen*.

[14] See particularly *Politisch-kulturelle Zeitschriften in den deutschen Besatzungszonen 1945-1949: Eine Sammlung bibliographischer Daten*, ed. by Iris Vielberg and Ingrid Laurien (Göttingen: [n. pub.], 1986); Janet K. King, *Literarische Zeitschriften 1945-1970* (Stuttgart: J. B. Metzlersche Verlagsbuchhandlung & Carl Ernst Poeschel Verlag, 1974); and *Als der Krieg zu Ende war: Literarisch-politische Publizistik 1945-1950. Eine Ausstellung des Deutschen Literaturarchivs*, ed. by Bernhard Zeller (Stuttgart: Klett, 1973).

where they exist, they are often incomplete. Uncertainty exists as to whether some information, particularly in the East, has been deliberately hidden or destroyed. Cataloguing, in for example the Institut für Zeitgeschichte, has only recently been updated. In addition, relevant material has often been dispersed. For example, some documents pertaining to *Der Monat* were taken to America and have found their way into the archives of the Congress for Cultural Freedom in Chicago University Library, while other material is possibly in Paris, with the original editor, Melvin Lasky, ignorant of its contents. The archives of the journal *Aufbau* relating to this time were destroyed in a flood in the basement of its publishing house.

For documentation and correspondence on *Der Ruf*, I had access to the personal archives of editors Alfred Andersch and Hans Werner Richter and to the archive of the Gruppe 47, all housed in the West Berlin Akademie der Künste. Information on the literary scene in the Eastern Zone and the GDR was consulted in the former Akademie der Künste in East Berlin before its merger with its western equivalent. Here, I was also able to see some personal papers of *Ost und West* editor, Alfred Kantorowicz. These documents had been seized by the Stasi after he fled to the West in 1957 and, as he was branded a traitor, had remained untouched until the 'Wende'. After re-unification, legal ownership of this archive was contested and it is now held with the rest of his bequest in the Universitäts- und Staatsbibliothek Hamburg. Access is still restricted and what was found there is published here for the first time. Insights into the press politics of the US Zone were provided by the files of the American Military Government in Germany (OMGUS) from 1945 to 1949, held in the Institut für Zeitgeschichte. That institute also houses personal records documenting the western cultural scene since 1945; these were particularly helpful in profiling editors and researching the political background to the western journals. The SED archive in the former Institut für Marxismus-Leninismus provided information about the Eastern Zone press and general cultural politics. Its files also contained specific references to *Aufbau* and *Ost und West*. In addition to these central party archives, the archive of the Kulturbund, brought to the same location after unification, provided important background information, particularly on *Aufbau*, as documents held there shed light on the political scrutiny to which this journal was subject.

Oral evidence also provided invaluable insights. Personal reminiscences, particularly those of Melvin Lasky, but also of Günter Caspar, have added vitality to archival material. This evidence too is of course incomplete, with Melvin Lasky the sole survivor of the editors. Widows and relatives remain, but are naturally protective of reputations. Also, even first-hand accounts, after the lapse of fifty years, cannot be assumed to be 100 per cent accurate.

The journals

Aufbau appeared in East Berlin in September 1945; *Frankfurter Hefte* in Frankfurt in April 1946; *Der Ruf* in Munich in August 1946; *Ost und West* in East Berlin in July 1947; and *Der Monat* in West Berlin in October 1948. By 1950, both *Der Ruf* and *Ost und West* had been suppressed. The others survived into later years, with the *Frankfurter Hefte* still appearing today after amalgamation with another journal.

The five were selected for their exposure of the most significant trends, the most revealing political attitudes and manoeuvres, and the central players. While other journals of the time, most notably *Die Gegenwart* and *Die Wandlung*, deserve as much attention individually, these five taken together offer the most broadly representative sample.[15] They occupy different points on the political spectrum and reveal what was symptomatic of each position. At the same time, they map areas of common ground which conflict with any narrow categorisations.

[15] *Die Wandlung*, edited by Dolf Sternberger, appeared under US licence in November 1945; *Die Gegenwart*, edited by Benno Reifenberg, appeared under French licence in December 1945.

The order of presentation of the journals, with the Eastern Zone journals first, traces this spectrum from left to right.

The aim is not, then, to compare Allied press policies or to reduce comparisons to East-West oppositions, but to reveal the scope and nature of German expression during occupation and before formal division. Together, they illustrate all shades of German debate. What all shared was an idealism which emphasizes the tragedy of the impending disunity.

CHAPTER ONE
CULTURAL POLITICS AND THE PRESS

Cultural Politics

Of the factors distinguishing the peace of 1945 from that after World War One, two are perhaps particularly significant. The first is obvious: the Soviet Union did not take part in the 1918 peacemaking process. The second is more subtle; the implementation of cultural politics. As one cultural historian has pointed out, 'il n'y a pas eu d'actions sérieuses des Etats dans le domaine culturel des relations internationales après la première guerre mondiale.'[1] Not only was this a new phenomenon as a peace measure, it was also to become an integral part of post-war strategic planning. There were two reasons for this: firstly, the triumph over Nazi cultural barbarism had to be consolidated; secondly, cultural measures had to be adopted to balance those of the opposing ideological bloc.

In the East, the cultural campaign initially appeared innocuous. The Kulturbund took over the building on the Schlüterstrasse which had previously been the site of the Reichskulturkammer and broadcast daily programmes on the Berliner Rundfunk — 'Die Stimme des Kulturbundes'.[2] Behind the scenes, however, the emphasis placed on culture by politicians was soon apparent. On 3 February 1946, at the first cultural meeting of the KPD, Wilhelm Pieck called for the 'Erneuerung der deutschen Kultur', while Anton Ackermann referred to

---

[1] Jacques Bariéty, 'Deux Après-Guerres: Recherches d'Une Politique Culturelle Française en Allemagne après les Déceptions des Années 1920 et 1930', in *Frankreichs Kulturpolitik in Deutschland 1945-1950*, ed. by Franz Knipping and Jacques Le Rider (Tübingen: Attempto, 1987), pp.3-8 (p.3).

[2] Kulturbund-Archiv, 'Präsidialrat Protokolle 1945', 97/498, sheet 92; and 908, sheet 204, 'Bericht über die Arbeit des Kulturbundes seit seiner Gründung gegeben auf der Präsidialratssitzung vom 9.1.46.

'unsere kultur-politische Sendung'.[3] Politically, the work of the *Kulturschaffenden* was promoted as a source of vital support to the working class and its party. Within the political agencies of the KPD's Agitation und Propaganda section, and its successor in the SED, there was clear pursuit of political ends through cultural means. Overall, the campaign mounted in the Eastern Zone was far more sophisticated and unified than that in the West.

In the West, each zone pursued its own cultural programme. In the American Zone, OMGUS set up Amerikahäuser as cultural centres for American literature and information services. The Amerika-Haus was envisaged as a bridge between Germany and the outside world.[4] Soon these were followed by broadcasting campaigns — the establishment of RIAS, then 'Stimme Amerikas', 'Radio Free Europe' and 'Radio Liberty'. The US organised exchanges with professors, students, artists and scientists. The British also established cultural centres in Germany, the Brücken, but these were in place until 1949. Like the Amerikahäuser, they were intended to bring Germany closer to the West, through classes, lectures, films and exchanges.[5] The British emphasis was on education, which was particularly progressive in the British Zone, where responsibility for this sphere was delegated to the Germans in January 1947.[6] In the French Zone, the emphasis was clearly on rapprochement.[7] The Rencontres de Genève, for example, brought together German Existentialists, led by Karl Jaspers, and their

---

[3] *Kulturpolitik in der Bundesrepublik von 1949 bis zur Gegenwart*, ed. by Erna Heckel and others (Köln: Pahl-Rugenstein, 1987), p.10; and ZPA, 'Erinnerungen', EAO 888/5, p.5 respectively.

[4] Manfred Strack, 'Amerikanische Kulturbeziehungen zu (West-)Deutschland 1945-1955', *ZfK* (1987/2), 283-300 (p.297).

[5] See M. Boulby, 'Aspects of the Work of the 'Brücken' in Germany', *GLL*, 7 (1953/1954), 3 (April 1954), 207-09.

[6] ibid.

[7] See, for example, Percy W. Bidwell, 'Emphasis on Culture in the French Zone', *Foreign Affairs*, (October 1948), 78-85; *Frankreichs Kulturpolitik*, ed. by Knipping and Le Rider; and *Die Deutschlandpolitik Frankreichs und die Französische Zone 1945-1949*, ed. by Claus Scharf and Hans-Jürgen Schröder (Wiesbaden: Franz Steiner, 1983).

French counterparts.[8] Cultural efforts in the western zones in many ways reflected the progress from re-education politics to reorientation.

Native German expression was limited to the Churches, the politicians and the press. The Churches had relatively limited influence given low congregation figures, and the politicians were not fully trusted, and in any case, had little power. The press was the means to communicate directly with the public and writers enjoyed a special position. The Nazi years had seen the splintering of German intellectual leadership. Many writers had been in exile in Russia, America, Britain or Mexico. German identity now depended significantly on the spiritual leadership of these returning exiles. They were welcomed by the Allies as anti-fascist and by the Germans as representative of 'another Germany'. But although Allied re-education policy preached the broadening of minds, even these returning exiles were restricted in their political and cultural activities. Their return to occupied Germany was not always straightforward, and once there, they often suffered constraints on their movements.[9] The OMGUS files contain reports 'transmitting biographical data on German political, cultural, diplomatic figures, scientists, university professors, church leaders and theologians, businessmen, trade union leaders, journalists', which reveal the importance placed by the occupying powers on the activity of these personalities.[10] The ostensible reason for gathering much of this information was the allocation of interzonal passes, which could be refused on the basis of these reports. Since communication between the zones was difficult, the 'other Germany' was handicapped in making its contribution to Germany's transition.

Despite this, these exiles became the literary elite. Emerging politically unscathed from the evils of National Socialism, they represented a limit to the

[8] Stephen Spender, *Journal*, p.93.

[9] Bark and Gress, p.136.

[10] Institut für Zeitgeschichte, OMGUS, POLAD (803-14) [National Archives of the United States: RG 84/OMGUS], no.765023.

charge of collective guilt. This elite was soon divided, however. On the whole, whereas in totalitarian systems the cultural elite must support the political leadership, in western democracies the cultural elite questions it. Accordingly, writers in the Eastern Zone were gradually incorporated into the political effort, while in the western zones they were, at least theoretically, freer to question the political situation. Yet the majority had been exiled because of their socialist convictions, and many, believing that Soviet-sponsored socialism presented the real alternative to fascism, chose to return to the Eastern Zone. Despite the divisions, a certain empathy remained between them and those in the western zones because of their common left-of-centre background.

Realizing that a change in political thought could only occur within the context of free and open debate, these intellectual leaders sought initially to prevent the division of *Geist* and *Macht* traditionally attributed to German society. Although many perceived their role as instigating debate, some saw silence as their only possible contribution. Theodor Adorno was the most famous cynic: 'Der Gedanke, daß nach diesem Krieg das Leben "normal" weitergehen oder gar die Kultur "wiederaufgebaut" werden könnte (...) ist idiotisch'.[11] Obstacles to a renewal of German thought were certainly considerable: the Nazi corruption of the notion of 'Germanness'; the selective analysis of history and literature in the fascist years; and the manipulation of language and literature. The result was that, while literature which had been banned, particularly foreign literature, flooded the market, production of new German literature after 1945 was meagre. Those writers who did produce novels or poetry in the early post-war years attempted to adopt a new style free of Nazi hyperbole. In this respect, the western zones saw more radicalism in literary style than the East, where writers were an integral part

---

[11] *Minima Moralia: Reflexionen aus dem beschädigten Leben* (Frankfurt: 1984), p.65, quoted by Hermann Glaser, 'Kultur und Gesellschaft in der Bundesrepublik: Eine Profilskizze 1945-1990', *Aus Politik und Zeitgeschichte*, 1-2 (1991), (p.3).

of the community. In the West a more combative spirit was evident, things were less structured, and writers still struggled with the past. The Kahlschlag movement developed from this sense of literary vacuum. Here, if anywhere, one might talk of a 'zero hour' approach. Wolfdietrich Schnurre, Alfred Andersch and Heinrich Böll were hailed as the bringers of 'der neuen deutschen Prosa'.[12] These 'pioneers' stood in marked contrast to their counterparts in the Eastern Zone.[13] As there was no politically organized focus for literature in the West, some degree of political subversion existed. The Gruppe 47 imparted a radical and satirical nature to literature and literary criticism in the FRG. Today there is debate as to whether the criticism of post-war society contained in the works of Walser, Koeppen, Böll and Grass, for example, had parallels in the GDR. In some sense, however, cultural activity in the East conveyed a sense of true departure from the past. It did not just celebrate socialist revolution, it communicated idealistic aims and optimism for the future.

The first Writers' Congress after the war was held in Berlin in 1947. This was greeted enthusiastically as an opportunity for writers from all over Germany to meet together. It was described by Gunter Groll as 'ein Parlament der Intellektuellen' — 'das erste deutsche Parlament' since the Third Reich.[14] Groll's words underline the absence over years of representation of all Germans which contributed to the involvement of writers in political affairs. The equal status of the delegates, whether returned exiles or not, was emphasized in the conference manifesto, which described them as 'Schriftsteller, die, sei es in der Emigration, sei es in der Heimat, die Integrität und Würde der deutschen Literatur bewahrt haben'.[15] Although the proceedings were embarked upon with enthusiasm, some

---

[12] Wolfgang Weyrauch, introduction to *Sammlung neuer deutscher Geschichten* (Rowohlt, 1949), quoted by Doderer, 'Über Zielsetzungen', (p.9).
[13] ibid., (pp.9-10).
[14] 'Wir gehören zusammen', *Ost und West*, 1 (1947), H.5, 89-90 (p.90).
[15] Alfred-Kantorowicz-Nachlaß, 65, *Manifest des ersten deutschen Schriftstellerkongresses*.

disquiet as to the residual contamination of German literature by Nazi thought was expressed: 'Axel Eggebrecht vom NWDR bedauerte, daß er die Frage: "Ist der Nazismus in der Literatur noch vorhanden?" zwei Jahre nach der Niederringung des Nationalsozialismus mit "Ja" beantworten müsse'.[16] Ricarda Huch made emotional appeals for unity among the writers themselves, for this to be the symbol of their shared concern for their country.[17] Alfred Kantorowicz pointed to their diversity not as contrary to unity, but as Germany's real strength and potential: 'Es gibt unter ihnen Männer und Frauen konservativer Weltanschauung, Liberale, Sozialisten und Kommunisten und sehr viele, (...) die sich Zeit ihres Lebens von jeder parteiisch politischen Bindung freigehalten haben.'[18] It was for the dramatic display of Cold War antagonism, however, that the conference is remembered. Günter Birkenfeld condemned the Western ban on the Kulturbund as an attack on the free movement of thought and literature.[19] Even more dramatic was Melvin Lasky's complaint that writers in the Soviet Union had to contend with the secret police. The following year's conference saw nearly all the seats of the Eastern Zone delegates empty.[20]

It was primarily in the press, however, that the writers' involvement with the political struggle was played out.

The press

Allied interest converged on the German media from an early date. As well as dismantling the machinery of Nazi propaganda, the Allies could use the media for

---

[16] 'D. F.', 'Wer falsch spricht, denkt falsch', in *Telegraf*, 8 October 1947 (AKN).

[17] Ricarda Huch, 'Begrüßung', *Ost und West*, 1 (1947), H.4, 25-28.

[18] A. K., 'Gruß an den 1. Deutschen Schriftstellerkongreß', *Ost und West*, 1 (1947), H.3, 93-94 (p.93); see also *Der erste gesamtdeutsche Schriftstellerkongreß nach dem Zweiten Weltkrieg im Ostsektor Berlins vom 4. bis 8. Oktober 1947*, ed. by Waltraud Wende-Hohenberger (Frankfurt a. M.: Lang, 1988).

[19] L., 'Der Dichter und seine Verantwortung', *Tägliche Rundschau*, 9 October 1947, (AKN, 65).

[20] Günther Rüther, *"Greif zur Feder, Kumpel": Schriftsteller, Literatur und Politik in der DDR 1949-1990* (Düsseldorf: Droste, 1991), p.34.

re-education purposes. During the last two years of the war, SHAEF's Psychological Warfare Division (PWD) prepared for this task. The PWD devised a three-step scheme to be implemented as Allied forces occupied the country.[21] First, a complete information blackout was to follow liberation. All broadcasting and all publication of printed material would be prohibited, unless authorized by Allied Military Control. Then, as soon as was practicable, official broadsheets were to be produced and distributed by Allied Forces. The third phase was the establishment of licensing procedures. On 12 May 1945, Law No. 191 or Nachrichtenkontroll-Vorschrift no. 1 of the Military Government of Germany denied Germans the right to use any form of public communication without a licence.[22] In many areas, Allied newssheets had already been dropped over enemy lines in advance of the troops. Mobile press units, including German-speaking newsmen and printers recruited by the PWD, accompanied the advancing troops. As towns fell, newspaper plants, printing works and publishing houses were all requisitioned. The newssheets became *Heeresgruppenzeitungen* and, from these, plans often emerged for a local or regional newspaper.

Press licensing was the most public implementation of the re-education policy agreed by all four Allies, controlling German exposure to information.[23] All publications carried a licence and political allegiance was often required. Only politically sound Germans were permitted to publish and, if procedure was not approved, licences were withheld or withdrawn. Generally, the exclusion of

---

[21] See *Manual for the Control of German Informations Services*, 12.5.1945, based on the plan of the PWD.

[22] Helmut Brandt, 'Lizenz und Presse', in *Handbuch der Lizenzen Deutscher Verlage: Zeitungen, Zeitschriften, Buchverlage* (Berlin: de Gruyter, 1947), V-XIV (pp.VIII-X); and *Börsenblatt für den deutschen Buchhandel* (Wiesbaden), 1 (6 Oktober 1945).

[23] On Allied press policy and the licensed press, see Harold Hurwitz, 'Die Pressepolitik der Alliierten', in *Deutsche Presse seit 1945*, ed. by Harry Pross (Bern: Scherz, 1965), pp.27-55; Rüdiger Liedtke, *Die verschenkte Presse: Die Geschichte der Lizenzierung von Zeitungen nach 1945* (Berlin: Verlag für Ausbildung und Studium in der Elefanten Presse, 1982); and Hermann Meyn, *Massenmedien in der Bundesrepublik Deutschland* (Berlin: Colloquium, 1968; repr. 1974), p.35ff.

Altverleger (representatives of politically compromised publishing businesses) was strictly adhered to, though it has been claimed that some publishing firms from the Nazi era were able to resurface with front men, 'Strohmännern', as licence-holders.[24]

The first guidelines on media practice were issued in a SHAEF directive on 22 May 1945. It revealed the emphasis placed by the Allies on collective guilt: 'der erste Schritt zur *reeducation* wird sich streng darauf beschränken, den Deutschen die unwiderlegbaren Tatsachen zu unterbreiten, die sie von ihrer Kriegsschuld überzeugen und von ihrer Kollektivschuld an Verbrechen, wie sie in den Konzentrationslagern praktiziert wurden.'[25] The press, regarded as the main tool of re-education, was not only expected to affirm collective guilt; it was also to teach the Germans to distinguish between opinion and news, and to further distinguish between different opinions. Inevitably, the occupying powers imposed their own ideas.

As the head of the Reichsministerium für Propaganda und Aufklärung, Goebbels had masterminded the exploitation of German press and radio. The media had been a central instrument in the establishment and maintenance of dictatorship. The purposes of indoctrination and incitement had engendered a type of journalistic practice which clearly had to be erased. By harnessing the information services in their turn, the Allies ensured maximum control over German political and social recovery. The press officers of the military authorities were particularly influential in this. Both the Americans and the Russians had re-educated some exiled German journalists in their own countries and now employed them in the restructuring of the system.[26] Captured German soldiers who had been in American camps were enrolled in OMGUS.

---

[24] See Doderer, 'Über Zielsetzungen', (p.13).

[25] Directive No.1 PWD/SHAEF, quoted by Hurwitz, 'Die Pressepolitik', (p.31).

[26] For personal records of OMGUS press officers, see Peter de Mendelssohn, *Zeitungsstadt Berlin: Menschen und Mächte in der Geschichte der deutschen Presse* (Berlin: 1959); and Hans

The first newspaper in 'post-war' Germany appeared well before the capitulation. The *Aachener Nachrichten*, a British-German collaboration, came out on 24 January 1945, three months before the last Nazi publication (*Der Panzerbär*) ceased.[27] Such collaborative effort was typical of subsequent newspaper planning and leading newspapers were in general representative of the official stance: *Die Tägliche Rundschau* in the Russian Zone, *Die Neue Zeitung* in the American Zone, *Nouvelles de France* in the French Zone, and *Die Welt* in the British Zone. The Allies had planned that the Germans should resume control of the press at an early stage, not least because they thought that wider communication among Germans would facilitate re-education. However, there was some variation both in their licensing procedures and in the rigour with which these were applied.

Differing press traditions and perceptions of the role of the press in society dictated patterns in the individual zones. The model for the British press was parliamentary, with a variety of publications expressing different views and all vying for readership. The Americans, on the other hand, envisaged each individual publication or editorial group as a microcosm of the democratic process, where people with different views had to reach democratic decisions on material and presentation. They favoured editorial teams of three or more people of different political stances. The Russians saw the press as a political unifier, supporting a socialist people's party. Nor did the French encourage a variety of opinions. Fear of their neighbour had induced a tough line on German political expression. Inevitably, efforts to construct a press for Germany became directed towards an Eastern or Western-style press. Procedure varied most in the matter of allowing

---

Habe, *Im Jahre Null: Ein Beitrag zur Geschichte der deutschen Presse* (München: Kurt Desch, 1966).

[27] The last edition of *Der Panzerbär: Kampfblatt für die Verteidiger Groß-Berlins* was dated 29 April 1945: see *Hauptsache Frieden: Kriegsende, Befreiung, Neubeginn: Vom antifaschistischen Konsens zum Grundgesetz 1949*, ed. by Peter Altmann (Frankfurt a. M.: Röderberg, 1985), p.155.

political parties to have their own publications. The US authorities were reluctant to license party publications and preferred to keep to their overall policy of awarding licences to varied groups of screened individuals. It was 1948 before publications with fixed political or ideological programmes were permitted in the American Zone.[28] The French were also initially reluctant, while the Russians sanctioned political publications immediately.

The US arguably had the most clinical approach to press restructuring. They pursued Western security with a detached interest. Their policy also attracted most German opposition. This was particularly evident in Bavaria, where political parties protested against their treatment. For detachment did not mean leniency. Even *Die Neue Zeitung*, seen as an organ of OMGUS, received official censure. It was charged with being too self-critical or too frank towards the German people.[29] This occasioned interest all over Germany and delight on the part of the eastern press. Questions were naturally raised about US control of other publications. Responses to US press practice in general vary from the accusation that American practices were imposed on another culture to an excessive degree, to its praise as true democratic procedure. Kurt Koszyk identified in the Americans an impatience for change and questioned their motivation, arguing that their aim was 'sich der lästigen Kontrollaufgaben zu entledigen und die Deutschen medienpolitisch, wie ganz allgemein, dauerhaft in den Westen zu integrieren'.[30] This description, cynical though it appears, is undoubtedly true. Whatever its bias, Norbert Frei has identified this American

---

[28] Emil Dovifat, 'Eine erste Pressestatistik', in *Lizenzenhandbuch Deutscher Verlage 1949: Zeitungen, Zeitschriften, Buchverlage* (Berlin: de Gruyter, 1949), pp.XIX-XXV (p.XXI).

[29] See Hurwitz, 'Die Pressepolitik', (p.34); and the editorials in the *Neue Zeitung* by Hans Habe (8 March 1946), and Hans Wallenberg (2 May 1946) for their responses.

[30] Kurt Koszyk, *Pressepolitik für Deutsche 1945-1949: Geschichte der deutschen Presse Teil IV* (Berlin: Colloquium Verlag, 1986), p.11.

'*panel*-Modell' as 'eine wirkliche Neuerung'.[31] He has, however, criticized American policy for hindering progress from the second to the third stage — the introduction of new German licensed publications. He blamed the 'Habe-Presse', maintaining that Hans Habe, the OMGUS press officer, had essentially regionalized army publications, giving them local names and thus circumventing the need for licensed German newspapers.[32]

At the time the British Zone was regarded as having the most innovative media set-up, one which was expected to be a blueprint for the future. The British had initially agreed with the Americans' plans for the press but, through their Information Services Control Branch, were to demonstrate a different approach from summer 1945.[33] BMG hoped that a mild form of control, easing gradually, would encourage the Germans to adopt mild, democratic behaviour themselves. They encouraged the expression of partisan views and licensed official publications by political parties and other organisations, so that the Germans were exposed to a variety of viewpoints within the press. The major parties were accorded licences for publications in all the important cities of the British Zone.

The French effectively transferred their journalistic practices over the border to their zone. Their wartime situation had excluded the possibility of any pre-victory planning, especially as their full participation in the occupation was under question for a considerable time. Perhaps as a result of this, problems in communication arose between the officers in the zone and the central authorities in Paris.

The Russian Zone established the most dramatic break from past German practices. Berlin had been the centre of journalistic activity in the Third Reich.

---

[31] 'Amerikanische Pressepolitik im Nachkriegsdeutschland', *ZfK* 37 (1987/2), 306-18 (pp.307-08). The term 'panel' was clearly used by the Americans: see Hurwitz, 'Die Pressepolitik', (p.37).

[32] ibid., (p.306).

[33] Koszyk, *Pressepolitik*, p.11.

The last edition of the fascist newspaper, the *Völkische Beobachter*, appeared there on 27 April 1945. On 30 April, Hitler committed suicide; on 2 May, the Soviet flag flew on the *Reichstag*; and on 3 May, the first issue of the Soviet authorities' news-sheet, *Nachrichtenblatt für die deutsche Bevölkerung*, appeared. Issue fifteen of this announced a ban on publishing and printing — the first step in press politics in the German capital.[34] Yet by the time the Allies reached Berlin, four new newspapers had appeared. The Russians, together with the 'Moscow Germans' flown in on 30 April, had moved quickly to locate usable printing works and to find Berliners suitable for employment in the press.[35] To what degree this was an aggressive political move is uncertain: SHAEF and the PWD plan were products of American and British thinking. It is possible that the Russians resented this Western planning for Germany and chose to ignore it. In any case, they took full advantage of their situation in the capital. When the Western Allies arrived in their sectors, they had to make an immediate start at phase three of the plan and set up licensed papers to compete with those already in circulation.

The first newspaper to appear in Berlin, printed in Neukölln on 15 May, was the *Tägliche Rundschau*, the Russian-German collaboration which became the major daily of the Soviet Zone. It had access only to the TASS news agency and was interpreted accordingly either as a friendly publication with German co-workers, or as a 'klägliche Rundschau'. This last criticism was based on its restricted content: praise of things Russian, a tiny foreign section and mundane

---

[34] See Jochen Vorfelder, 'Der Neuaufbau der Berliner Tagespresse zwischen April und Dezember 1945 durch die alliierten Siegermächte' (unpublished master's thesis, Freie Universität Berlin, 1985).

[35] Gerhard L. Weinberg, 'From Confrontation to Cooperation: Germany and the United States, 1933-1949', in *America and the Germans: An Assessment of a Three-Hundred-Year History*, ed. by Frank Trommler and Joseph McVeigh (Philadelphia: University of Pennsylvania Press, 1983), II: *The Relationship in the Twentieth Century*, (p.54).

local announcements.[36] But in the judgement of the GDR writer Günter Raue, it was the 'erste Sammelbecken des demokratischen deutschen Journalismus'.[37]

The divergence of press patterns in East and West was soon apparent. In the West, there was a gradual and monitored re-establishment of a privately owned, commercial press structure. In the East, control and censorship were more ruthlessly achieved, but surprisingly the authorities' ever tighter grip on the press and publishing community was not so apparent. This was because control in the East was exercised before publication, whereas in the western zones it came after publication, in the form of withdrawal of licences or forced personnel changes, and was of course much more noticeable. In the British Zone, for example, there were several instances of licence withdrawal in connection with the Berlin crisis of 1948.[38] Western commentators have argued that the policies pursued by the ISC and by the different western military authorities must be set 'against the background of political developments in the Russian Zone'.[39] In other words, measures had to be taken against Russian propaganda or 'aggression'. Censorship was aimed against the East, rather than against the Germans.

In the first few weeks after capitulation, the Soviet military authorities had set up in their zone of occupation political structures (communal administration, political parties and a *Stadtverwaltung*), forming a network which the incoming Allies could neither avoid nor ignore. However, while the principal positions of authority were blatantly given to candidates loyal to Moscow, a situation bound to provoke confrontation, the SMAD (Soviet Military Administration) was nonetheless acting within the framework agreed by the Allies. Accordingly, when

---

36 Margret Boveri, *Tage des Überlebens* (Munich: 1968), pp.159 and 268, quoted by Vorfelder, 'Der Neuaufbau', p.32.

37 Raue, *Im Dienste der Wahrheit*, p.133.

38 Kurt Koszyk, 'The Press in the British Zone of Germany', in *The Political Re-education of Germany and her Allies after World War II*, ed. by Nicholas Pronay and Keith Wilson (London: Croom Helm, 1985), pp.107-38 (p.136, note 62).

39 ibid., (p.121).

the Allied Kommandatur met for the first time, the measures taken by the SMAD could only be ratified.[40] Concerned at developments in Berlin and particularly about the press, the Western Allies sent press officers to Berlin on 7 July with the task of mitigating the Soviet advantage.[41] Communist propaganda, however, accelerated. By October 1947, after the establishment of the zone's unity party, the SED, its Abteilung Werbung, Presse, Rundfunk was clearly targeting the media as part of the party's propaganda effort. An SED in-house memo of 21 February 1948 to this department recommended the production of 'Agitationsbroschüren'. Later in 1948, the SED's Agitation department produced propaganda on the subject of the Berlin blockade. This, referred to as 'Aufklärung', placed the blame for the situation firmly on the West: 'Indem die Befehlshaber der Bizone am 24. Juni 1948 die Lieferungen an die sowjetische Besatzungszone sperrten, sperrten sie damit auch die Lieferungen der sowjetischen Besatzungszone an Berlin, verhängten also die Blockade über Berlin'.[42] By 1950, the manipulation of the press for ideological ends in the Eastern Zone was publicly acknowledged in party publications.[43]

On 23 September 1949, Allied Command announced the end of licensing. The Western Allies and the USSR were each satisfied that they had a basis for a democratic press. Two different press systems had, however, been constructed.

Surprisingly, the withdrawal of licensing provoked some disagreement within the German community. A resolution of the Bavarian Landtag, passed in October 1948, urged that the military government's licensing powers be transferred to German authorities. German politicians in Hesse supported this

---

40 Vorfelder, 'Der Neuaufbau', p.53.

41 ibid., p.55.

42 ZPA, SED ZK, Agitation, IV 2/9.02/2, 'Vorschläge für die Aufklärung über die Berliner Fragen', signed by Otto Winzer.

43 See, for example, *Unsere Presse — die scharfste Waffe der Partei: Referate und Diskussionsreden auf der Konferenz des Parteivorstandes der SED v. 9./10.2.1950 in Berlin* (Berlin: 1950).

move to maintain licensing legislation by transferring it to German control, rather than phasing it out.[44] Some elements of the German press, however, voiced opposition. They feared neo-Nazism, overweening government power, competition from the older journalistic establishment, and litigation by owners of printing facilities which the Allies had commandeered and which were now being used by licensees.[45] The end of licensing brought a sharp increase in the number of publications and the return in the West of the *Altverleger*, which compounded the rivalry of the occupation years between them and other journalists. Despite their return, most licensed papers survived, and the distinction in society between licensed and new publications faded.[46]

Later, the licensing system was to be criticized in the West, and German journalists who participated in it were slighted as collaborators. Even before the revisionist mood of the sixties, when the Allied occupation came under scrutiny, possession of a licence was equated with collaboration, and the term *Lizenz-Presse* acquired a pejorative meaning.[47] At the time, however, participation was not seen as any kind of betrayal. As a commentator in a professional press publication underlined: 'die Lizenz von heute (...) ist *ein positiver Auftrag mit politischen Aufgaben.*' He agreed with the words of an American occupation officer: 'Mit ihr werde *Vertrauen* begründet. Sie verkörpere den Glauben, den die Besatzungsmacht in die Lizenzträger als die Sprecher eines zukünftigen demokratischen Deutschlands setze.'[48] The accusation of collaboration was not heard in the East, where German-Russian co-operation was celebrated.

---

[44] Henry P. Pilgert, *Press, Radio and Film in West Germany 1945-1953* (HICOG Historical Division, 1953), pp.24-25.
[45] ibid., p.24.
[46] Kenneth E. Olson, *The History Makers: The Press of Europe from its Beginnings through 1965* (Louisiana State University Press, 1966), p.125.
[47] IfZ, OMGUS, ODI, 7/42-3/1-2 (11.1949-4.1950) Weekly Intelligence Report No.15, Trend Report, part IV (20 January 1950) (secret), p.14.
[48] Brandt, 'Lizenz und Presse', (p.XI), (Brandt's emphasis).

Political-cultural journals

Within this period of transition for the German press, there was a boom in periodicals, all keen to contribute to the new freedom of debate. Journals have always been viewed as providing considered and informed critical analysis; a later description of *Encounter* underlines this perception: 'a monthly review (...) creating when the world is destroying, helping where it is hindering'.[49] The critical distance associated with much journal production emphasizes in the case of these journals the unfairness of summary accusations of collaboration based on licensing. From 1946, the number of journals rose rapidly. At the beginning of 1947 there were 661, in 1948 there were over 1300.[50] By 1949 the numbers of new titles had steadied. Journals benefited from the cash surplus of the first two post-war years; reading material was guaranteed to sell out. Often, publications would be bought for non-reading purposes as consumer goods were so scarce.[51] As time went on, the paper shortage worsened, and the economic reforms of 1948 had an adverse effect on publishing all over Germany. In addition, the economic progress of Bizonia and Trizonia brought greater demand for specialized journals and less for those of a more aesthetic nature. According to contemporary analyses, theological publications were the most numerous. Then came the industrial and trades periodicals. The third largest category was 'Politik — Kulturpolitik — Politisch-satirische Blätter'.[52] While the primary goal was political discussion, many of this latter category in particular devoted considerable space to literary matters; they sought to inform the German population of developments in foreign literature and culture and to distract them from the grim reality around them. In addition, then,

---

[49] Cyril Connolly, quoted by Melvin J. Lasky in his preface to *Encounters: An Anthology from the First Ten Years of Encounter Magazine* (London: Weidenfeld and Nicolson, 1963).

[50] *Lizenzen-Handbuch Deutscher Verlage 1949.*

[51] Pilgert, *Press, Radio and Film*, pp.18-19.

[52] *Lizenzen-Handbuch Deutscher Verlage 1949.*

to their central role in political (re-)education, these journals' importance for literary re-education was inestimable; this was already evident to contemporary assessments.[53]

Political-cultural journals were particularly successful and prominent in the American Zone, where the party political press was insignificant.[54] The British Zone, with its revived party press, had relatively fewer journals with a political flavour. The Russian Zone had a comparatively small number of journals. There, licences were only granted to journals with a political interest if this slant coincided with the politics of the zonal authorities. In the French Zone too, political-cultural periodicals were less numerous, and the political angle was overshadowed by the French desire to instil *l'esprit français* in German culture. The political-cultural journals could not be fully representative of the party political debate in Germany. Zonal differences, the general limitations of licensing, and even the perception of 'Lizenzzwang', prevented this.[55] However, they undoubtedly made an elementary and most representative contribution to 'das Gespräch der Zeit', contributing, along with the political parties and the broadcasting system, to the German political effort.[56] They facilitated and influenced the discussion of political conditions and political aims. They also offered uniquely varied discussion of Germany's possible future. Emil Dovifat, the respected academic commentator on journalism, pointed to this breadth in his explanation of the flood of journals onto the market:

Die ersten Nachkriegsjahre hatten im politisch-weltanschaulichen Kampf, im Neuwerden der Parteien und anderer politischer Gesinnungsgruppen eine große Zahl von Zeitschriften entstehen lassen, die in der Zeit allgemeinen Lesehungers

---

[53] Leonard Forster, *German Poetry 1944-1948* (Cambridge: Bowes and Bowes, 1950) (first pub. 1949).

[54] *Handbuch der Lizenzen Deutscher Verlage* (1947).

[55] Heinz-Dietrich Fischer, *Parteien und Presse in Deutschland seit 1945* (Bremen: 1971).

[56] Gerhard Menz, 'Deutschlands Neue Zeitschriften', in *Handbuch Deutsche Presse*, ed. by Norwestdeutscher Zeitungsverleger-Verein (Bielefeld: Deutscher Zeitungs-Verlag, 1947), pp.130-32 (p.131).

und doktrinär erregter Startdebatten des neuen geistigen Lebens sicheren Absatz fanden.[57]

Another commentator has claimed that they had a 'monopoly' on the discussion of German questions.[58] The journals of the 1945-49 period provide an unparalleled view of Germany between the Second World War and the Cold War. Central, then, to any understanding of this fraught period of transition is what Melvin Lasky called 'the journals war'.[59]

---

57 'Eine erste Pressestatistik', (p.XXIV).

58 Helga Grebing, 'Demokratie ohne Demokraten?: Politisches Denken, Einstellungen und Mentalitäten in der Nachkriegszeit', in *Wie neu war der Neubeginn?: zum deutschen Kontinuitätsproblem nach 1945: Wissenschaftliche Tagung am 7. und 8. Juli 1989 im Kollegeinhaus Universität Erlangen Nürnberg*, ed. by Helga Grebing, Erlanger Forschungen, 50 (Erlangen: Universitätsbibliothek, 1989), pp.6-19 (p.7).

59 Interview with Melvin Lasky.

CHAPTER TWO
AUFBAU

Aufbau was the first licensed journal to be published in post-war Germany, appearing in Berlin in September 1945. As the first official organ of the *Kulturbund*, it was at the forefront of the literary revival in the Soviet Zone and of the journalistic campaign there in particular. *Aufbau* had two namesakes: '*Der Aufbau*' had been the journal for the trade organisation of Nazi Germany; and another '*Aufbau*' had appeared during the war among German exiles in New York. The latter publication was quick to complain.[1] The choice of name was deliberate. It echoed the dedication of the KPD 'zum Aufbau eines neuen demokratischen Deutschlands'. It was not, however, intended to be exclusive, but to unite all those opposed to fascism in the reconstruction of Germany. As an underground railway advertisement of the time announced, the aim was to encourage people to 'Bau auf mit Aufbau'.[2]

The journal was launched in tandem with the Aufbau-Verlag, which was founded on 16 August 1945 and became the leading publishing house for contemporary German literature in the Eastern Zone. Its head, Kurt Wilhelm, had some influence on the early journal, as did Heinz Willmann, the general secretary of the Kulturbund.[3] Members of the journal's staff, many of whom were well-known writers and editors, were predominantly socialist in their thinking, but the number of staff members actively involved in the communist campaign increased over the years from 1945 until 1949. The editorial team included the prominent Marxist theoretician, Alexander Abusch; the socialist literary critic, Herbert Jhering; the CDU politician, Ernst Lemmer; the academic and Kulturbund official

---

[1] KA, uncatalogued.
[2] Interview with Günter Caspar.
[3] KA, 495/844, *Präsidialrat* meeting, 12 November 1948, p.21.

Alfred Meusel; one of the founders of the Kulturbund, Paul Wiegler; the young socialist writer, Stephan Hermlin; and the publisher, Max Schroeder. Three others were of prime importance: Klaus Gysi, Bodo Uhse, and, most famously of all, Johannes R. Becher. Gysi was the editor of the journal during the first few crucial years. His role, although not as well known as Becher's, was central in the day-to-day running of the journal. At a meeting of the newly elected Kulturbund council on 31 May 1947, he was appointed chief editor.[4] It was he who proposed the membership of the journal's advisory committee and determined the frequency of its meetings. Gysi had been one of the founding members of the Kulturbund and, as he became increasingly caught up in its activities, his involvement with the journal quickly diminished. Later he worked for the government, eventually becoming a diplomat. He was succeeded as editor by Bodo Uhse in 1948, by which time the structure of the journal was largely in place. Uhse's appointment followed immediately on his return from exile in Mexico, and was undoubtedly influenced by his editorship of *Neues Deutschland*, the Mexican exile journal. He remained as editor until the journal's demise in 1958. *Aufbau*'s most important figurehead, however, was Johannes Becher. He became the literary role model for the whole Eastern Zone, epitomizing the returning revolutionary, determined to reform Germany, and representative of the 'other' Germany: 'die Stimme des "anderen Deutschland", die dem Imperialismus und dem Krieg unerschütterlich feindlich ist, klingt laut in seinen Versen und Rundfunkreden, die in Moskau und Mittelasien entstanden sind.'[5] Although he played a central role in the journal's image, his participation in the practical, day-to-day management was limited. His presence at editorial meetings was not always guaranteed and the decision-making was left to others from the start. He too was a committee member of the

---

[4] KA, 909, sheet 186.

[5] Alexander Dymschitz, 'Johannes R. Becher über den sozialistischen Realismus', *Aufbau*, 14 (1958), H.7, 778-83 (p.778).

Kulturbund and was also a member of the central committee of the SED. He later became Minister of Culture of the GDR. His political career necessarily restricted his involvement with *Aufbau*, and his influence on the staff and journal undoubtedly waned, although he himself was probably unaware of this.[6]

Aufbau's circulation figures can be estimated only roughly. Archival documents suggest that 50,000 copies of the first issue sold out within a few days.[7] Elsewhere, the figure of 100,000 is quoted for each of the first three issues.[8] The first issue of 1946 is reported as running to 120,000, and the following five issues to 150,000.[9] Thereafter, differing figures are contained in the handbooks, but it seems probable that the average for 1947 was about 100,000 per issue.[10] The paper shortage was at its most severe at this time, however: the paper allocation to SED publications alone dropped by 45%.[11] What is clear is that *Aufbau*, as a quasi-official publication, received preferential treatment, being financed through the Soviet Military Authorities. Readership figures must be judged in the light of the fixed quota system and also of the resultant practice of passing round reading material.[12] Another unknown factor in these calculations is the effect on Kulturbund publications of the action of the West in proscribing its activities.

Aufbau ceased publication in 1958. Its demise was rumoured to have been the result of political intervention, and there is certainly evidence to support this. Tension in the GDR had increased, and there had been a clampdown on the voicing of alternative socio-political ideas. After the introduction in 1953 of the GDR's policy of 'Sozialisierung', a system of information control was gradually

---

[6] Interview with Caspar.
[7] KA, 97/498, *Präsidialrat* meeting 17 October 1945, p.91.
[8] Karen Kiwus, 'Die politische Funktion des *Aufbau* in der antifaschistisch-demokratischen Periode der SBZ 1945-1948' (unpublished master's thesis, Freie Universität Berlin, 1970), p.16.
[9] ibid.; and *Handbuch Deutsche Presse* (1947).
[10] King, p.77.
[11] ZPA, SED ZK, W. Pieck, NL 36/750, 102-05.
[12] Interview with Carsten Wurm.

set up. Dissident voices were increasingly heard in the cultural sphere and by 1957 the SED was taking measures to suppress them. In the same year there were accusations that anti-socialist groups had emerged in *Aufbau-Verlag* and in *Sonntag*, *Aufbau*'s sister publication.[13] The conclusion that *Aufbau* was forcibly discontinued has therefore been widely accepted. The explanation for its disappearance, however, is almost certainly simpler. It is said that Bodo Uhse simply lost enthusiasm, and wanted to devote more time to his own writing.[14] There is also no material in the last issues of *Aufbau* which might have caused official disapproval. It is unlikely then, that the journal was the victim of political alienation. On the contrary, it was actively mourned, and there were even calls within the Kulturbund for a suitable replacement.

The 'humanistisches Erbe'

The first issue of *Aufbau* appeared on 21 September 1945 as advertised in the *Tägliche Rundschau* two days earlier.[15] In this first edition, the manifesto of the Kulturbund itself was presented as the journal's programme. In its introduction, it identified its task as awakening and uniting all the 'aufbauenden Kräfte' within the cultural sphere and thereby promoting Germany's 'geistige Neugeburt'.[16] In a powerful opening article, Becher dealt with the preoccupations of the time — Germany's recent past, her guilt, hopes and fears for the future, and most of all, the role of culture. Becher argued that the 'moralische Katastrophe' of Nazism was the product of over five decades of German history. He described those years as a 'geistig-moralischer Auflösungs- und Fäulnisprozeß' and their impact as 'Die

---

[13] See, for example, Alexander Abusch's complaints at the 'Kulturkonferenz der SED' (23-24.10.1957): ZPA, SED ZK, Konferenzen und Beratungen des ZK der SED, IV 2/1.01/407, 26.

[14] Interview with Caspar; this view is corroborated by Rolf Schneider, 'Unvollkommene Versuche, einen Schriftsteller zu beschreiben', *Sinn und Form*, 24 (1972), H.4, 798-807 (p.803).

[15] Carsten Wurm, *Das Haus in der Französischen Strasse: Eine Verlagsgeschichte in Bildern. Aufbau-Verlag Berlin und Weimar* (Berlin: Aufbau-Verlag, 1990), p.3.

[16] 'Zum Geleit', *Aufbau*, 1 (1945), H.1, 1.

Zerstörung der Vernunft'.[17] Becher's perception of the wider 'deutsche Tragödie' was of a consolidation over centuries of a 'Widerspruch zwischen dem deutschen Wesen, wie es sich im Kulturellen ausdrückt, und seiner politischen Erscheinungsform'.[18] These two historical developments — the recent moral decadence and the separation of politics and culture — had to be reversed. The utter devastation of the immediate post-war situation, vividly described by Becher, necessitated a radical new cultural beginning. He supported the idea of a zero hour, but presented it as a *moral* zero hour — the 'Trümmerlandschaft der deutschen Seele'.[19] In this, the opening article of the first journal to appear in post-war Germany, Becher mixed harsh realism with proposals for humanistic progress. His approach was at times grim: 'So haben wir Berge von Haß unter allen Völkern gegen uns aufgetürmt. Berge von Haß und Verachtung umlagern, ummauern uns. Einsam sind wir.' This was countered by nostalgia engendered by his exile in Russia, and by his hopes for a socialist future. He proposed the construction of a truly democratic, peaceful state, and friendly co-operation with all nations. Using a religious metaphor, he encouraged the German people's 'Auferstehung' by arguing that the whole population could be 'converted': 'Auch ein ganzes Volk kann sich wandeln, kann anders werden.'[20] Becher was convinced that an overall strategy for recovery required advances in thinking, that national and political recovery must be based on moral recovery: 'Ohne Enttrümmerung, ohne eine Erneuerungsbewegung auf geistigem Gebiet, ohne eine moralische Neugeburt unseres Volkes muß jeder materielle Neuaufbau über kurz oder lang zum Scheitern verurteilt sein.'[21] Contributing to this re-definition of morality would be 'die deutsche Klassik' and 'der deutsche Humanismus'. In common with

---

[17] Johannes R. Becher, 'Deutsches Bekenntnis', *Aufbau*, 1 (1945), H.1, 2-12 (p.3).
[18] ibid., (p.4).
[19] ibid., (p.7).
[20] ibid., (p.6).
[21] ibid., (p.10).

many other commentators of the time, Becher regretted the neglect of the classical tradition, in particular Goethe and Hegel. Quoting from *Faust* to underline his condemnation of the destructive pursuit of self-interest, demonstrated so extremely in Nazi Germany, Becher reinstated Goethe as 'dieser große Menschheitserzieher zur Wahrheit'. Becher tried to provide not just commentary, but also solutions. He not only asked, but also offered an answer to the question 'was sollen wir tun?'.[22] Becher saw this new start as an opportunity to redress past failure and to create a better, socialist future for Germany: 'Es gilt das zu tun, was seit 100 Jahren, seit dem Jahre 1848, wir zu tun verabsäumten.'[23] Fortunately, Germans could also learn from another tradition, that of the German 'Freiheitshelden'. Under this heading Becher grouped heroes of the 1848 revolution, the workers' movement and the martyrs of the resistance to Hitler. The political catchwords used here for the revitalization of Germany were not uncommon at the time: 'Demokratie, Sozialismus und Christentum'.[24] The inclusion of Christianity, or of religion more generally, in this and subsequent articles in *Aufbau* reflects the deliberate compromise of communist thought in the interests of a wider appeal at this early stage. The religious theme emerged again when Becher referred to the task facing the German people as 'das Reformationswerk'. He concluded with a poetical rallying cry to his readers: '"Baut auf!" Und baue, deutsches Volk, dich frei'.[25]

The first issue also brought an extract from a letter written in 1879 by the French thinker, Ernest Renan. Publication of this letter, praising Germany's positive achievements, exemplified the journal's approach. By reminding the old and informing the young of Germany's past glories, *Aufbau* hoped to strengthen

---

[22] ibid., (p.9).
[23] ibid.
[24] ibid., (p.11).
[25] ibid., (p.12).

the resolve and enthusiasm of the people. Renan's letter offered a reminder of Germany's long humanistic tradition:

Wir alle, wie wir da sind, verdanken ihm viel — diesem großen, klugen und tiefgründigen Deutschland, das uns durch Fichte den Idealismus lehrte, durch Herder den Glauben an die Menschlichkeit, durch Schiller die Poesie des Moralischen, durch Kant die abstrakte Pflicht.[26]

The litany of past heroes in Renan's letter is of some interest. That certain of the names, for example Fichte, had been used for less admirable purposes, was left to the reader to ponder. It could be argued, then, that the extract was not only educative, but also re-educative, in that it challenged patterns of thought prevalent in 1945. The letter was intended to inspire; past respect for Germany's intellectual achievements suggested that the nation might recover its reputation: 'Der deutsche Genius ist groß und machtvoll; er bleibt eines der wichtigsten Organe des menschlichen Geistes.'[27] At a time when Germans found it difficult to think positively about themselves as a nation, Renan's remarks must have served as encouragement.

The 'heroes' of Germany's most immediate past were condemned when the journal unquestioningly supported the forthcoming Nürnberg Trials: 'Bald werden die ehemals "führenden" Gestalten des Dritten Reiches in ihrer ganzen Feigheit und Jämmerlichkeit vor den Schranken des Gerichtes stehen, das im Namen der freiheitliebenden Menschheit, im Namen der ungezählten Opfer Rechenschaft von ihnen fordern wird.'[28]

This very first *Aufbau* is a unique record of the immediate post-war days and efforts to deal with them. The two subsequent issues of 1945 were in the same vein — bringing comment on the failure of the German people to live up to the ideals of its great writers and thinkers. Typically in one article, where Germany

---

[26] Ernest Renan, 'Brief an einen deutschen Freund', *Aufbau*, 1 (1945), H.1, 12-14 (pp.12-13).
[27] ibid., (p.14).
[28] Die Redaktion, *Aufbau*, 1 (1945), H.1, 64.

was depicted as the 'armes, törichtes deutsches Volk, betäubt von seinem eigenen Weihrauch!', Bernhard Kellermann concluded that 'sein Hochmut stürzte es in die Tiefe, und heute ist es zum verachtetsten Bettler der Welt geworden!'.[29] Yet in the very same article Kellermann reminded the German people that they were 'das Volk eines Goethe und Schiller, eines Kant, eines Beethoven und Mozart, ehedem eines der geachtetsten Völker der Erde'.[30] *Aufbau* thus presented a mixture of realism and optimism, facing up to the disasters of the time, while reminding Germans of their former glory which was also a promise of future potential.

The journal followed the same pattern over the following years. Allusions to the German classics, humanism, the positive outlook of 'another' Germany, and socialist anti-fascism, were accompanied by the pragmatic recognition of national guilt. Becher's unquestioning acceptance of the 'Mitschuld' of the German people was of particular significance. In his view, no excuse held any water. Such responses as 'we only wanted the best' or 'we know nothing of politics' were scornfully dismissed: 'Wer sich als unpolitisch erklärt, erklärt damit: "Ich will mit meinem Volk nichts zu tun haben".'[31] This uncompromising attitude was at variance with his views, expressed elsewhere, of faith in 'another Germany', free from shared guilt. With the passage of time, the journal was increasingly to display the dichotomy between acceptance of collective guilt and pursuing reforms led by 'other' Germans who had opposed the Third Reich.

On guilt

The early launch of *Aufbau* is undoubtedly connected to Becher's determined acceptance of collective guilt, since his approach modified with time. Initially, the debate on guilt had a strongly religious tenor. Both the psychological and the

---

[29] Bernhard Kellermann, 'Gewogen und zu leicht befunden', *Aufbau*, 1 (1945), H.2, 90-94 (p.91).
[30] ibid.
[31] Becher, 'Deutsches Bekenntnis', (p.8).

religious aspects of collective guilt were explored with reference to thinkers such as C.G. Jung.[32] In 1945 Paul Ronge stated that 'redemption' depended on all Germans confessing their guilt: 'Das dritte Reich ist innerlich beim deutschen Volke erst dann endgültig vorbei, wenn sich jeder auch über seine Erbärmlichkeit im Letzten Rechenschaft abgelegt hat.'[33] Manfred Hausmann similarly emphasized the recognition of individual guilt as essential for recovery: 'so lange der Mensch nicht eingesehen hat, daß er vor sich selbst, vor seinem Volk, vor der Welt und vor Gott mehr oder weniger schuldig geworden ist [...], so lange kann er auf keine Rettung hoffen.'[34] F.W. Krummacher, citing Luther as inspiration, described renewal as inseparable from the admission of guilt: 'Von Schuld zu reden bleibt zwecklos, wenn nicht aus ehrlicher Erkenntnis der Schuld ein getroster und mannhafter Neuanfang des Lebens erwächst.'[35] Krummacher's reference to victory over humanity's guilt in God's kingdom, however, broadened the focus from individual to universal. In so doing, he sought to encourage the German people to overcome their own 'transient' guilt: 'In dem "Mitleiden" Christi findet die Gesamtschuld ihre tiefste Bejahung und zugleich ihre Überwindung.'[36] Elsewhere, Werner Ziegenfuß questioned the idea of innate guilt, arguing that, as man was not the creator of evil, man was, therefore, not solely responsible for it.[37] Using Goethe ('ohne Mephisto kein Faust') to support his point, he proposed that evil was valuable in one respect — in that it could stimulate goodness.[38] Georg Lukács, in one of the most impressive early contributions to the debate about guilt,

---

[32] W. Schellworth, 'Ein Tiefenpsychologe blickt in die deutsche Seele', *Aufbau*, 2 (1946), H.7, 766-67.

[33] Paul Ronge, 'Ob es sich gelohnt hat?', *Aufbau*, 2 (1946), H.4, 423-25 (p.425).

[34] Manfred Hausmann, 'Jugend zwischen gestern und morgen', *Aufbau*, 2 (1946), H.7, 667-74 (p.670).

[35] F. W. Krummacher, 'Luthers bleibendes Wort für unsere Zeit', *Aufbau*, 2 (1946), H.3, 235-44 (p.237).

[36] ibid.

[37] Werner Ziegenfuß, 'Wozu ist das Böse gut?', *Aufbau*, 2 (1946), H.7, 706-11 (p.706).

[38] ibid., (p.710).

provided a perceptive analysis of the nation's involvement in Nazism. Acknowledging that the Nazi system of oppression had ensured that those sections of the German people who were not fanaticized or hypnotized were made powerless and forced into silence, he pointed out that this silence also was blameworthy. Lukács argued, however, that there was no case for equating Nazism with Germanness: 'Aus dieser einzigartigen Lage ist jene — trotz allem — falsche Auffassung entstanden, die den Nazismus mit dem deutschen Volk gleichsetzt.'[39] In 1947 Fritz Kirchheimer identified the standard-bearers of Hitler's ideology as bearing the greatest guilt and called on them to show humility and acceptance of this guilt: 'Wo bleibt das Gefühl für die Mitschuld an dem namenlosen Unglück? Die Vergangenheit ist diesen Herren aus dem Gedächtnis geschwunden.'[40] This allocation of blame to the leaders is evidence of a shift in emphasis from collective guilt to that of a narrower category of Germans. By 1947 guilt was associated in *Aufbau* almost solely with Nazi leaders. National guilt had been reduced to pockets, as if the burden itself had gradually induced redrawing or rejection of guilt.

Becher's own approach was a striking reflection of this. After his eloquent acceptance of collective guilt in 1945, his attitude changed within a year to one of complete rejection. His essay of 1946, 'Deutschland klagt an!', was a virulent attack on the Nazi era, but the feisty approach, reflected in the title, was in stark contrast to his earlier tone of remorse. Now he betrayed a more ambivalent attitude to responsibility. He restricted guilt to Nazi leaders and absolved the bulk of the German people. They were presented as victims rather than perpetrators. Becher went further still: not only had the German people suffered from the criminal actions and policies of the Nazis — their suffering was equated with that

39 Georg Lukács, 'Der Rassenwahn als Feind des menschlichen Fortschritts', *Aufbau*, 1 (1945), H.2, 100-14 (p.102).
40 F. Kirchheimer, 'Die Flucht aus der Verantwortung', *Aufbau*, 3 (1947), H.3, 269-70 (p.270).

of the Jews: 'Was den Juden angetan wurde, wurde *uns* angetan.'[41] Although this might be another instance of drawing on Christian messages (suffering in brotherhood), to apparently equate, and thereby mitigate, was spectacular. Implicit in this change of approach are certain indicators of wider developments. Firstly, the basis of re-education policy was being redrawn, or rejected, in the Eastern Zone. Secondly, this re-allocation of blame enabled the rejection of National Socialism as a precursor to the eastern, socialist German community; this aim, along with *Aufbau*'s vaguely contradictory promotion of Germany as a cultural unit, reflected wider zonal shifts. Becher's lamenting of the loss of 'bester Deutscher' and his combative style paved the way for the portrayal of the Soviet Zone as the assembly point for anti-fascists, free from the guilt of Nazi involvement and entitled therefore to disclaim responsibility.[42] There were few other references to the Jews, and the contribution of Jewish voices was minimal. One reviewer described their situation: 'Die Mehrzahl ist eines qualvollen Todes gestorben, und die Übriggebliebenen starren noch ungläubig aus ihren verweinten Augen in das Licht eines unbarmherzigen Tages. Wie sollen sie da schon Zeugnis ablegen für das, was ihnen geschehen ist?'[43] References to other Nazi victims, for example homosexuals, freemasons, religious groups, were also sparse; Paul Ronge was one of the few commentators in *Aufbau*, or indeed in any of the journals of the time, to mention them.[44]

Much condemnation of National Socialism centred on its racism. In his essay, 'Der Rassenwahn als Feind des menschlichen Fortschritts', Georg Lukács, a frequent contributor in the early editions, followed *Aufbau*'s prescribed formula:

Jedenfalls sind — wissend oder unwissend — breite Schichten durch die Rassentheorie zu aktiven oder passiven Mitschuldigen an den Greueltaten der Nazis geworden; mit Hilfe der Rassentheorie ist der Anschein entstanden, als wäre

---

[41] Johannes R. Becher, 'Deutschland klagt an!', *Aufbau*, 2 (1946), H.1, 9-18.
[42] ibid., (p.11).
[43] Erich Lichtenstein, 'Jüdische Klage', *Aufbau*, 4 (1948), 166-68 (p.166).
[44] Paul Ronge, 'Das Problem der "Anderen"', *Aufbau*, 3 (1947), H.8, 121-24 (p.124).

ein so großes Volk wie das deutsche, ein Volk mit einer so glorreichen Vergangenheit, zu einer Bande von Henkern, Räubern, Mördern und Mordbrennern erniedrigt worden.[45]

Lukács illustrated the spurious nature of this racist philosophy: 'Die Rassentheorie blieb im wesentlichen ein Geheimnis, ein Mysterium, ein Mythos, wenngleich ihr auch ununterbrochen eine dilettantische, pseudowissenschaftliche Begründung zu geben versucht wurde.'[46] He dismissed the theory as 'wissenschaftlich betrachtet, eine lächerliche Karikatur' and concluded that the destruction of Nazism represented 'die Rettung des deutschen Volkes aus seiner tiefsten politischen und moralischen Erniedrigung'.[47]

Within the debate about fascism and its origins, the question arose as to whether there was a 'Volkscharakter' which made the Germans especially vulnerable to anti-Semitism.[48] Citing the Dreyfuss affair in France, Arnold Bauer argued that these tendencies were also manifest in the histories of other nations — not just Germany. He reminded readers of happier things in the past with his eloquent evocation of the contrast: 'Welche Abgründe zwischen den geistigen und moralischen Welten: das durch die Klassik bestimmte Bildungserlebnis des deutschen Bürgers der Goethezeit auf der einen Seite und das neurasthenische Bildungsprotzentum, das der faschistischen Götzendämmerung vorausging, auf der anderen!'[49] Literary decadence was frequently blamed, with certain philosophers and writers (most notably Nietzsche), 'die in dem Bösen [...] Gewalt sehen und loben', figuring prominently.[50] Nietzsche's idea of the 'Supermensch' (sic) was linked to theories of racial supremacy, and one article explored the varying roles of

---

[45] Lukács, 'Der Rassenwahn' (pp.100-01).
[46] ibid., (p.104).
[47] ibid., (pp.105 and 114).
[48] Arnold Bauer, 'Der Einbruch des Antisemitismus im deutschen Denken', *Aufbau*, 2 (1946), H.2, 152-64.
[49] ibid., (p.152).
[50] Ziegenfuß, 'Wozu ist das Böse gut?', (p.709).

Nietzsche, Schiller, Fichte, Langbehn and Moeller van den Bruck in the rise of nationalist thought.[51] On the first anniversary of the foundation of the Kulturbund, Becher again focused on the German character. He maintained that Germans were not essentially different from other peoples. He believed that there was both good and bad in all Germans, producing a kind of split personality. The good German was not free of the disastrous characteristics of the German people, but the bad was not irredeemable. According to Becher, the peculiarity of the German case lay in the combination of events: 'Ist dieser "Zweiseelenkampf" spezifisch deutsch? Nein! Es handelt sich "nur" um eine spezifisch deutsche geschichtlich bedingte Form eines allgemeinen Menschheitsproblems, aber dieses "nur" der spezifisch deutschen Form ist ein besonders tragisches.'[52] Generally, the origins of fascism were presented as entirely political. It was 'ein Kind des Imperialismus'.[53] National Socialism, as its German manifestation, was the reaction of the bourgeoisie to the possibility of socialism in Germany.[54] Both imperialism and fascism were continuously described in the journal as by-products of capitalism. In 1949 it was argued that Germany was still poisoned by imperialism and fascism, and that, consequently, it still presented a danger to itself and to the world.[55] Clearly, the West was the target here and the moral charge of national betrayal now part of their ammunition.

---

[51] Ernst Niekisch, 'Im Vorraum des Faschismus', *Aufbau*, 2 (1946), H.2, 122-37.
[52] Johannes R. Becher, 'Auf eine andere Art so grosse Hoffnung: Rede zum Jahrestag der Gründung des Kulturbundes', *Aufbau*, 2 (1946), H.7, 675-81 (p.679).
[53] Martin Hoffmann, 'Zur Vorgeschichte des Faschismus', *Aufbau*, 2 (1946), H.12, 1187-98 (p.1198).
[54] Alfons Kauffeldt, 'Zurück zum deutschen Bildungsideal', *Aufbau*, 2 (1946), H.1, 31-36 (p.35).
[55] Max Schroeder, 'Zur neuen Lage', *Aufbau*, 5 (1949), H.11, 980-81 (p.981).

Historical accounts

As part of the analysis of Nazism, resistance to it was examined and celebrated. Günther Weisenborn argued that it had to be shown that resistance had existed.[56] He had been a member of the 'Schulze-Boysen-Harnack' resistance group and in an address identified with political prisoners recently released from the Sachsenhausen concentration camp.[57] Particular mention was also made in the journal of both Adam Kuckhoff and Arvid Harnack, and the Rote Kappelle, formed from the co-operation between the Schulze-Boysen-Harnack group and the spy network working for the Russians.[58] Both the Protestant and Catholic Churches were presented as anti-fascist forces. Mostly, such contributions by theologians came with no comment on the part of the editorial staff, but they chose to introduce an article on the Catholic Church as a valuable contribution in the appraisal of the Nazi past and to simultaneously publicize a forthcoming book by Kardinal von Preysing.[59] There was, however, some criticism of the Protestant Church. Whether this can be seen as evidence of the growing gulf between socialism and the Church is unclear; while one might speculate that Lutheranism was more significant than Roman Catholicism in the Eastern Zone and therefore attracted greater suspicion, the early date of this article does not support its use as evidence of deliberate targeting. The author, Aurel von Jüchen, accused the Evangelical Church of narrow-mindedness and self-interest during the Third Reich. He judged it to have been too concerned with the fate of the Church in public life

---

[56] Günther Weisenborn, 'Rede über die deutsche Widerstandsbewegung', *Aufbau*, 2 (1946), H.6, 571-78 (p.571).

[57] Günther Weisenborn, 'Tag und Traum: Aus dem unveröffentlichten Memorial', *Aufbau*, 3 (1947), H.2, 136-49.

[58] See Friedrich Lenz, 'In memoriam', *Aufbau*, 2 (1946), H.12, 1234-38; Adam Kuckhoff, 'Das Weltpanorama: Aus dem Nachlaß', *Aufbau*, 3 (1947), H.8, 108-09; 'Adam Kuckhoff sechzig Jahre — Biographische Notizen', *Aufbau*, 3 (1947), H.8, 110; and Greta Kuckhoff, 'Rote Kappelle', *Aufbau*, 4 (1948), H.1, 30-37.

[59] 'Die nationalsozialistische Christenverfolgung: Kurze Darstellung des Kampfes der katholischen Kirche gegen den Nationalsozialismus', *Aufbau*, 4 (1947), H.10, 236-39.

and not enough with real Christian action. Consequently, its commitment to opposition was also insufficient. This criticism was extended to the Confessing Church, the breakaway resistance group of the Evangelical Church: 'Warum aber hat auch die Bekennende Kirche die im Wesen der Sache liegende Unvereinbarkeit von Christentum und Nationalismus nicht gelehrt? [...] Sie hat vielmehr weithin bedauert, daß der Nationalsozialismus die Kirche aus dem öffentlichen Leben verdrängte.'[60] Jüchen identified the Church's failure as a betrayal of its fundamental tenets: 'Sie hatte vergessen, daß nach Luthers Überzeugung nicht nur die Lehre des "geistlichen", sondern auch des "bürgerlichen Lebens" aus dem Worte Gottes fließt.'[61] It was precisely this acceptance of secular authority that had led to the horrific extent of Germany's wrongdoing. Georg Lukács claimed that the most vehement opposition to racism came from the atheistic communist and the pious Catholic.[62] These two, he suggested, could work together because of the strength of their beliefs. They differed only in advocating different roads towards humanity and equality.

Strategies for Germany's recovery included the merger of political with religious theory. The 1945 article, 'Der Dienst der evangelischen Kirche am Aufbau unseres Volkes', illustrated the early toleration of political comment from religious sources.[63] It saw a political role for the Protestant Church. It was argued that, while ministers of the Church should care for the soul and be above party politics, this did not mean that they should be apolitical. On the contrary, it was clear that 'politische Abstinenz bedeutet historische Impotenz'.[64] The Protestant Church had a particular role to play, and the forces of Christianity and

---

[60] Aurel von Jüchen, 'Protestantismus und Selbstverantwortlichkeit', *Aufbau*, 2 (1946), H.10, 1008-15 (p.1011).
[61] ibid., (p.1012).
[62] Lukács, 'Der Rassenwahn'.
[63] Friedrich Wilhelm Krummacher, 'Der Dienst der evangelischen Kirche am Aufbau unseres Volkes', *Aufbau*, 1 (1945), H.2, 116-22.
[64] ibid., (p.117)

the Reformation would contribute to the renewal of culture: 'Die Erneuerung unserer Kultur wird auch zu einer Neubesinnung auf die positiven und negativen Verflechtungen der deutschen Geschichte, der Kultur und der Literatur mit den Kräften des Christentums und der Reformation führen müssen.'[65] The article ended, 'Die evangelische Kirche gehört, mit ihrem besonderen Auftrag, mit in die Front dieser aufbauwilligen Kräfte!'[66] In these early days, there was considerable effort to marry religion with socialist idealism. One article in particular promoted Christianity as a force which ought to be active alongside socialism.[67] Religious socialists should not be disillusioned; on the contrary, they should be part of the campaign. Any thought of contradiction or conflict was dismissed in the language of partnership. The clear need for co-operation between the two was advanced by considerable theoretical advocacy, including the argument that Christian ethics constituted 'das stärkste Gegengewicht gegen alle Verirrungen und Übersteigerungen politischer Extreme'.[68] Furthermore, this partnership was to be a lasting one, advertised as the force of the future: 'In Harmonie gemeinsam wirkend sind sie die Zukunftsträger.'[69] Nowhere else in *Aufbau* was there such a vivid promotion of Christian belief in society, and the publication of this article as late as 1948 invites speculation as to whether aspirations for plurality were by then desperate or whether this was Eastern Zone window-dressing and, given the appearance in the interim of more overtly political publications, *Aufbau* was still the place for this inclusive approach.

Assessment of recent historical events took place as part of a wider exploration of the German *Sonderweg*. It was not just an abstruse intellectual

---

65 ibid., (p.121).
66 ibid., (p.122).
67 Max Greiner, 'Christentum und Sozialismus: Aus den Lebenserfahrungen eines Pfarrers', *Aufbau*, 4 (1948), H.1, 5-10.
68 ibid., (p.10).
69 ibid.

exercise, but was considered vital to guide the country into the future. According to Ernst Niekisch, German history was full of extreme and short-lived trends in philosophy, and he argued that there was a need for continuity, balance and solidity.[70] Meanwhile, Heinz Gatermann called for the denazification of 'Urgeschichte'. Concepts such as 'Volk, Nation, Rasse, Kultur-, Sprach- und Religionsgruppe', which had been corrupted by National Socialism, had to be rehabilitated.[71] Historical events were used as sources of inspiration for future political action. 1947 was celebrated in the Eastern Zone as marking two anniversaries: the thirtieth anniversary of the October revolution and the twenty-ninth anniversary of the 1918 German revolution. This approach was reflected in the SED propaganda slogan, '2 Revolutionen — 2 Wege'.[72] In 1948, a similar link was made with the revolution of 1848. Alexander Abusch claimed that the bond between the two was the desire for 'eine *klassische demokratische Politik*', and Klaus Gysi argued that urgent attention be given to the lessons of the past: 'es handelt sich diesmal nicht nur um eine einfache Hundertjahrfeier, sondern unser Jahr 1948 liegt, historisch gesehen, im Brennpunkt des Kampfes um die deutsche Einheit und um eine deutsche Demokratie.'[73] Meanwhile, a more subtle change in the dicussion of historical ideas was taking place and more specifically socialist historical theory became more evident. History had to reveal the 'truths' of historical conflict, and in so doing, be redefined.[74] Alexander Abusch's response to Friedrich Meinicke's *Die Deutsche Katastrophe* typified the diverging approaches to historical analysis in East and West.[75] Laying stress on *social* rather than political history, he objected strongly to Meinicke's approach, and in

---

[70] Niekisch, 'Im Vorraum des Faschismus', (p.131).

[71] Heinz Gatermann, 'Rehabilitierung der Urgeschichte', *Aufbau*, 4 (1948), H.7, 559-62 (p.561).

[72] ZPA, SED ZK, Agitation, IV 2/9.02/2.

[73] Alexander Abusch, 'Geistige Folgen der unvollendeten Revolution', *Aufbau*, 4 (1948), H.4, 275-81 (p.280) (Abusch's emphasis); and K. G., '1848-1948', *Aufbau*, 4 (1948), H.1, 1-4 (p.1).

[74] 'Um die Erneuerung des Geschichtsbildes: Ein Streitgespräch zwischen Alexander Abusch, Günther Birkenfeld und Jürgen Kuczynski', *Aufbau*, 3 (1947), H.3, 243-46.

particular to his reference to Germany's potential for becoming 'ein Glied der abendländischen Kulturgemeinschaft'.[76] Abusch regarded this concept of 'Abendland' as symptomatic of dangerous Western historicization. He recommended his own recent book *Der Irrweg einer Nation* as an example of literature which would set the record straight.[77] Emphasis on social history continued in *Aufbau* in an article defining the unhappy aspects of German history as social illness.[78] In this, the work of Jürgen Kuczynski with its references to the class struggle was particularly praised. The author encouraged the adoption of ideological jargon, arguing that, while the terms 'Ausbeutung' and 'Klassenkampf' might be initially off-putting, Kuczynski's work justified their use.[79] In 1947 the journal published a debate in which Kuczynski, Abusch, and Günther Birkenfeld presented varying ideas on historical theory. While Birkenfeld defended 'Ideengeschichte', Kuczynski and Abusch upheld their view that history in general was the history of the masses, whatever the era.[80] Kuczynski advocated the study of economic history as the most directly informative, while Abusch based his argument for historical objectivity on Marx, Engels and Lenin.[81] The Marxist reading of history, the history of class conflict and dialectical materialism, was therefore dominant in this debate. The discussion illustrated the campaign for 'ein neues Geschichtsbild' and is indicative of the ideological convictions gaining currency in the political sphere.[82]

---

[75] Alexander Abusch, 'Die deutsche Katastrophe', *Aufbau*, 3 (1947), H.1, 2-8.
[76] ibid., (p.8).
[77] ibid., (p.6).
[78] Hans W. Aust, 'Die soziale Krankheitsgeschichte des deutschen Volkes', *Aufbau*, 3 (1947), H.2, 156-59.
[79] ibid., (p.159).
[80] 'Um die Erneuerung des Geschichtsbildes', (p.245).
[81] ibid., (pp.244 and 246).
[82] ibid., (p.245).

On politics and ideologies

The regular appearance of Abusch and Kuczynski as contributors lent a sharp political edge to *Aufbau*. Together with Wolfgang Harich, they were amongst the most prominent thinkers behind the political reconstruction in the East, and their cogent intellectual arguments were more powerful than the official communiqués. Abusch had been editor, from 1935 until 1939, of the exile KPD newspaper *Die Rote Fahne*, originally founded in 1918 by Luxemburg and Liebknecht. Kuczynski was a young academic who became increasingly important in the intellectual life of the GDR.[83] Harich, a philosophy lecturer, was later to become a critic of the GDR régime. The appearance of such figures as Abusch, Alfred Meusel and Paul Wiegler on the editorial board during the early years influenced the journal's political development. Bourgeois writers became fewer and communist contributors more prominent as anti-fascist collaboration lost ground. Georg Lukács's early popularity declined after his political reputation suffered in the 1947 'Lukács-Streit'. The mounting tension was acknowledged by Gysi in 1947, when he stated 'daß es heute nicht mehr in erster Linie auf den Kampf gegen die Naziideologie ankommt, sondern auf den Kampf gegen den Marxismus als einer Weltanschauung ganz bestimmter politischer Wirksamkeit und Konsequenz'.[84] By 1948, *Aufbau* had become markedly more partisan.

Perhaps the most telling contribution to the ideological debate between Germans appeared in 1946. Harich's review of Erik Reger's *Union der festen Hand* was not only of the greatest interest in ideological terms; it also revisited old arguments. It represented a personal attack by a German journalist of the East on a German journalist of the West. Reger's text had first appeared in 1931, was then

---

[83] See, for example, Jürgen Kuczynski, 'Warum studieren wir deutsche Wirtschaftsgeschichte?', *Aufbau*, 2 (1946), H.4, 356-61.
[84] Klaus Gysi, 'Überparteilichkeit und Diskussion', *Aufbau*, 3 (1947), H.6, 460-61 (p.460).

banned under Hitler, and was currently being republished by Aufbau-Verlag.[85] To Harich, Reger's book remained 'ein bewundernswürdiges Kunstwerk nüchterner, realistischer Wahrhaftigkeit, eine Analyse der gesellschaftlichen Wirklichkeit'.[86] Harich used the text to illustrate how the working class was responsible, through their disunity, for political developments. Rather than fulfilling Marx's prophesy of their 'historische Sendung', it had again failed through divided leadership of the working population: 'in allen geschichtlich entscheidenden Momenten versagte sie.'[87] The task was now clear, Harich argued; the working class had to unite all the people into a 'demokratischer Block' to fight capitalism.[88] By this time, the merger of the SPD and the KPD in the Eastern Zone had already occurred, but as Harich's piece shows, arguments for unity in socialist effort continued. Harich bitterly criticized Reger for allying himself to the capitalist West after 1945. Reger, Harich stated, 'macht sich zum Anwalt eben jener Kräfte, deren abscheuliche Ziele sein Buch enthüllt'.[89] He attacked Reger's recent rejection of what Harich regarded as the proper conclusions from the teachings of history, judging it 'grotesque' that Reger was now a defender of the Berlin SPD in opposition to the KPD-SPD merger in the East. That merger, Harich insisted, symbolized the unity of the working classes. His disgust emphasizes the perception in the East that the SPD in the West was making the same mistake as before — 'die Aufrechterhaltung der proletarischen Entzweiung'. He argued that the nature of the SPD's failures in both 1918 and 1946 was the same: 'die Vorwände wechselten, die Sache blieb dieselbe.'[90] Harich's call for working class unity found favour in a later article in 1946, entitled 'Demokratisches

---

[85] Wolfgang Harich, 'Union der festen Hand: Einsicht und Konsequenz', *Aufbau*, 2 (1946), H.8, 808-27.
[86] ibid., (p.827).
[87] ibid., (p.821).
[88] ibid., (p.823).
[89] ibid.
[90] ibid., (p.824).

Blocksystem'.[91] Here it was argued that this system was preferable to proportional representation, which reminded Germans of the Weimar Republic and its failure, caused, according to socialist thinkers, by decadent capital-based democracy, and preferable too to any first-past-the-post system.[92] Responding to the Heidelberg campaign against proportional representation, Alfons Steiniger argued that true democracy entailed representation through trades unions and women's, youth and cultural organisations, as well as parties. This would ensure that political parties would not gain a monopoly.[93] Significantly, Ernst Lemmer, the head of the East Berlin CDU, in his article 'Demokratischer Block', also argued for the simplification of the political spectrum, again citing the Weimar years as a warning against a multiplicity of parties.[94] He regretted the 'partikularistische Tendenzen' of 1946 party politics and argued that fragmentation endangered German unity. He expressed the desire to see the Western zones develop along the lines of the Soviet Zone and voiced interest in the 'Verschmelzung' of the two socialist parties.[95] Ironically, implementation of this policy led to the demise of the CDU in East Berlin. In an earlier article, 'Vollzug eines historischen Gesetzes', Lemmer had supported the policy of land reform in a powerful argument for the progressive politics of the Eastern Zone.[96] He based his argument on historical parallels, ruling out all counter-interpretations and concluded that 'das historische Bild ist eindeutig'.[97] Referring to the reactionary influence of land ownership on politics, Lemmer asked:

Kann die Erde, die Deutschland verbleibt, die Deutschen ernähren? Eine der entscheidenden und zugleich primitivsten Fragen unserer Existenz ist gestellt. Der

---

[91] Alfons Steiniger, 'Demokratisches Blocksystem', *Aufbau*, 2 (1946), H.11, 1083-90.
[92] Alfons Steiniger, 'Aktion Heidelberg', *Aufbau*, 3 (1947), H.2, 102-10.
[93] ibid., (p.104).
[94] Ernst Lemmer, 'Demokratischer Block', *Aufbau*, 2 (1946), H.2, 117-21.
[95] ibid., (pp.118-19).
[96] Ernst Lemmer, 'Vollzug eines historischen Gesetzes', *Aufbau*, 1 (1945), H.2, 94-100.
[97] ibid., (p.98).

Entschluß zur Bodenreform ist der Beginn einer Antwort. Er ist nicht einmal das Resultat einer volkswirtschaftlichen oder soziologischen Doktrin. Der Entschluß ist nicht zuletzt ein Akt der Notwehr.[98]

He stated that the four political parties (in the Eastern Zone) agreed on the necessity of the policy. Referring to the misery of different sections of the German population, and particularly of displaced persons, Lemmer sought to enlist general support for what was a controversial communist policy.[99]

Although the general socialist agenda was prominent in *Aufbau*, for instance in its predictable handling of the subject of the trades unions, there was support for a non-party-political attitude, and efforts were made to minimise any display of bias.[100] This was especially evident in the press section, where extracts from other publications, often from the western zones, appeared. Readers were left to draw their own conclusions, although often the selection of these articles was pointed. In the 'Presseschau' of November 1948, an extract from *Frankfurter Hefte* reiterated the appeal of a French archbishop to combat the misery of the working classes.[101] This small section of *Aufbau* provided the most dramatic evidence of the ideological conflict which arose between East and West. Until October 1947 criticism of the West had been moderate. In that month, however, the overtly hostile headline, 'Totalitäre Kulturpolitik im Westen', appeared.[102] This article had been written by Colonel Dymschitz for the Russian daily *Tägliche Rundschau*, and was reprinted without comment. The Nürnberg trials had earlier provoked criticism of the West. There was disappointment that the German people were not allowed access, excluded, it was claimed, because of Western

---

[98] ibid., (p.95).

[99] ibid., (p.100).

[100] Henri Johansen, 'Brücken zur neuen Gesellschaft: die Bedeutung der Gewerkschaften', *Aufbau*, 3 (1947), H.8, 96-100.

[101] Kardinal Gerlier, 'Das Recht auf zureichenden Lohn', *Aufbau*, 4 (1948), H.11, 1013-14.

[102] *Aufbau*, 3 (1947), H.10, 290-93.

decisions.[103] A Soviet approach would have been much more constructive: 'Wenn es nach dem russischen Vorschlag gegangen wäre, dann hätte der Prozeß im Nürnberger Opernhaus stattgefunden — mit 2000 Zuschauern pro Tag. Man möchte es bedauern, daß diese Anregung von den englischen und amerikanischen Juristen abgelehnt wurde, die — vielleicht nicht ganz zu Unrecht — eine Beeinträchtigung der Würde des Gerichts befürchteten.'[104] Now the main criticism was levelled at Western propaganda. Harich objected to the anti-Eastern tone of the West Berlin daily, *Tagesspiegel*, edited by Erik Reger. Allegations appearing there, that the 'Enteignung der Kriegsverbrecher' was 'nazistisch' and that the FDJ was a new version of the HJ, were condemned as contrary to the interests of re-education.[105] In the same issue *Aufbau* published Thomas Mann's condemnation of anti-Bolshevism for the second time.[106] Meanwhile, criticism was directed at the Western brand of denazification. The situation for Jews in West Germany was described as almost worse than 1938; the lifting of the Nürnberg laws had allowed Nazis to reclaim their property and placed Jews and their previous persecutors on an equal footing.[107] Under the ironic pseudonym, 'Marsyas', the editors condemned the use of Ernst Jünger's *Atlantische Fahrt* as a text for German prisoners-of-war in British camps: 'Hurra — der eingefleischte SS-Mann wittert Morgenluft. Wo Jünger spuken darf, da wird auch Dwinger bald nicht fehlen. Und die "Reichskultursenatoren" Blunck und Johst warten nur darauf, durch neue Feldpost- (pardon! Lager-) Ausgaben wieder Leser und Anhänger zu gewinnen.'[108] The reference to Hans Friedrich Blunck and Hans Johst, leading writers of the Third Reich, reveals the already vitriolic nature of charges of Western restoration. The West's later categorization of Erich Edwin Dwinger as 'Mitläufer' was

---

[103] Curt Rieß, 'Grand Hotel Nürnberg', *Aufbau*, 2 (1946), H.2, 138-41.
[104] ibid., (p.141).
[105] Harich, 'Union der festen Hand', (p.825).
[106] Thomas Mann, 'Grundtorheit Bolschewismus', *Aufbau*, 2 (1946), H.8, 855-58.
[107] Werner Ilberg, 'Juden und Fortschritt', *Aufbau*, 3 (1947), H.9, 198-99.

condemned by Gysi.[109] This Nazi writer, tried in the American Zone, was treated leniently after pleading that National Socialism had represented for him a means to fight Bolshevism. Gysi objected that, for two years, the East had had to campaign against 'diesen schamlosen Trick einer Gleichsetzung von Faschismus und Sozialismus'.[110] The Dwinger affair provoked a later, more scathing attack on Western practices of denazification:

Die Geheimnisse der Entnazifizierung in den Westzonen Deutschlands scheinen unerforschlich. Ihre Prinzipien sind ungeklärt, ihre Grundlagen nicht erkennbar. Ihre Durchführung ist barbarisch-bürokratisch. Nur ihre Konsequenzen sind völlig klar. Sie laufen auf die Restauration hinaus.[111]

These followed previous complaints about the West's failure to prosecute anti-Semitic Nazi writers.[112] The most frequently criticized in all this were the British, whose attitude was regarded as light-weight.[113] In 1948 Gysi stated that the campaign for German unity, fronted by the Kulturbund, now had to be waged against the West.[114] Two months later, the *Tagesspiegel* was once more derided as a manipulator of the truth.[115] By 1948 *Aufbau* had identified a specific 'Ideologie der Westzone', characterized by dangerous superficiality.[116] This was due, according to *Aufbau*, to capitalist philosophy. Developments in the West had brought not a unified democratic society, but a 'Bündnis zwischen Junkertum, Militarismus und Großkapitalismus'.[117] Although the West was consistently

---

108 Marsyas, 'Ernst Jünger als Erzieher', *Aufbau*, 3 (1947), H.8, 133-34 (p.134).

109 K. G., 'Symptom', *Aufbau*, 4 (1948), H.8, 639-42 (p.639).

110 ibid.

111 Angelus Hartkopf, '"Mitläufer" Erich Edwin Dwinger', *Aufbau*, 4 (1948), H.9 807-08 (p.807).

112 Hermann Ahrens, 'Anklage gegen Artur Dinter', *Aufbau*, 3 (1947), H.3, 288-90.

113 See, for example, 'Widerstand der Widerspenstigen', *Aufbau*, 3 (1947), H.3, 291-92.

114 Klaus Gysi, 'Neue Entwicklungen', *Aufbau*, 4 (1948), H.7, 545-49 (p.545).

115 P., 'Bilanz von Breslau', *Aufbau*, 4 (1948), H.9, 735-37.

116 Hermann Kastner, 'Nach drei Jahren', *Aufbau*, 4 (1948), H.8, 643-49 (p.644).

117 Karl Obermann, 'Deutsche Säkularfeiern', *Aufbau*, 4 (1948), H.9, 738-44 (pp.743-44).

criticized for its imperialism, it was the German nationals in the West whom *Aufbau* held ultimately responsible for Germany's division. West German figures who appeared at official celebrations in the West, for example Adenauer and Brüning, were derided as representing continuity with the Nazi past.[118] The nature of German leadership in the West led to the expression of concern as to 'wie lange sich das deutsche Volk noch durch Männer repräsentieren läßt, die schon längst ihr Nationalbewußtsein verloren haben und im Auftrag der Besatzungsmächte Deutschland spalten'.[119] The accusation that West Germans represented the interests of the occupation powers rather than those of the German people gave power to the argument that the representation of the German nation and its interests — and above all its unity — was safer in the hands of Germans in the East. An article by Walter Dirks in 1948, entitled 'Ein falsches Europa', published in *Frankfurter Hefte*, precipitated another skirmish. In this article Dirks had expressed fears about effects of the Marshall Plan on Europe, and particularly the overwhelming American influence which might result. *Aufbau* described this as symptomatic of the failure of West German thinkers to preempt such risks: 'Wenn man die Gefahr des Marshall-Planes so klar erkennt, muß man den Zweijahresplan bejahen. Wenn man die Kriegshetze so klar sieht, muß man gemeinsam mit denen arbeiten, die sich für den Frieden erklärten.'[120] Dirks should act on his own conclusions. The journal condemned supporters of the Marshall Plan as 'die Herren der Rüstungsindustrie, der Monopole und Konzerne im Bunde mit Militaristen und Faschisten'.[121] The West German intellectual community was failing its people.

The steadily mounting criticism of the West was in stark contrast to the coverage of the East. Nowhere was there any real critical analysis of the Russian

---

118 ibid., (p.744).
119 ibid.
120 'Ein falsches Europa', *Aufbau*, 4 (1948), H.10, 831-34 (p.834).
121 ibid., (p.831).

occupation or of Russia itself. The journal reflected the Eastern socialist acceptance of the Russians as guides and mentors, and commitment to the Russo-German partnership. The change from collective obedience under the Nazis to collective social responsibility under socialism was proclaimed as a victory for harmonious comradeship, Ernst Bloch urging that 'das Kollektiv des kämpfenden Proletariats ist Protest gegen die privatkapitalistische Aneignung seiner Produktion'.[122] Becher's 1949 'Goethe-Rede', 'Die Freiheit der Persönlichkeit', combined Goethe's teachings with allusions to individual freedom within collective responsibility. Goethe's words were presented as an appropriate slogan of the new era: 'Jedes Lebendige ist kein Einzelnes, sondern eine Mehrheit.'[123] According to Heinrich Mann, the acquisition of true freedom still remained a challenge, despite all that was known about parliamentary forms.[124] Yet *Aufbau*'s attitude was clear. German intellectuals in the East espoused socialist free thinking, while those in the West were already ineffectual.

Enrolling culture

In line with Marxist theory, cultural recovery in eastern Germany was tailored towards the creation of a socialist society. Socialist positivism extended to all areas of the arts, and *Aufbau* reflected this. It also reflected the competing claims of newfound freedom of creativity and the artist's duty to society. The liberation of their country had freed artists from the ideological shackles of the Nazi era and their socialist home in the East, many believed, would make them truly free. They did not acknowledge that their duty to society would require them still to direct their creative effort along specific lines, and that this and the implicit separation from Western society threatened their ideals of freedom and unity. For Eastern

---

[122] Ernst Bloch, 'Ich und Wir', *Aufbau*, 5 (1949), H.9, 785-91 (p.787).

[123] Johannes R. Becher, 'Die Freiheit der Persönlichkeit', *Aufbau*, 5 (1949), H.9, 771-76 (p.773).

[124] Heinrich Mann, 'Ein Volk begreift seine Freiheit', *Aufbau*, 5 (1949), H.9, (p.777).

artists, the eternal 'Kampf zwischen den schöpferischen Künstlern und der dekadenten Ideologie der Bourgeoisie' was over, and they could turn their minds to the future: 'In der heutigen Zeit tritt die Menschheit in eine neue Periode ihrer Entwicklung ein, in der entsprechend neue Perspektiven für die Kunst auftauchen.'[125] There was a sense of pioneering, and a camaraderie in promoting altruism. The opening up of new vistas for the arts was regarded as crucial for the rebirth of the culture, Uhse referred to 'ein neues Kunstbedürfnis'; composer Hanns Eisler called for a 'new and different' music to reflect the new society.[126] The superior level of artistic endeavour in the Soviet Union was indicative of that country's superior social and political morality: 'die Volkskunst [...] ist auf einer höheren sozialen Stufe.'[127] This was contrasted with the artistic reflection of the perceived decadence of capitalist states: 'Hingegen ist das Streben nach Volkstümlichkeit in den hochkapitalistischen Ländern nichts als der Wunsch nach möglichst leichter Verständlichkeit.'[128] Art and culture in the West were simplistic and reflected social failure. Eisler's view was shared by André Bonnard. In the West, Bonnard argued, literature and art opposed society, the root cause lying in its very disorder.[129] He conjured up the vision of a harmonious Eastern socialist community and compared it with the artist/authority conflict in the West. In his view, the artist had a responsibility to promote peaceful co-existence.[130] Later in the same article, Bonnard's veneration of Soviet writers verged on the dogmatic. In reply to the suggestion that a writer in a communist state should refrain from propaganda, he asked why should he, (when) he knows he is right. Bonnard

---

125 See Max Schröder, 'Renaissance des Realismus?', *Aufbau*, 5 (1949), H.3, 209-17 (p.209); and Hanns Eisler, 'Hörer und Komponist', *Aufbau*, 5 (1949), H.3, 200-08 (p.200) respectively.

126 Bodo Uhse, 'Von der Bedeutung des Auftrags', *Aufbau*, 5 (1949), H.3, 224-31 (p.230); Eisler, 'Hörer und Komponist', (p.200).

127 Eisler, 'Hörer und Komponist', (p.205).

128 ibid.

129 André Bonnard, 'Von den Russen und von den Griechen', *Aufbau*, 5 (1949), H.3, 233-35.

130 ibid., (p.234).

promoted the writer to the role of evangelist: 'Der Schriftsteller hat die Aufgabe, das Volk zu erziehen.'[131]

The difficulties facing German writers in the contemporary climate were vividly expressed by Wolfgang Weyrauch:

> Nach 1945 ist alles auseinandergefallen. Die Realität, das Unmittelbare darin. Die Sprache wird sich zweifellos anschließen. Wirklichkeit und Sprache zu bündeln, sie beide mit den Katarakten der uns umgebenden Erde zu kommunizieren, wird eine höllische Aufgabe für die deutschen Schriftsteller und Dichter sein. Die Aufgabe wird leichter sein, wenn sie bedenken, daß auch dies eine Wiedergutmachung ist.[132]

Within the climate of accusation and shame, who should write and who should not was a further problem. *Aufbau* largely celebrated exile literature.[133] This was not surprising, as many influential members of the Eastern community, and of the journal's staff, had been in exile during the Nazi years. The émigré community as a whole was regarded as representative of the 'other' Germany. Uhse himself had been acclaimed in the journal as the writer of one of the few great anti-Nazi novels, *Leutnant Bertram*, alongside Anna Seghers and her celebrated exile work, *Das siebte Kreuz*.[134] Experience of exile was presented as a positive and formative influence. Annie Voigtländer alluded to Feuchtwanger's opinion that exile writers had become wiser and 'renewed'; for him life in exile was 'jenes Stirb und Werde'.[135] This allusion to Goethe evoked the classical tradition so important to the cultural revival, and such allusions helped to create a mythology around these

---

131 ibid., (p.235).

132 Wolfgang Weyrauch, 'Realismus des Unmittelbaren', *Aufbau*, 2 (1946), H.7, 701-06 (p.706). See also Wolfgang Weyrauch, 'Neue Lyrik', *Aufbau*, 2 (1946), H.12, 1246-50; and Stephan Hermlin, 'Wo bleibt die junge Dichtung?' *Aufbau*, 3 (1947), H.11, 340-43.

133 See, for example, Paul E. H. Lüth, 'Deutsche Dichtung in der Verbannung', *Aufbau*, 3 (1947), H.9, 207-09.

134 Alexander Abusch, 'Deutsche Menschen unter Hitler: Zu Bodo Uhses Roman "Leutnant Bertram"', *Aufbau*, 3 (1947), H.11, 359-60.

135 A. Voigtländer, 'Von Büchern und Autoren', *Aufbau*, 5 (1949), H.3, 278-82.

exiles. *Aufbau* supported not just 'outer' but 'inner' émigrés, and foresaw a role for both in the new literature. Abusch in particular heralded a 'Zusammenfluß der beiden, während zwölf Jahren getrennten Ströme der deutschen Literatur'.[136] Inner émigrés published in *Aufbau* included Manfred Hausmann and Ernst Wiechert, and one of the heroes of German literature in the Eastern Zone, Gerhart Hauptmann. On Hauptmann's death in 1946, there were generous tributes to him, even from such official sources as the Kulturbund, despite his controversial role during the Third Reich.[137] There were, however, limits to this advocacy on behalf of inner émigrés. Abusch felt it necessary to qualify his definition of inner emigration: he accepted the sincerity of the inner émigrés provided they actually merited that description — 'soweit sie diesen Namen zu Recht tragen'.[138] He rejected literature which had turned its back on reality: 'Die Grenze der Inneren Emigration verschwamm dort, wo sie literarisch zur einfachen Flucht in eine weltfremde Innerlichkeit ward.'[139] Sensitivity to fascist backgrounds could, however, flare up, as when Wilhelm Raabe prize was awarded in Braunschweig to Werner Bergengruen and Ina Seidel. Bergengruen's conversion to Catholicism had caused his exclusion from the Reichsschrifttumskammer in 1937 and he was therefore exonerated. But Seidel had written verse honouring Hitler, and although she expressed regret, *Aufbau* protested that her active involvement in the Third Reich should have excluded her from being awarded the prize.[140] *Aufbau* published (apparently at the behest of readers) the statement of support for the Reich signed in 1933 by 88 writers, among them Gottfried Benn.[141] Frank Thieß

---

[136] Alexander Abusch, 'Die Begegnung: Die innere und die äußere Emigration in der deutschen Literatur', *Aufbau*, 3 (1947), H.10, 223-26 (p.226).
[137] See *Aufbau*, 2 (1946), H.6, 551-52; and C. F. W. Behl, Ivo Hauptmann and Gerhart Pohl, 'Letzter deutscher Klassiker: Bekenntnisse zu Gerhart Hauptmann', *Aufbau*, 2 (1946), H.11, 1091-98.
[138] Abusch, 'Die Begegnung', (p.225).
[139] ibid.
[140] Lukian (Gerhart Pohl), 'Im Zeichen Wilhelm Raabes?', *Aufbau*, 4 (1948), H.10, 905-06.
[141] 'Kundgebung deutscher Schriftsteller', *Aufbau*, 2 (1946), H.9, 972.

rebutted criticism of inner émigrés by attacking exiles, including Thomas Mann.[142] Yet questions raised at the time about Thieß, Ernst Jünger and Dwinger contributed to the impression that *Aufbau* had modified its support for inner émigrés. Jünger remained the most controversial figure in this debate. Harich was scathing about this writer's attempts to justify his war-time activities and accused him of trivialising the legacy of National Socialism: 'Jünger versenkt die deutsche Schuld in einer mystischen Weltschuld, stempelt den Krieg zum "allgemeinen Werk der ganzen Menschheit".'[143] *Aufbau* opposed his immediate acceptance into the new German society: his suggestion of a 'Paneuropa' was, it was said, reminiscent of past nationalism; he regarded fascism and Bolshevism as related phenomena; and he lobbied for a 'Westblock' against the Soviet Union, with Germany as a buffer zone.[144] Jünger's literary themes of 'Liebe, Frömmigkeit und "metaphysischer Stärkung"' were further reasons to question his thinking and intentions.[145] The core question remained, 'Hat der Nihilist Ernst Jünger sich wirklich gewandelt?'[146]

Of all the 'acceptable' writers of the time, Becher was pre-eminent. The second issue published his poem 'Heimkehr', which accepted the guilt of the German people ('Ich halte über meine Zeit Gericht, | Wobei mein "Schuldig!" auch mich schuldig spricht'). The poem clearly portrays his nostalgia for his homeland during his exile years in Russia:

Wenn ich ein Trümmerland auch wiederfand,
Bist du es doch, mein Deutschland, Vaterland.

---

142 Frank Thieß, 'Frank Thieß an Johannes R. Becher'; and Alexander Abusch, 'Antwort an Frank Thieß', *Aufbau*, 4 (1948), H.5, 454-55 and 455-56 respectively.

143 Wolfgang Harich, 'Ernst Jünger und der Frieden', *Aufbau*, 2 (1946), H.6, 556-70 (p.565).

144 ibid., (p.568).

145 Klaus Herrmann, 'Ernst Jünger und der deutsche Nihilismus', *Aufbau*, 4 (1948), H.1, 42-51, (p.51).

146 ibid.

Fand ich dich auch verarmt und sterbensbleich,
Bist du es doch: Deutschland, mein Märchenreich.

Fand ich dich auch verhärmt und ohne Ruh,
Bist du es doch: Heimat und Mutter du![147]

His style contrasted with the deliberate avoidance of pathos found at this time among younger or 'inner exile' writers. The use of patriotic and mystical references was apparently acceptable from progressive sources.

The reclamation of literature from the German past was an important cultural theme. Using past heroes provided role-models without creating unfamiliarity. Using the words of Schiller, *Aufbau* cited Jakob and Wilhelm Grimm's opposition to an absolutist monarch as an example for the German people of 'bei uns leider so seltenen Männerstolz vor Königsthronen'.[148] The journal sought to restore Heine's reputation by exposing the 'falsche These' that Heine had no love for Germany.[149] Forgotten heroes were rehabilitated. Fritz Reuter was praised as a 'Volksdichter' and 'Freiheitskämpfer'. He joined the ranks of standard-bearers for the cultural revival: 'Scott, Dickens und Irving, [...] Heine und Hauptmann, Puschkin und Dostojewski, Tolstoi, Gogol und Maxim Gorki'.[150] Justus Moeser, a little-known contemporary of Goethe, was praised as a 'Vorkämpfer der Demokratie' and described as 'nicht nur ein glänzender Erzähler, sondern ein Erzieher der Deutschen zu volkstümlicher Demokratie und damit ein wirklicher Humanist'.[151] Literary criticism provided a vehicle for political theory. Lukács twice used Goethe's *Faust* as a source of political education: firstly, to

---

[147] Johannes R. Becher, 'Heimkehr', *Aufbau*, 1 (1945), H.2, 172-74.
[148] Introduction to Ferdinand Deml, 'Jakob Grimm über seine Entlassung', *Aufbau*, 3 (1947), H.7, 57.
[149] Heinrich Heine, 'Deutschland und die Deutschen', *Aufbau*, 2 (1946), H.1, 79-83.
[150] Willi Finger, 'Fritz Reuters nachgelassenes Werk: Herr von Hakensterz und seine Leibeigenen', *Aufbau*, 4 (1948), H.9, 771-76 (p.776).
[151] Raimund Pissin, 'Vorkämpfer der Demokratie: Justus Moeser', *Aufbau*, 2 (1946), H.9, 928-30 (p.930).

explore the social aspects of Gretchen's fall; and secondly, to contribute to the debate on capitalism.[152] Goethe was by far the most prominent literary figure in *Aufbau*'s recall of the humanistic tradition. Becher referred to Goethe as 'der Dichter, der Seher, und der Erzieher deutscher Nation' and highlighted the 'Sendung' Goethe had perceived for the German people: 'Weltempfangend und weltbeschenkend, die Herzen offen jeder fruchtbaren Bewunderung, groß durch Verstand und Liebe, durch Mittlertum und Geist —, so sollten sie sein, und das ist ihre Bestimmung; nicht als Original-Nation sich zu verstocken, in abgeschmackter Selbstbetrachtung und Selbstverherrlichung sich zu verdummen und gar in Dummheit herrschen über die Welt.'[153] Goethe's importance to the journal was reflected in the fact that a whole issue was devoted to him.[154] Schiller also was revered, Lutz Besch praising his work for its breadth, its exploration of freedom within society, and its exposure of the dilemma between political desire and political reality.[155] The literature of the generation that had lived through the Nazi years, the 'Zwischengeneration', was also part of the cultural inheritance. Gerhart Pohl provocatively described this as 'Magischer Realismus' and defined it as realism with a certain mythical, mystical or irrational touch.[156] His analysis sparked controversy, as this irrational element seemed to be at odds with realism, and moreover suggested a similarity to Nazi literature, but by referring to the influence of cultural inheritance, he could argue that this literature was acceptable: 'Ihr geistiger und sittlicher Gehalt entstammte dem humanistischen deutschen Erbe: Christentum, Weimarer Humanität, Sozialismus.'[157] The crucial reference to

---

[152] Georg Lukács, 'Die Gretchen-Tragödie', *Aufbau*, 2 (1946), H.9, 904-16; and 'Faust und Mephistopheles' *Aufbau*, 3 (1947), H.7, 33-48.
[153] Becher, 'Auf eine andere Art', (p.681).
[154] See, for example, Heinz-Winfried Sabais, 'Goethe in dieser Zeit', *Aufbau*, 4 (1948), H.8, 664-68.
[155] Lutz Besch, 'Der politische Schiller', *Aufbau*, 4 (1948), H.12, 1048-52.
[156] Gerhart Pohl, 'Magischer Realismus?', *Aufbau*, 4 (1948), H.8, 650-53.
[157] ibid., (p.651); and 'Leserstimmen' in next two numbers, for example 'Hat magischer Realismus Gegenwartswert?', H.10, 923-26.

the heritage of German humanist culture was clearly emerging as the key cultural policy of Eastern Germany. This development reflected the literary alignment with communist theory in the repetition of certain key themes compatible with socialist ideals and in the clear message that writers contributed to socialist-democratic thought. As well as underlining the role of writers in the new socialist community, these trends created a point of reference for subsequent literary criticism.

For *Aufbau*, the key inspiration for literary endeavour was the German humanistic tradition. In his speech to the Writers' Congress in 1947, reprinted in *Aufbau*, Becher referred to the task and hope of the Germans — 'das Vermächtnis unserer großen deutschen Tradition [zu] erfüllen'.[158] He argued that the young generation should be largely absolved from guilt by the occupation authorities so that it could move on.[159] The dearth of new young writers was identified by Stephan Hermlin: 'Wo bleibt die junge Dichtung?'.[160] In an effort to overcome the problem, Manfred Hausmann warned the older generation against telling the younger what to do: 'Erwachsene mit erhobenem Zeigefinger, besserwissende, schulmeisternde Erwachsene sind ihnen einfach ein Greuel. Heute mehr als je'.[161] One new writer who did emerge was the Brandenburg poet Peter Huchel, who was described as following in the footsteps of Becher and Brecht.[162] This lineage clearly heralded his political suitability, and Huchel was indeed soon a hero of East German literature. One contributor, now obscure, was effusively welcomed by *Aufbau* as representing both the young generation and humanism.[163] The quest for

---

158 Johannes R. Becher, 'Vom Willen zum Frieden', *Aufbau*, 3 (1947), H.11, 321-32 (p.321).
159 ibid.
160 Hermlin, 'Wo bleibt die junge Dichtung?'.
161 Hausmann, 'Jugend zwischen gestern und morgen', (p.667).
162 Ernst Reißig, 'Der Lyriker Peter Huchel', *Aufbau*, 5 (1949), H.11, 1013-18 (p.1017).
163 Heinz-Winfried Sabais, 'Vom klassischen zum modernen Humanismus (1)', *Aufbau*, 2 (1947), H.8, 75-81.

literary inspiration went hand in hand with attempts to inspire the nation's young.[164]

Alfons Kauffeldt argued that educated youth had a special role in political responsibility: 'wir alle und insbesondere die Studenten müssen die zentrale Bedeutung des Politischen erkennen'.[165] He drew a distinction between the concept of democracy in bourgeois and in socialist societies: 'So notwendig es nun für uns ist, die Demokratie bürgerlicher Prägung eingehend zu studieren, so notwendig ist es, auch die Demokratie sozialistischer Prägung, so wie sie in Rußland Gestalt angenommen hat, kennenzulernen und zu studieren'.[166] His conclusion was that socialism was the only option. He added that there was a need in society for 'geistige Führung', whose continuity would be ensured by the education of a further 'geistige Elite'.[167] This description of Party and leaders is not unusual, yet the terms remain striking in their ideological implications.

Major developments in contemporary thought were interpreted by *Aufbau* in the context of socialism. For instance, significant space was devoted to the changing role of women in Eastern Germany. *Aufbau* reminded its female readers of women's contribution to anti-Nazi resistance and urged them to play their part in the construction of a new democratic Germany.[168] It recommended August Bebel's *Die Frau und der Sozialismus* as 'ein Lehrbuch'.[169] It presented Russian women as role-models. Edith Krull noted that the Russian Revolution had enabled

---

164 See, for example, Dr. Alfons Kauffeldt, 'Deutsche Jugend: Versuch einer Analyse', *Aufbau*, 2 (1946), H.6, 648-52.
165 Kauffeldt, 'Zurück zum deutschen Bildungsideal', (pp.31 and 34).
166 ibid., (pp.34-35).
167 ibid., (pp.35-36).
168 See Elfriede Paul, 'Frauen aus der Widerstandsbewegung', *Aufbau*, 3 (1947), H.2, 172-73; Helmut Vogt, 'Was wir den Frauen schuldig blieben', *Aufbau*, 3 (1947), H.7, 60-62; and Charlotte Heinrichs, 'Die Frau im Neubau der Gesellschaft', *Aufbau*, 2 (1946), H.12, 1264-65.
169 Review of Bebel's *Die Frau und der Sozialismus*, *Aufbau*, 4 (1948), H.1, 80-81.

women to become active in the literary scene.[170] Russian literature in general was praised as a 'school for life', with its didactic element as important as its artistic one.[171] Articles and features on Turgenev, Gorky and Ehrenburg widened exposure. In January 1948, the 'Presseschau' section featured a debate about Socialist Realism. A cynical Western view of the term was countered by an article demonstrating the humanistic, progressive aims of Socialist Realism.[172] French literature presented an opportunity to learn from past events (as, for example in an article stressing the lessons of the French Revolution).[173] It also offered a source of humanist writing and anti-fascist campaigning. Romain Rolland's homage to Lenin established the link between progressive French thought and socialism seen also, it was stated, in such writers as Baudelaire, Éluard, Valéry and Balzac.[174] Paul Wiegler's focus on the 'Repräsentanten des französischen Geistes' further elevated the reputation of French cultural tradition in eastern Germany.[175] Sartrian Existentialism and the wider phenomenon of nihilism, however, caused problems. Existentialism was of considerable contemporary interest, but was incompatible with the tenets of communism. Sartrian nihilism was presented as an 'extreme' variety of individualism, and the mystical retreat into the soul or ego which this entailed, had to be exposed.[176] Herbert Jhering argued that attention should be given to existentialist literature, and the plays of Sartre and Anouillh be performed, so that the advantages of the opposite, 'positivism', would be clearly

---

[170] Edith Krull, 'Die Stimme der Frau in der neuen russischen Dichtung', *Aufbau*, 4 (1948), H.9, 754-60.

[171] Michael Hell, 'Wege in literarisches Neuland', *Aufbau*, 4 (1948), H.7, 563-68.

[172] 'Um den sozialistischen Realismus: Eine Diskussion in Berliner Zeitungen', *Aufbau*, 4 (1948), H.1, 84-87.

[173] Karl Obermann, 'Deutsche Jugend zur Zeit der Französischen Revolution', *Aufbau*, 2 (1946), H.7, 687-701.

[174] See Romain Rolland, 'Lenin', *Aufbau*, 2 (1946), H.2, 165-68; and *Aufbau*, 4 (1948), H.1, 23-29 and 70-73.

[175] Paul Wiegler, 'Repräsentanten des französischen Geistes', *Aufbau*, 4 (1948), H.6, 486-90.

[176] D. Müller-Hegemann, 'Psychotherapie in der modernen Gesellschaft', *Aufbau*, 5 (1949), H.9, 817-30 (p.829).

discernible.[177] *Aufbau* saw Existentialism and nihilism as essentially decadent, and, to emphasize their danger, published an article from a New York journal which criticized the nihilism of existentialist philosophers as perilous to the development of post-war order.[178] Further rejection of individualism was contained in an article on psychotherapy, where regret was expressed that the work of Freud had not been used to improve the life of the working class.[179] People should be taught that psychological problems were manifestations of social rather than individual illness. It was alleged that the problems afflicting American society had at their root the 'niedere Instinkte' that were by-products of capitalism (pornography, mass psychosis, lynch justice and warmongering), and that the management of these problems did not recognize these aetiological factors. In Russia, by contrast, diagnosis and treatment were rightly based on social analysis.[180] This approach had led to community support within education, professional and marriage advisory services, and youth organisations.[181] The humanistic standards of the East were thus superior, and a partnership with Russia desirable.

To Herbert Jhering, Becher already symbolized this partnership: 'Jetzt, in den zwölf Jahren, schufen das Erlebnis Sowjetrußland und das Erlebnis Deutschland eine der ergreifendsten Entwicklungen der Literaturgeschichte.'[182] In Western Germany, Jhering claimed, 'nazistische Restbestände' and 'ein militärischer Geist' persisted.[183] He expressed anxiety that Zuckmayer's *Des Teufels General* would be misunderstood and encourage denial of responsibility. His message was clear: such attitudes could be induced by literature. By 1949,

---

[177] Herbert Jhering, 'Entscheidungsjahre des deutschen Theaters: Rede vor den Intendanten der Ostzone', *Aufbau*, 4 (1948), H.9, 777-87, (p.784).
[178] J. Alvarez del Vayo, 'Die Existenzialphilosophie und ihre politischen Folgen', *Aufbau*, 2 (1946), H.11, 1158-61.
[179] Müller-Hegemann, 'Psychotherapie', (p.820).
[180] ibid., (p.826).
[181] ibid., (p.828).
[182] H. Jh., 'Julius Hay und das deutsche Theater', *Aufbau*, 1 (1945), H.2, 189-92.
[183] Jhering, 'Entscheidungsjahre des deutschen Theaters', (p.778).

there was condemnation of the whole Western literary scene and of a system which was said to commission and produce literature for mass consumption, thereby lowering the quality of that literature, the population's expectations and degrading the role of the writer.[184]

Unity

Above all, *Aufbau* was devoted to German unity. Together with the political planks of socialism — land reform, reversal of bourgeois education, state ownership — unity featured as a clear political aim. Revered by Eastern commentators for the intellectual integrity of its pursuit of 'konsequente Demokratisierung', *Aufbau* also managed to convey an almost spiritual longing for unity.[185] *Aufbau*'s role in the pursuit of national unity was reinforced at a meeting of the Kulturbund Präsidialrat in October 1945. At this meeting members expressed their concern that, in the absence of national consensus, the overall political situation might dissolve into chaos. Fears were even expressed that the Kulturbund itself might appear divided. Although some members felt that the Kulturbund's thrust should be wider, to include for example the production of a twice-monthly aimed at a Western market and to present a less rigid view of the Eastern movement, the majority were against dilution of representation, provided at that point by *Aufbau*.[186] The Präsidialrat decided that preservation of unity was more important than a partisan stance: 'Wir wollen die Einheit Deutschlands unter allen Umständen als geistige Einheit repräsentieren durch unsere Zeitschrift'.[187] Cultural unity was essential for the promotion of peace, and *Aufbau* was the best

---

[184] Franz Joseph Pootmann,'Das Elend der Literatur in Westdeutschland', *Aufbau*, 5 (1949), 976-79.
[185] Dieter Noll, 'Vorwort', in *Aufbau Berlin 1945-1958: Bibliographie einer Zeitschrift*, ed. by Dieter Noll (Berlin and Weimar: Aufbau, 1978), pp.5-28 (p.7).
[186] KA, 907, PR-Protokolle 1945, 'PR Sitzung 17.10.45', sheet 96.
[187] ibid., sheet 98 (Becher's words).

journal to pursue this: 'Der "Aufbau" ist eine Zeitschrift, die weder östlich, westlich, südlich, nördlich, noch irgendwie anders orientiert ist, als auf Deutschland.'[188] Applications to produce local journals in Thüringen, Sachsen and Schwerin were thus rejected, and distribution of the journal in the West was recommended as an essential step towards the maintaining of cultural unity. The Präsidialrat urged maximum co-operation between *Aufbau* and the Kulturbund and recommended that the journal try to attract a wide range of contributors from all over Germany as well as from abroad.[189] The journal tried to achieve this primarily by fostering communication between the cultural sectors of both East and West Germany. From 1945 until 1949, its publishing of Western press articles in 'Presseschau' conveyed some effort towards a national balance. In 1949 its 'Rundfrage' engaged writers from East and West in discussion of East and West. Pursuing unity, according to Becher, would set the best example for the youth of tomorrow.[190] Unity could not be achieved by individuals, but by a community: 'Es müssen viele, es müssen alle, es muß ganz Deutschland sein. Und es muß ein in sich einiges, einheitliches Deutschland sein.'[191] Despite *Aufbau*'s avowed non-partisanship, promotion of unity as stemming from the East in fact formed part of the political campaign against the West. The West was presented as the bringer of division. It was running a campaign of insult and belligerence, evidence not only of insatiable warmongering, but also of immature statesmanship. Zweig indicted these as 'infantile' forces.[192] Comparing the behaviour of the West to that of primitive communities, he argued that the central dynamic in this behaviour was narcissism: 'Das Kampfgeschrei gegen den Bolschewismus [...] befriedigt aufs

---

188 ibid.
189 ibid., 96-98.
190 Becher, 'Auf eine andere Art', (p.680).
191 ibid., (p.681).
192 Arnold Zweig, 'Spaltgeist', *Aufbau*, 5 (1949), H.3, 195-97 (p.196).

tiefste den Narzismus.'[193] He reminded readers that 'Deutschlands Unglück begann immer mit Deutschlands Spaltungen' — a warning reiterated by Bodo Uhse, who blamed past disunity for the flourishing of National Socialism.[194] Gysi argued that the disunity imposed by the West was encouraging the appearance of anti-democratic forces: 'Das Wiederaufleben antihumanistischer Strömungen, ihr zunehmender Einfluß auf die Kulturpolitik in den Westzonen wäre nicht möglich gewesen ohne die Zerreißung Deutschlands.'[195] Gysi argued that the Western 'Tendenz zur Zerreißung' was already evident in the series of divisive reforms which had taken place: 'Das Verbot des Kulturbundes in den westlichen Sektoren Berlins war der Beginn einer Entwicklung, die über den Versuch einer Spaltung der Universität, einer Spaltung der Gewerkschaften bis zur Spaltung der Währung in Berlin führte.'[196] Presented in direct contrast was the 'vorbildliche, beispielhafte demokratische Kulturarbeit' of the East.

Aufbau continued to plead for peace and unity. In July 1949, it embarked on a series of conversations between East and West on the subject of peace.[197] This ongoing 'Gespräch' was later described by Max Schroeder as a genuine effort to achieve dialogue and unity in face of the onslaught from the West.[198] He blamed Bonn for bringing about new division with the establishment of a government. The East's reciprocal move was a necessary response to this, but was described as temporary.[199] He insisted that, as permanent peace depended on German unity, the East was still determined to oppose division.[200] In October 1949 Bodo Uhse repeated the accusation that the West Germans, and not the

---

193 ibid., (pp.196-97).
194 ibid., (p.195); and Schroeder, 'Zur neuen Lage', (p.980).
195 Gysi, 'Neue Entwicklungen', (p.545).
196 ibid., (p.548).
197 'Gespräch um den Frieden', *Aufbau*, 5 (1949), H.7, 646-57.
198 Schroeder, 'Zur neuen Lage', (p.980).
199 ibid.
200 ibid.

Allies, were ultimately responsible for the country's division. In his view, they should have seized the political initiative after the Western Allies had failed to embrace unity at the Paris conference: 'Es ist ein wohl merkwürdiges, weit mehr aber noch erschreckendes Symptom, daß die maßgeblichen politischen Kräfte Westdeutschlands diese geringe Chance zu selbständigem nationalem Handeln nicht wahrnehmen wollten.'[201] Alongside this essay, *Aufbau* published another in its series, 'Frieden und Einheit', in which Reinhold Schneider disputed the harsh judgement on western politicians as undeserved.[202] *Aufbau* gave tacit support to this, suggesting that representatives from all over Germany, if given the chance, could provide proper leadership: 'Wollte man auf allen Seiten ernstlich ein Gesamtdeutschland wahrhaben, fiele es nicht schwer, aus West und Ost die zuverlässige deutsche Stimme zu bilden, die mit den Siegern das Gespräch über einen ehrlichen Frieden beginnen könnte.'[203] Even with *Aufbau*'s announcement of the new German Democratic Republic, the journal's call to peace and unity was repeated. In the same issue, there was a contribution from the West on 'das Herz Europas'. This article, resonant with the fear of war and concern that Germany might starve, reminded readers that recent developments were not irreversible and promoted the middle ground ideal of a 'Vermittlerrolle' for Germany.[204] *Aufbau*'s aspirations for peace and unity were expressed by its editor, Uhse, who urged that there had to be co-operation — 'schließen wir uns wie Brüder zusammen'.[205]

Aufbau's high-profile campaign for German unity continued even after 1949, when it became a campaign for the *re*-establishment of German unity — '*Wieder*herstellung der deutschen Einheit'.[206] Despite the sectarian rhetoric in

---

201 Bodo Uhse, 'Betrachtung zur Zeit', *Aufbau*, 5 (1949), H.10, 867-74 (p.868).
202 Reinhold Schneider, 'Die Macht des Gewissens', *Aufbau*, 5 (1949), H.10, 875-77 (p.875).
203 Emil Belzner, 'Die große Gegenprüfung', *Aufbau*, 5 (1949), H.10, 883-84 (p.884).
204 Hulda Pankok, 'Das Herz Europas', *Aufbau*, 5 (1949), H.11, 965-69 (p.965).
205 Uhse, 'Betrachtung zur Zeit', (p.874).
206 Noll, 'Vorwort', p.6 (my italics).

which the whole concept had become entrapped something more profound could be detected. *Aufbau*'s editor, Uhse, maintained that achievement of unity would restore the honour of the German name, and was, therefore, a national duty.[207]

The idea of unity within Europe was presented as simply an extension of the unity of Germany. Logically, if Germany were divided, Europe would be also. One contributor, Paul Distelbarth, described much of the discussion as nonsensical; as long as Russia and America were at odds, there would be a European problem, and consequently a German problem.[208] He declared that a new European order had to be created and that a unified Europe would have a role to play in the nuclear power game. As a 'dritte Kraft', Europe could prevent a build-up of dangerous tensions.[209] The Bavarian writer, Johannes Tralow, stated that for the Germans to have to choose East or West was wrong — there was, as he put it, 'eine dritte Entscheidung'.[210] Ulrich Noack argued that only neutrality could now reverse the fact that there were two Europes.[211] Another contributor stated that Germany was the heart of Europe — 'Hört es auf zu schlagen, ist Europa tot'.[212] Arnold Zweig declared 'Wir sind Europäer und heute mehr als Europäer' — an avowal which acknowledged the change in German self-perception from aggressor to new citizen.[213]

The tragic incompatibility of the journal's campaign for unity with its approval of the new eastern state and its criticism of the West, was striking. In October 1949 its series 'Frieden und Einheit' was advertised as 'Ein Gespräch zwischen Ost und West', in November as 'Deutsche aus West und Ost sprechen zur neuen Lage'. In both issues, *Aufbau* continued its pursuit of German unity and

---

207 Uhse, 'Betrachtung zur Zeit', (p.874).
208 Paul H. Distelbarth, 'Frieden und Einheit', *Aufbau*, 5 (1949), H.10, 877-83 (p.882).
209 ibid.
210 Johannes Tralow, Die Wunde an der Elbe', *Aufbau*, 5 (1949), H.11, 969-72 (p.970).
211 Ulrich Noack, 'Die Neutralisierung Deutschlands', *Aufbau*, 5 (1949), H.5, 404- 10 (p.404).
212 Pankok, 'Das Herz Europas', (p.965).
213 Arnold Zweig, 'Worte an die Freunde', *Aufbau*, 4 (1948), H.11, 928-34 (p.932).

dialogue between East and West, yet also celebrated the birth of the new republic. This echoed its earlier challenge — 'der Aufbau eines neuen Deutschland und die Wahrung der deutschen Einheit'.[214] *Aufbau* welcomed in the GDR just as it had opened its first issue, with a Becher poem. 'Der Staat' heralded 'Ein Reich des Menschen und ein Menschen-Staat'.

Aufbau continued in publication until 1958. Its last issue emphasized how its own history charted the creation of socialist Eastern Germany. Fittingly, it concluded with a tribute to Becher:

> Wir trauern um Johannes R. Becher,
> den großen Dichter des Friedens,
> der uns lehrte,
> den Krieg zu hassen
> und den Frieden zu erzwingen.[215]

Comment

Created as the organ of the Kulturbund, *Aufbau* was designed to assist the cultural recovery, and its intellectual character became in many ways synonymous with this political function. To communist sympathisers, *Aufbau* represented the successful application of their ideals to the task of creating a new German culture: 'Die Zeitschrift "Aufbau" war von Anfang an von größter Bedeutung im Kampf um den Aufbau einer neuen deutschen Kulturbewegung.'[216] To intellectuals who declared their allegiance to humanism, it symbolized political-cultural renaissance: 'Aufbau est véritablement le porte-parole de la nouvelle Allemagne humaniste, et mériterait l'audience internationale la plus large.'[217] The journal illustrates the early idealism, but also the firm grip which the communists — Russian and German — held on the cultural activities in the zone. In the West *Aufbau* mostly had a reputation for

---

214 Kauffeldt, 'Zurück zum deutschen Bildungsideal', (p.33).

215 'Aus dem Nachruf des Deutschen Kulturbundes', *Aufbau*, 14 (1958), H.7.

216 Walter Janka, 'Zehn Jahre Aufbau-Verlag', *Aufbau*, 11 (1955), H.8, 678-80 (p. 679).

217 Joël Lefebvre, 'La vie intellectuelle dans la République Démocratique Allemande', *La Pensée*, n.s.50 (September/October 1953), 139-41 (p.141).

being a vehicle for propaganda, increasingly so after the onset of the Cold War: 'Ab 1948 wird der Ton erheblich schärfer'.[218]

As part of the initial cultural campaign, many German intellectuals gravitated towards the Kulturbund, and from there to its voice, *Aufbau*. The Kulturbund, described as the 'Verband der fortschrittlichen deutschen Intelligenz', was publicized as a non-partisan organisation and as its official organ *Aufbau* was supposedly non-partisan too.[219] After the forced merger of the SPD and the KPD to form the SED in 1946, however, the Kulturbund, as one of the mass organisations, was required to help lead the campaign for unified socialism. This National Front policy imposed conformity on the Kulturbund, and *Aufbau* could scarcely escape echoing this rallying-cry. Listed among the members of the founding committee of the Kulturbund were Becher, Gysi, Harich, Jhering, Wiegler, Ackermann, Lemmer, Bennedik, and Weisenborn — the incestuous relationship between *Aufbau* and the Kulturbund is patent.[220] *Aufbau*'s first issue opened with the Kulturbund's manifesto, adopted as its programme. It reported on Kulturbund meetings and on the progress of the Aufbau-Verlag.[221] It transmitted messages of approval and congratulations to the Kulturbund and celebrated its role in the recovery.[222] The close relationship between the two is also notable in the proceedings of Kulturbund council meetings in 1947, which contain details of a new advisory committee for the journal, including Gysi's proposals for membership and for arrangements for monthly meetings.[223]

---

[218] King, p.77.

[219] Dymschitz, 'Johannes R. Becher über den sozialistischen Realismus', (p. 778).

[220] KA, 907, 'Protokoll der Gründungskonferenz des Kulturbundes zur demokratischen Erneuerung Deutschlands am 8. August 1945', sheet 245.

[221] (W.), 'Zwei Jahre Aufbau-Verlag', *Aufbau*, 3 (1947), H.9, 212.

[222] 'Gruss und Anerkennung aus aller Welt', *Aufbau*, 2 (1946), H.3, 221-34.

[223] KA, 909, 'Protokoll der 1. Sitzung des neugewählten Präsidialrates am 31. Mai 1947 im Klubhaus', sheets 186 and 263-65.

This committee, it emerged in the ensuing discussion, had been formed as a response to 'Angriffe aus der gegnerischen Presse'.[224] Its editorial board had been judged too one-sided in its constitution.[225] At a meeting of the Präsidialrat on 31 May 1947, Heinz Willmann stated that the validity of the Kulturbund's original 1945 Russian licence was being disputed by the Americans and British. The Kulturbund was now a major political target: 'Es wäre eine Anweisung von der amerikanischen Behörde gegeben worden, dass der Kulturbund systematisch behindert werden soll'.[226] By 5 November the Präsidialrat was publicly expressing its regret at the obstacles which had been placed in the way of the Kulturbund in the American sector during the preceding six months. Its work would now be made completely impossible.[227] In *Aufbau* Abusch expressed grief at the ban on all traffic of Soviet-licensed literature, including that of the Kulturbund, from East to West. For Abusch, this suppression of literary activity displayed 'unsere tragische deutsche Lage'.[228]

In addition to *Aufbau*'s expressions of solidarity with the Kulturbund, it seems that the journal may initially have been subject to censorship. One piece of evidence perhaps justifies the West's suspicions. Within the Präsidialrat, Professor Hoffmann expressed concern that the heavy hand of censorship in Eastern Germany aroused suspicion in the American and English zones.[229] Replying to this, Becher urged patience with the procedure which he stated was improving; the second issue, he said, had encountered only half the problems of the first.[230] The transcript of this meeting is unfortunately incomplete. Nevertheless, it offers clear

---

224 ibid., 265.
225 ibid., 264.
226 ibid., 189.
227 KA, 909, 'Erklärung des Präsidialrates', sheets 336-37.
228 Abusch, 'Geistige Folgen der unvollendeten Revolution', (p.280).
229 KA, 907, sheet 99.
230 ibid.

evidence that *Aufbau* was politically manipulated by the Kulturbund and, through it, by the political élite.

To categorize it as a communist journal is, however, to tell only half the story. Firstly, *Aufbau* was committed to encouraging discussion across political boundaries and across disciplines. This aim was emphasized at a meeting of the Präsidialrat on 24 August 1945, where, on discussing an early progress report on the journal, members expressed their expectations. Willmann argued 'Jeder muß das Gefühl haben, das ist *meine* Zeitschrift, ich bin zwar nicht mit allem einverstanden, aber das ist ein Weg, hier wird etwas gesagt, zu dem ich stehen kann.' Becher was ambitious for the quality of discussion which diversity would bring: 'Wir müssen in der Zeitschrift zu geistigen Auseinandersetzungen kommen.'[231] These ideals were seen in practice. On occasion, the editorial staff distanced itself from something it published, stating that the piece was included for the purpose of stimulating discussion.

Secondly, newly available evidence reveals the relationship between *Aufbau* and the Kulturbund to have been more complex than one might assume. At the meeting which approved the journal's advisory committee in 1947, Gysi was adamant that this committee must not be a protective shield against criticism or the new public face of *Aufbau*: 'Es ist uns nicht daran gelegen, vor den Aufbau ein Schutzschild von repräsentativen Persönlichkeiten verschiedener politischer Prägung zu stellen, um damit den überparteilichen Charakter zu dokumentieren.'[232] The journal did not need this. The function of the committee was rather to improve communications between the journal and the Kulturbund: 'der eigentliche Gedanke war der, dass wir sozusagen zwischen dem Kulturbund und der verantwortlichen Redaktion ein Zwischenglied schaffen wollten.'[233] The

---

[231] KA, 907, 'Sitzung des Präsidialrates am 24. August 1945', sheet 74.
[232] KA, 909, sheet 266.
[233] ibid., 265.

implication here was that there was already a certain distance, if not dissatisfaction. Yet the fact that the journal was criticized implies that it had freedom of action. In January 1946, after just three issues, *Aufbau* was judged to have taken its task of targeting bourgeois intellectuals too seriously: 'Unsere Zeitschrift ist auf einem außerordentlich hohen Niveau, mir persönlich auf einem zu hohen, und zwar nicht in dem was sie sagt, sondern in der Form, wie sie es sagt.'[234] It did, however, escape the criticism levelled at *Sonntag* in 1947 of having become too left-wing. *Aufbau*, on the contrary, was deemed immune to 'solche Entgleisungen'.[235] This question of political tameness may of course explain some members' dissatisfaction. Further proof that it did not always meet with full approval came in 1948 and 1949, when there were complaints that *Aufbau* was not fulfilling its task as the central organ of the Kulturbund.[236] All this evidence suggests that *Aufbau* was not as closely controlled by the Kulturbund as might have been expected. Dieter Noll, who worked with *Aufbau* from the fifties, later judged that: 'Man muß sich, bei der Durchsicht der ersten 4 Jahrgänge des "Aufbau", immer wieder vor Augen halten, daß es damals nicht um die Entwicklung sozialistischer Gesinnung ging.'[237] Finally, three later communications point to a certain distance between the Kulturbund and the journal. The editor, Uhse, in a letter to Erich Wendt in 1951 expressed his hope that the Kulturbund would approve his suggestions for the changes in the Redaktionsbeirat.[238] A letter from Alfred Meusel of the Kulturbund to Uhse announced the former's intention to withdraw from the committee. He objected to the fact 'daß mein Name in jeder Nummer des AUFBAU steht' given his minimal involvement.[239] While this is a later incident

234 KA, 'Präsidialrat Protokolle 1945-1948', 10/112, sheet 188 (Professor Bennedik).
235 KA, 373/715.
236 KA, 15/211, and 495/844, p.27.
237 Noll, 'Vorwort', (p.13).
238 KA, Aufbau-Verlag, 530/782,1, 41.
239 KA, 782, letter from Professor Meusel to Bodo Uhse, (10 November 1951).

and suggests he wanted to leave a condemned ship, it nonetheless points to the redundant nature of this committee. A third letter, from Uhse consulting Wendt, Abusch and Hermlin about the format of one of the issues, suggests that this was a question of courtesy rather than a necessary request for permission from a political master.[240] The overall impression is emphatically not one of a dictatorial Kulturbund and a subservient journal.

The Kulturbund itself was of relatively minor importance among the mass organisations. It was not always represented at official meetings of these organisations with the SED, and its representation in election lists was well below that of the FDGB and the FDJ. The SED had its own official publications, which fulfilled a more clearly defined political role. Furthermore, by contrast with other journals, the Russian occupation authorities are scarcely mentioned in *Aufbau*. Where contact between the Kulturbund and the Russians is reported, it appears to be unforced — one report describes Sokolowski, the head of the Soviet Military authorities, arranging for a meeting with the 'Geistesarbeiter' to discuss the tasks still to be undertaken, 'um den kulturellen Wiederaufbau zu fördern'.[241] The idea that *Aufbau* was a link, via the Kulturbund, between the SMAD or the German political authorities (the KPD Zentralsekretariat, or thereafter the SED), and the population, is untenable.

For these reasons, categorization of *Aufbau* as a communist journal, with the political connotations therein, is simplistic.

Conclusions

Aufbau was the first journal to appear in Germany after the war, and provides the most comprehensive coverage, in terms of time, of this period of most intense unrest. Established as the official organ of the Kulturbund, and thereby

240 KA, Aufbau-Verlag, 530/782,2.
241 'Gruss und Anerkennung aus aller Welt', (p.221).

representing the cultural elite of the East, the journal's reputation in the West was of a straightforward propaganda blurb. The manifesto of the Kulturbund was printed in its first issue as *Aufbau*'s programme. It pledged to further the Kulturbund's main aim: 'die große deutsche Kultur, den Stolz unseres Vaterlandes wiederzuerwecken und ein neues deutsches Geistesleben zu begründen'.[242] As its name suggests, it was to unite all anti-fascists, particularly in the pursuit of German unity. The major personalities behind *Aufbau* were main office-bearers in the Kulturbund, and of these Johannes R. Becher, Klaus Gysi and Bodo Uhse were the most important. The study of *Aufbau* reveals looser control by the Kulturbund and greater independence of the Kulturbund itself than is often assumed. With the impending division, the journal's aim, especially in terms of literature, was focussed more on the idea of cultural inheritance, an idea Germany shared with Russia. It is almost impossible to disentangle the literary contributions of the journal from its political content and background. As the division became established, the dichotomy of *Aufbau*'s approach to the East and to unity was vivid. However, this was a purely German journal, controlled by Germans, and actively promoting German unity. All this, and its openness to suggestions for a 'Third Way', confirms that *Aufbau* was a more independent, discursive forum than categorization as a communist journal could possibly convey.

---

[242] KA, 908, 'Bericht über die Arbeit des Kulturbundes seit seiner Gründung gegeben auf der Präsidialratssitzung vom 9.1.46', sheet 204.

CHAPTER THREE
OST UND WEST

Ost und West appeared in Berlin in July 1947. As the title suggests, it was to look to both East and West. This reflected the dual interests of its creator and editor, Alfred Kantorowicz. Kantorowicz had been born in Berlin in 1899 into a middle class Jewish family. Aged seventeen, he had volunteered for service in the First World War and had been sent with occupation troops to Russia. He was awarded the Iron Cross.[1] In the twenties, he started work in the cultural section of the *Vossische Zeitung*. Subsequently he worked as cultural editor and theatre critic with the *Neue Badische Landeszeitung*, but then rejoined the *Vossische Zeitung* as its cultural correspondent in Paris. On his promotion in 1929, he returned to Berlin. In 1931 he joined the Communist Party and, following a raid by the SA two years later on his apartment in the 'Red Block', fled to France.[2] Here, he joined the campaign being mounted against the Nazis by the German community in exile. He founded the Schutzverband Deutscher Schriftsteller im Exil and in 1934 helped to set up the internationally backed 'Library of the Burned Books' or 'Deutsche Freiheitsbibliothek', later becoming its General Secretary.[3] In 1935 he joined the International Brigade in the Spanish Civil War, thereby becoming one of a community of writers and war correspondents which included Ernest Hemingway.[4] Back in France, Kantorowicz was forced to flee to the South, where, together with other Germans, he suffered increasing persecution at the

---

1 'Professor Kantorowicz: Rechenschaft', *Die Zeit: Sonderdruck aus den Ausgaben Nr.36/37/38 vom 5.12.19. September 1957*, 1-6 (p.1); and Heinz Joachim Heydorn, 'Wache im Niemandsland', in *Wache im Niemandsland: Zum 70. Geburtstag von Alfred Kantorowicz*, ed. by Heinz Joachim Heydorn, (Köln: Verlag Wissenschaft und Politik, 1969), (p.8).

2 IfZ, Sammlung W. Hammer, ED 106, Band 33.

3 See Richard Drews and Alfred Kantorowicz, *Verboten und Verbrannt deutsche Literatur: Deutsche Literatur 12 Jahre unterdrückt* (Berlin: Ullstein-Kindler, 1947).

4 See Alfred Kantorowicz, *Spanisches Kriegstagebuch* (Köln: Verlag Wissenschaft und Politik, 1966; repr. Fischer-Taschenbuch-Verlag, 1982).

hands of the French authorities.[5] Eventually released from detention, Kantorowicz, with his wife, Friedl, and some friends (among them Anna Seghers, who went on to Mexico), fled to the United States. There he was employed by the CBS for a time. He continued his fight against National Socialism, becoming a signatory to the declaration of the 'Council for a Democratic Germany, 1944-1946'. Another signatory was Maximilian Scheer, who later became his co-editor on *Ost und West*.[6] A Jew, a writer, a member of the Communist Party, on all these counts Kantorowicz was regarded as an enemy of National Socialism. His name appeared in the first 'brown list', in which 'anti-nationalist traitors' — politicians, writers and others — were identified.[7] In a secret SS document dated June 1939, he was described as one of the 'übelsten Hetzer gegen das neue Deutschland'.[8]

In all Kantorowicz spent more than thirteen years in exile. When he returned to Germany in 1945, he found it 'fremd', but nevertheless he felt himself to be in an ideal position to help in its rebuilding.[9] Not only had he acquired a positive attitude to the West, in particular its brand of democracy, he still remained a committed socialist. He was determined that his homeland should become neither the pawn nor quisling of either power bloc. He felt that Germany could re-emerge in a special central role as mediator between East and West. His initial idea to call his journal 'Die Brücke' encapsulates his whole philosophy.

Writing just prior to the launch of *Ost und West*, Kantorowicz expressed his belief that the battle for Germany had not ended.[10] It was not enough that German evil had been defeated, German victory had to be won, the victory of the

---

[5] See Alfred Kantorowicz, *Exil in Frankreich: Merkwürdigkeiten und Denkwürdigkeiten* (Bremen: Schünemann Universitätsverlag, 1971).

[6] IfZ, Sammlung Glaser, ED 202, Band 2.

[7] See Alfred Kantorowicz, *Deutsches Tagebuch Band 1* (München: 1959).

[8] IfZ, Dc 15.02, No. 173 (Geheim) (Der Reichsführer-SS; Der Chef des Sicherheitshauptamtes).

[9] Kantorowicz, *Deutsches Tagebuch Band 1*, p.212.

[10] *Neue Zeitung*, 14 February 1947, in Alfred Kantorowicz, *Vom moralischen Gewinn der Niederlage: Artikel und Ansprachen* (Berlin: Aufbau-Verlag, 1949).

'other' Germany. In his article, 'Mein Platz ist in Deutschland', he laid the responsibility for this on the Germans themselves: 'Der Sieg des besseren, des schöpferischen, friedliebenden Deutschland ist noch zu erkämpfen. Dieser Kampf muß hier im Lande ausgetragen werden, unter uns Deutschen.'[11] To achieve this inner metamorphosis, Kantorowicz prescribed cultural renewal. This would nullify the effects of Hitlerism and national defeat, and would also open up a vista of the future. His conviction that only the Germans could reconstruct Germany made him passionately committed to independence of German thought and expression. An immediate obstacle to this lay in the Allied licensing procedure. It had overtones of dependence rather than independence, a fact which necessarily betokened a degree of polarisation:

> Der Fakt, daß jede Publikation von einer der vier Besatzungsmächte lizensiert werden muß, behaftet, wenn auch oft zu Unrecht, die Äußerungen der Publizisten mit dem Stigma, als schrieben sie nicht nur mit der Zustimmung, sondern mehr oder minder im direkten oder indirekten Dienst jener Besatzungsmacht, die der Zeitung oder Zeitschrift, für die sie schreiben, die Lizens erteilt hat.[12]

To mitigate the effects of this, Kantorowicz applied to all four powers for a licence. The Russian authorities alone granted one, with the paper allowance set at a circulation level of 50,000.[13] An advertising campaign before the journal's appearance led to the recommendation by the Druckerei- und Vertriebs-Gesellschaft that a higher circulation of 83,000 might be more appropriate.[14] This body also suggested that there might be more interest in the western zones than in the East. Later documents on the journal's financial situation confirm this. A breakdown of the 53,000 circulation in June 1948 gave details: 'Sowjetische Zone'

---

[11] ibid.

[12] From *Ost und West*'s licence application, quoted by Kantorowicz in Der Herausgeber, 'Einführung', *Ost und West*, 1 (1947), H.1, 3-8 (pp.6-7).

[13] Ost-AdK, Alfred-Kantorowicz-Nachlaß, 69.

[14] Ost-AdK, AKN, letter dated 3 July 1947.

40%; Berlin 12%; and 'Westzonen' 48%'.[15] Yet difficulties in reaching this western readership were prevalent throughout 1948 and 1949. There was evidence that delivery was being deliberately hindered in the West, particularly from April 1948 onwards.[16] In January 1949 Kantorowicz was forced to write to the Military Government in Steglitz in West Berlin, requesting the release of four thousand impounded copies of the journal, explaining that the route taken by the driver through the American sector had been against the publishers' instructions.[17] Despite economic reform, postal delays, and the ban on Eastern literature, interest in the West persisted.[18] Kantorowicz's own figures suggest a peak of 70,000 before the economic reform in the West in June 1948. They then dropped to approximately 30,000 and decreased steadily until, by October 1949, the figure was about 1,000 in the West, and 5,000 in the East.[19] The consequent financial problems which the journal encountered were largely overcome by subsidies from Kantorowicz's publishing businesses, the Ost-und-West Verlag and the Alfred-Kantorowicz-Verlag, founded, he later claimed, specifically for this purpose.[20] It became necessary, however, to seek support through guaranteed sponsorship in the East.[21]

The exiled literary community, of which Kantorowicz had been a part, was the source of many contributors to the journal. Rudolf Olden, Lion Feuchtwanger, Heinrich Mann were all personal friends of Kantorowicz. *Ost und West* was heavily laced with extracts from Kantorowicz's own writings, often couched in

---

15 AKN, 'Zur wirtschaftlichen Lage der Zeitschrift OST UND WEST', enclosed with letter dated 24 June 1948.

16 AKN, letter dated 24 June 1948.

17 AKN, letter dated 24 January 1949.

18 AKN, 'Zur wirtschaftlichen Lage der Zeitschrift OST UND WEST'.

19 AKN, 92, letter from Alfred Kantorowicz to SED, dated 21 October 1949.

20 Alfred Kantorowicz, *Deutsches Tagebuch: Zweiter Teil* (Berlin: Verlag Anpassung und Widerstand, 1979), p.11.

21 AKN, letter dated 24 June 1948.

personal tones, as for instance, 'aus meinem spanischen Tagebuch'.[22] In the first twelve months twenty articles were published under Kantorowicz's name, thirteen were by Maximilian Scheer and five by Max Schroeder, head of the Aufbau-Verlag. The majority of contributors, however, had only one entry. *Ost und West* was Kantorowicz's personal possession.

As the Cold War progressed, it became increasingly clear that the political aims expressed by Kantorowicz were unachievable. Yet many Germans still harboured the ideal of a socialist — but independent — Germany, and *Ost und West* continued to support that ideal as a legitimate, even if latterly apparently unrealistic, proposition. In so doing, the journal attracted a readership extending well beyond Germany's borders.[23] The fact, however, that it had been licensed by the Russian authorities and that it was overtly socialist, inevitably attracted left-wing writers. As division became imminent, the German people, and prominent figures in particular, were under increasing pressure to opt for either communism or capitalism. Adherents of both sides became more outspoken. Western contributors to the journal were apparently punished in terms of access to Western markets and material advantage.[24] Articles of a polemic nature became more numerous, and the appearance of establishment figures more regular. Kantorowicz's 'bridge' was collapsing. In the new climate of the GDR, journals regarded as being of questionable alignment were unwelcome, and *Ost und West* was finally suppressed, appearing for the last time in December 1949.

---

22 Alfred Kantorowicz, 'Begegnung in Bel Alcazar', *Ost und West*, 2 (1948), H.7, 6-18 (p.6).

23 See correspondence in IfZ showing exchange of journals between exiles and contacts in Germany, ED 119/10.

24 Christian Heinschke, '*Ost und West* oder die Eintracht der Literaten', in *Zur literarischen Situation 1945-1949*, ed. by Gerhard Hay, (Kronberg: Athenäum-Verlag, 1977), pp.189-202 (p.200).

The guilty and the young

The first issue of *Ost und West* opened with Kantorowicz describing the philosophy underlying the journal.[25] First, neither the American nor the Soviet political model was appropriate for Germany. Germans had to find their own solution — a 'Third Way'. Second, Germany was geographically neither western, nor eastern, but was situated in between, occupying the middle ground, in an ideal place to mediate, or form a bridge, between the two blocs. Although this concept of a bridge was political in origin, the journal was to be primarily literary, and Kantorowicz's main thrust was to make foreign writing known in Germany: 'Über die Brücken, die hinüber- und herüberführen werden, wird zunächst nicht so sehr an einen Export deutschen Geisteslebens gedacht als an den Import geistiger Güter, die uns seit 1933 vorenthalten worden sind.'[26] A crucial part of his programme was to involve his readers in discussion. In keeping with his idea that the Germans themselves had to develop their own ideas for the future of their country, Kantorowicz demanded that the readers participate in the intellectual effort of the journal:

> Sie wendet sich an Leser, die nicht nur auf billige, von unseren Sorgen ablenkende Unterhaltung bedacht sind, sondern bereit, den Gefahren und Prüfungen, durch die wir alle gemeinsam noch zu gehen haben, ins Auge zu sehen, Leser, die sich nicht vor der Anstrengung des Nachdenkens fürchten.[27]

To encourage this participation he tried to create a comfortable and relaxed tone. This opening article was conciliatory, and he announced that no room would be given to the expression of enmity or hate towards any of the occupation powers. This opening piece, 'Einführung', lays out Kantorowicz's ideas and the journal's policies.

Ost und West's attempts to engage the readership met a major contemporary problem — that of silence. Much space was given in all publications

---

[25] 'Einführung'.
[26] ibid., (p.4).
[27] ibid., (p.6).

of the time to this problem, and *Ost und West* was no different. In correspondence with a reader, Kantorowicz expressed his hope that his journal would help to overcome this: 'nichts besseres erhoffen wir von unseren Lesern als diese geistige Auseinandersetzung mit dem, was wir darbieten.'[28] Even as late as January 1948, Kantorowicz noted that 'das Gespräch, das zwischen Deutschen geführt werden muß, hat noch kaum begonnen'.[29] Among the possible causes for the silence was, of course, the idea of guilt. Maximilian Scheer challenged Germans to address this question:

Warum schweigen die Menschen? Warum klagen sie oft über das Heute und erwähnen das Gestern, welches das Heute verschuldete, nie? Wollen sie das Gestern vergessen? Wollen sie ihre frühere Haltung verbergen? Wollen sie das Morgen auf einer Verheimlichung des Gestern aufbauen? Dann bauen sie auf einer Lüge auf und vergiften nicht nur sich selber, sondern die deutsche Jugend.[30]

His use of the collective noun 'Menschen' implies that the problem was a collective one, that the failure was broadly inclusive:

Es scheint sehr einfach zu sein, zu sagen: Ich habe davon nichts gewußt. Es scheint der leichteste Weg zu sein, mit dem Grauen fertig zu werden. In Wahrheit ist der der schwerste Weg. Er verhindert die Klärung, verhindert die Reinigung, verhindert die eigene Befreiung von einer Last.[31]

Kantorowicz, however, in a major article, 'Wie Hitler zur Macht kam', perhaps implied some escape from collective guilt in his conclusion that the blame lay with particular individuals: 'Schwerindustriellen, Bankiers, machtgierigen Politikern und gewissenlosen Demagogen'.[32] Heinrich Mann pointed to the preservation of the nation's 'conscience' in resistance efforts, appearing by this to mitigate the guilt of the nation as a whole.[33] Despite Scheer's exhortation to clarify and cleanse, the

---

28 'Ost- und West-Leser schreiben', *Ost und West*, 1 (1947), H.5, 92-95 (p.93).
29 Kantorowicz, 'Suchende Jugend', *Ost und West*, 2 (1948), H.2, 85-91 (p.87).
30 Maximilian Scheer, 'Berliner Mosaik', *Ost und West*, 2 (1948), H.1, 62-66 (p.65).
31 ibid., (pp.65-66).
32 Alfred Kantorowicz, 'Wie Hitler zur Macht kam', *Ost und West*, 2 (1948), H.2, 22-25 (p.25).
33 Heinrich Mann, 'Widerstehe dem Übel', *Ost und West*, 2 (1948), H.7, 19-24 (p.19).

journal itself was relatively silent about the evils of the Third Reich, an omission surprisingly unrecognized by Scheer, when he again referred, a year later, to the unwillingness of many Germans to face up to what had happened.[34]

Scheer's reference to the danger which denial posed to German youth indicates a major concern of *Ost und West* — the young generation. *Ost und West*'s targeting of this generation, which it defined as 'etwa die heute 18- bis 35jährigen', precipitated much discussion.[35] One reader wrote to the journal criticizing the general impatience with the young. He was thirty years old, an age which, in view of the times, betokened 'eine gewisse Frühreife'.[36] Another reader seemed to imply that definition by age was of less importance than shared experience, for example 'die erschütternde innere und äußere Armut unserer Generation, die ich bitter und schmerzlich genug täglich erfahre'.[37] Another letter blamed the older generation for the difficulties facing the young: 'Mann kann die Frage nach der jungen Generation nicht stellen, ohne nicht auch zugleich die nach der alten Generation zu stellen.'[38] Kantorowicz himself responded to this letter, stressing the importance of the problems raised: 'Es wird von der Lösung dieser Fragen abhängen, ob Deutschland noch eine Zukunft haben wird und wie diese Zukunft aussehen wird.'[39] He stated that moral and spiritual leaders were essential to guide their transformation from a misguided, confused nation in a vacuous society, to strong and convinced democrats. He proposed his literary hero, Heinrich Mann, as 'ein echter geistiger Führer, unser Mentor'.[40] While displaying a sensitive awareness of the plight of the young, Kantorowicz failed to address directly the question of the older generation. Another letter the following month

---

34 Maximilian Scheer, 'Mord', *Ost und West*, 3 (1949), H.2, 37-40 (p.39).
35 Kantorowicz, 'Suchende Jugend', (p.87).
36 'Drei Briefe', *Ost und West*, 2 (1948), H.7, 89-90 (p.89).
37 'Ost- und West-Leser schreiben', *Ost und West*, 2 (1948), H.5, 90-96 (p.96).
38 Käte Fuchs, Suchende Jugend', (p.85).
39 Kantorowicz, 'Suchende Jugend', (p.87).
40 ibid., (p.88).

raised the same problem: 'Wie kann sich ein Achtzehnjähriger heute, nach solch veränderter Situation, in die Gedankenwelt seiner, meinetwegen zehn Jahre älteren Kameraden versetzen?'[41] The question as to the age at which innocence stopped, and guilt began was unanswerable. The charge of passivity levelled against the young was rebutted in another letter, which argued that 'die junge Generation durch die falsche Politik der Älteren bereits einmal zum Prügelknaben wurde und eine Wiederholung dessen nur durch uns selbst vermieden werden kann'.[42] Another defence mounted by a young writer was based on their crucial role as bearers of future values: 'Auch müssen wir jungen Schriftsteller in der literarischen Produktion alles Feige und Haltlose ablehnen. Wir sind eine Vorhut.'[43] The section in *Ost und West* devoted to young writers, 'Tribüne junger Autoren', begun in April 1948, was a particular focus of attention. In keeping with the overall aim of the journal, it was to be 'ein Ansporn, eine Ermutigung zu sich selbst und ein Anlaß zu gesunder Kritik und Selbstkritik'.[44] It also threw up much fascinating correspondence. One young reader, who had, he said, volunteered for national service in 1939 because the fatherland was in danger, continued, 'Die Begeisterung, mit der ich ins Feld zog, ist mir noch atemwarm gegenwärtig — sie war die gleiche, mit der ich heute den Frieden bejahe.'[45] Another section devoted to the young, 'Tribüne der Jungen', brought comments on the disappearance of the tight bonds of comradeship. The transition from childhood through the Hitler-Jugend to the army had established an order which had now vanished. Claus Katschinski regretted 'das Aufhören gegenseitiger Unterstützung', but stated that the 'Kameradschaftsgefühl' had already in fact been betrayed.[46] Mistrust had

---

[41] 'Ost- und West-Leser schreiben', *Ost und West*, 2 (1948), H.3, 92-95 (p.92).
[42] 'Ost- und West-Leser schreiben', *Ost und West*, 2 (1948), H.1, 92.
[43] 'Ost- und West-Leser schreiben', *Ost und West*, 2 (1948), H.5, 90-96 (p.96).
[44] 'Tribüne junger Autoren', *Ost und West*, 2 (1948), H.4, 90-91 (p.90).
[45] 'Tribüne junger Autoren', *Ost und West*, 2 (1948), H.6, 89-92 (p.90).
[46] Claus Katschinski, 'Zusammenbruch der Kameradschaft', *Ost und West*, 2 (1948), H.7, 81-84 (p.81-82).

replaced the initial support. Theft, embezzlement and corruption, gangs and lynchings had been rife. This breakdown in community spirit had been caused not by anarchic elements, but by the officer corps, 'das unter der ersten Maske der Disziplin und der zweiten Maske der Despotie sich mehr und mehr einer genußsüchtigen und ungehemmten Vorsintflut-Stimmung hingab'.[47] Even the end of hostilities brought 'Kampf aller gegen alle'. His final despairing conclusion was that his 'Kameraden' had not been friends, but part of the Nazi 'Gemeinschaftsidee', artificially organized by exploiting 'Nationalgefühl'.[48] Katschinski also implicated academics and members of organized religions. The few who had retained their integrity had been non-conformists, mostly young, and, even more interestingly, aspiring Europeans:

Eines ihrer Hauptmerkmale war, daß sie keiner der herrschenden Ideologien anhingen, sondern mit großem Ernst nach dem Gedanken unterwegs waren, der die Zukunft enthalte, und daß sie vor allem davon überzeugt waren, daß dieser ein europäischer Gedanke sein müsse. Ich fand also im Bewußtsein des einzigen Typus, der widerstanden hatte, die europäische Idee in gärenden, noch ungestalten Formen.[49]

Another correspondent from the 'Heimkehrergeneration', Hans Losecaat v. Nouhoys, while admitting that the young had, as yet, no definite political stance, insisted that this was no fault of their own.[50] He complained bitterly that those who were writing about the problem of the young were the self-same teachers and other professionals who had previously been in positions of authority over them. He regretted that they had not checked what they had been told by 'schmierige Hinterhauspolitiker'. They had not been thinking of the young, but of themselves: 'Man zwang uns in die HJ, man warf uns, als wir noch Kinder waren, in das

---

47 ibid.

48 ibid., (p.83).

49 ibid., (p.84).

50 Hans Losecaat v. Nouhuys, 'Leben, nicht Tod', *Ost und West*, 2 (1948), H.7, 86-89 (p.86).

Inferno eines irrsinnigen Krieges.'[51] His attitude was uncompromising: 'ich möchte nur betonen, daß ich diesen Menschen das Recht abspreche, über uns zu urteilen. [...] Wir haben es satt, uns von Leuten bevormunden zu lassen, die es scheinbar darauf abgesehen haben, uns jedesmal in eine neue Katastrophe zu stürzen.'[52] He wrote: 'Wir kamen zurück, nicht als die Helden und Supermänner, die der Nationalsozialismus aus uns gemacht hatte, wir kamen schlicht und einfach als die verlorenen Söhne unserer Eltern.'[53] Another young correspondent described their experience in even more sombre tones:

Haben wir denn von unserem zehnten bis fünfundzwanzigsten Lebensjahr etwas anderes gehört oder gesehen als Rassenlehre, Völkerhaß, Trommeln, Volk ohne Raum, Lagerleben, Deutschland, Deutschland über alles, Krieg, Nazismus, Faschismus und Millionenmord? Hatten wir je etwas anderes zum Vorbild als Demagogen, Massenmörder, Verbrecher und...Helden?[54]

On their return, bureaucracy absorbed their last energies, corruption stared them in the face, and they were reviled. They were used to hearing that they were the 'größte Schatz der Nation', and now they were described as 'verloren'.[55] They had become aliens. 'Ist dann verwunderlich,' Losecaat asked, 'daß wir so zum "Gesindel" wurden — wie uns der Frankfurter Polizeipräsident kürzlich bezeichnete — das heute die Bahnhöfe des Westens bevölkert? Blieb uns denn hier ein anderer Ausweg, als der des Schwarzen Marktes?'[56] Despite all this, politicians, often the self-same people as had held office before, were offering similar messages as before. As Losecaat's damning indictment stated:

Als wir zurückkamen, dachten wir, daß alles mit vereinten Kräften an den Wiederaufbau gehen würde, stattdessen aber fanden wir nur Parteikämpfe, die an die Zeit vor 1933 erinnerten. Als dann die Wahl vorbei war, blieb doch alles beim

---

51 ibid., (p.87).
52 ibid., (p.86).
53 ibid., (p.87).
54 'Drei Briefe', (p.89).
55 Losecaat v. Nouhuys, 'Leben, nicht Tod', (p.87).
56 ibid.

alten. Es wurde uns dann von den verschiedenen Parteiführern erklärt, daß wir falsch gewählt hätten.[57]

Remarking that there was even an American general expressing confidence that they were ready to die for the cause of democracy, Losecaat responded, 'Wir werden uns eins suchen, nach dem wir leben können und für das wir leben können.'[58] Another directly challenged the journal, 'Ich frage mit Ihnen: Wo bleibt die deutsche Publizistik?'[59] Out of the silence *Ost und West* seemed already to have established dialogue.

Historical explanations

Re-exploration of history was part of *Ost und West*'s effort to educate the young. One teacher wrote, expressing his appreciation: 'Meinen 16- bis 18jährigen Schülern kann ich durch diese wertvollen Beiträge eine neue Welt erschließen, die diesen jungen Menschen 12 Jahre vorenthalten wurde.'[60] In 1948, the journal commemorated the revolution of 1848 as an example of German liberalism in action. The anniversary provided sufficient material for two whole issues. It was a reminder of possible reasons for wrong turnings ('Der Deutsche glaubt an gar nichts, bedient sich aber nach Wunsch der gesellschaftlichen Vorurteile. Er ist an die kleinbürgerliche Zufriedenheit, an Wohlbehagen und Ruhe gewöhnt'), but also an encouragement in the current struggle: 'Alle deutschen Revolutionäre sind große Kosmopoliten, die den Standpunkt der Nationalität überwunden haben, und sie sind alle von äußerst reizbarem und sturem Patriotismus erfüllt (sic).' [61] Prose and poetry from the 1840s were included. The hope was expressed that 1948, hailed as 'das deutsche Schicksalsjahr', would set standards of humanism and

---

[57] ibid., (p.88).
[58] ibid., (p.89).
[59] 'Drei Briefe', (p.90).
[60] 'Ost- und West-Leser schreiben', *Ost und West*, 2 (1948), H.6, 92-94 (p.94).
[61] Alexander Herzen, 'Epilog', *Ost und West*, 2 (1948), H.2, 18-21 (p.19).

democracy for Germany's future.[62] The same device was used in Kantorowicz's handling of more recent history. Using the date 10 May, he gave a list of events: in 1932, Carl von Ossietzky had been imprisoned; in 1933, the book-burning had taken place on the Opernplatz in Berlin; and on 10 May 1940, Hitler's tanks had turned against the West. The first of these, 10 May 1932, was described by Kantorowicz as the 'Todestag der deutschen Republik'. It had seen the demise of a great liberal, the defeat of his supporters, whom Kantorowicz described as 'die Creme der deutschen Intelligenz', and, he stated, the loss of a future president.[63] Another man regarded as a hero by *Ost und West* was Hellmut von Gerlach. He had fled Germany in 1933 and died in exile two years later.[64] Informed by his experiences as a journalist during the First World War, when 'man glaubte Alles, was zugunsten der deutschen Sache vorgebracht wurde', Gerlach served as a reminder that war imposed expressions of nationalism on people and suppressed the freedom to report the truth where it was considered to be against the national interest: 'Lügen ist jetzt patriotische Pflicht!'[65] Disillusioned by this, Gerlach had turned to pacifism. *Ost und West* held that the redefinition of patriotism after the Third Reich could benefit from such reminders of positive manifestations of concern for the people.[66] *Ost und West* promoted humanism and, while rarely mentioning religion, suggested that humanism might incorporate it. One issue, with the leitmotif 'Besinnung auf einen neuen realen Humanismus', set up past models such as Theodor Lessing, Heinrich Heine, Thomas Jefferson and Alfred Kerr.[67] *Ost und West*'s dwelling on events and heroes of the past, however, came in for some criticism:

---

[62] Cover of *Ost und West*, 2 (1948), H.1.

[63] Alfred Kantorowicz, 'Der Zehnte Mai', *Ost und West*, 2 (1948), H.5, 4-10 (pp.4-5).

[64] Introduction to Hellmut v. Gerlach, 'Zeiten der Lüge', *Ost und West*, 2 (1948), H.8, 18-23 (p.18).

[65] ibid., (p.19).

[66] ibid., (p.18); and the introductory editorial to the issue, 'Die Nebelschwaden'.

[67] 'Zu unseren Beiträgen', *Ost und West*, 1 (1947), H.6.

Sie behandeln alle Gebiete, die uns die geschichtliche Entwicklung Deutschlands zeigen können, das ist recht und gut. Aber die Menschen des 20. Jahrhunderts und besonders die Deutschen nach dem Zusammenbruch von 1945 geht in erster Linie die Zeit bis heute an, also die letzten drei Jahre. Warum wird davon so wenig gesprochen?[68]

This reader blamed *Ost und West*'s writers ('müssen denn *nur*, immer nur Schriftsteller zu Wort kommen?'), suggesting that some were ill-equipped to address the contemporary crisis.[69] 'Der kleine Mann' should be involved more. These writers wrongly assumed that ordinary people did not have 'Verstand und Sinn genug [...], sich eine Meinung über die Fragen der Zeit zu machen'.[70] Hans-Günther Cwojdrak effectively supported this reader's protestations, similarly concluding that there was a certain inability, particularly among European intellectuals, to deal with some questions. What they should not be doing at the present time was shrinking from reality into mysticism: 'Bedarf es noch eines Beweises dafür, daß Romantik, Mystik und Irrationalismus die ersten Schritte auf dem Wege zur Bestialität und Herrschaft der Untermenschen sind?'[71] Kantorowicz also criticized this mystic approach, but described it as characterizing Western writers — here we note anti-West sentiments which were to appear frequently in subsequent issues. He objected in particular to the campaign for the 'Rettung der christlichen Zivilisation vor dem Bolschewismus'. Only bigotry, he declared, explained the survival of this 'prejudice' over three decades. According to him, the real moral campaigners were those who had fought for their convictions against fascism in the Spanish Civil War.[72]

---

68 'Ost- und West-Leser schreiben', *Ost und West*, 2 (1948), H.6, 92-94 (p.93).

69 ibid.

70 ibid., (pp.93-94).

71 Hans-Günther Cwojdrak, 'Hermann Kasack: "Die Stadt hinter dem Strom"',*Ost und West*, 2 (1948), H.4, 86-88 (p.88).

72 Alfred Kantorowicz, 'Glaubenshelden unserer Zeit', *Ost und West*, 1 (1947), H.1, 49-54 (p.50).

East-West division

The suggestion that *Ost und West*'s writers did not address current events was a little unfair. Kantorowicz addressed the complaint of the young that the contemporary political scene was now peopled by 'descendants' of those who had imprisoned Ossietzky and who had erred during the Third Reich. The irony was that this group justified their return to political activity on the grounds that they had had previous experience of politics before Hitler's seizure of power.[73] Again, the discussion was turned against the West. Kantorowicz compared its ban of *Kulturbund* publications with the 1933 book burning.[74] He saw in this the influence of fascism. Interestingly, Peter de Mendelssohn, the press advisor to the British Control Commission in Berlin, had himself earlier contributed to *Ost und West*.[75] The survival of fascism in the West was also part of Maximilian Scheer's proposition in his essay, 'An Rhein und Ruhr'. Its description of life in western Germany under occupation, contained grave allegations. It quoted one villager as saying:

Die Alliierten hätten in einem großen Schwung mit den Nazis aufräumen und das Fundament einer wirklichen Demokratie legen müssen; aber dann hätten sie uns auch in dieser neuen Demokratie die Möglichkeit geben müssen, uns aus dem Dreck herauszuarbeiten. Sie haben, wenigstens hier, weder das eine noch das andere getan.[76]

Scheer alleged that 'die Tönung richtet sich danach, von wem materiell das meiste zu erwarten ist und wer den alten Trott unter neuer Flagge am wenigsten stört'.[77] That the majority of the intake of Bonn university were former Nazis, he presented as confirmation of the West's unsatisfactory approach.[78] Scheer pinpointed the

---

[73] Kantorowicz, 'Der Zehnte Mai', (pp.4-5).

[74] ibid., (p.10).

[75] Peter de Mendelssohn, 'Jean Giono, das Problem des "Dummen Genies"', *Ost und West*, 1 (1947), H.5, 72-86.

[76] Maximilian Scheer, 'An Rhein und Ruhr', *Ost und West*, 2 (1948), H.2, 26-36 (p.31).

[77] Maximilian Scheer, 'Denken an Rhein und Ruhr', *Ost und West*, 2 (1948), H.3, 25-30 (p.25).

[78] Scheer, 'An Rhein und Ruhr', (pp.35-36).

West's emphasis on re-education, however, as the greatest hindrance to recovery: 'Als der Krieg zu Ende ging, sprach man im westlichen Ausland sehr viel von der Umerziehung des deutschen Volkes. Es war ein unglückliches Wort. Der erste Schritt ist nicht Umerziehung, sondern Besinnung.' 'Besinnung' meant for Scheer that 'ein Deutscher sich um Deutschland kümmert: um eine soziale und geistige Neuschöpfung Deutschlands'.[79] Re-education by the Western Allies was something imposed. Moreover, freedom of expression was not yet encouraged in the West, and this led to apathy. Scheer stated that 'Flucht aus dem Denken ist das Stigma der geistigen Situation an Rhein und Ruhr'.[80] Arnold Zweig joined in this condemnation when he wrote in a letter to *Ost und West*: 'Ich hasse das Wort "Umerziehung", weil die Kräfte selber nicht erzogen sind, die es den Deutschen verordnet haben.'[81]

Nowhere in *Ost und West* is there similar criticism of the Russian occupation. On the contrary, the Russians' less formal approach to re-education received support. In July 1948 *Ost und West* included a report on a prisoner-of-war camp in Tbilisi, where the authorities had encouraged participation in a range of performing arts. The artists were anti-fascists, and the author appreciated the gentle 'enlightened' approach: 'Die Veranstaltungen sollten das Musikalische, das gesprochene, vermittelnde Wort (und damit die Dichtung), und das Politische verbinden.'[82]

Scheer's famous report on the Rhein-Ruhr area also concerned itself with the West's economic philosophy. As this industrial centre was under the jurisdiction of the Western Allies, some writers in the East feared that a resurgence of capitalist practices there would hinder the development of democracy in the

---

[79] Scheer, 'Berliner Mosaik', (p.66).
[80] Scheer, 'Denken an Rhein und Ruhr', (p.26).
[81] 'Ost- und West-Leser schreiben', *Ost und West*, 2 (1948), H.1, 92-93 (p.92).
[82] Rolf Hartmann, 'Saatkorn im Gefangenenlager', *Ost und West*, 2 (1948), H.7, 85-86 (p.85).

western zones.[83] As another contributor put it, economic stability was a determinant of moral stability.[84] After the economic reform of 1948, *Ost und West*'s tone vis-à-vis the West became notably harsher. The journal's reaction was clear: the country had become 'deformiert' and Berlin was 'währungsgeteilt'. Stating that Germany was changing not just 'zu zwei Geldhälften', but into 'zwei politischen Hälften, zwei geographischen Hälften', the journal blamed the West for the split.[85]

America was increasingly criticised by the journal, despite, or perhaps because of the fact that both Kantorowicz and Scheer had spent time in exile there. In 1948 the journal published a suggestion made in 1945 by an American journalist that Berlin be razed to the ground.[86] When its inclusion was questioned by a reader, the journal claimed it was illustrative of current American thinking — that 'der heutige amerikanische Kampf um Berlin nicht aus humanen Gründen geführt wird'.[87] America was now not the America of Roosevelt. Scheer acknowledged the help of the Allies in loosening the fascists' stranglehold on Europe and paid homage to America's tradition of helping the poor and needy, but Roosevelt's enemies had destroyed his land:

> Hochherzige Amerikaner, Erben einer humanen Tradition im frühen Asylland der Verfolgten, hatten Spanienkämpfer unterstützt, denen die Flucht über den Ozean gelungen war. Jeder wahre Amerikaner achtete sie, niemand behelligte sie. Dann starb Roosevelt, und seine Feinde im Land zerstörten sein Erbe.[88]

There was also an 'other' America. Henry Wallace, introduced as 'die Stimme des anderen Amerika', described the persecution of those who sought 'Verständigung

---

[83] 'Zu unseren Beiträgen', *Ost und West*, 2 (1948), H.2.

[84] Herbert Roch, 'Über den schwarzen Markt', *Ost und West*, 2 (1948), H.9, 86-88 (p.88).

[85] 'Besinnung!', *Ost und West*, 2 (1948), H.7.

[86] 'Berlin — vor drei Jahren', *Ost und West*, 2 (1948), H.8, 87.

[87] 'Ost- und West-Leser schreiben', *Ost und West*, 2 (1948), H.10, 96.

[88] Maximilian Scheer, 'Das Beispiel Albert Maltz', *Ost und West*, 2 (1948), H.8, 4-5 (p.4).

mit Rußland'.[89] Scheer brought the early McCarthy era to readers' attention by reporting that Hollywood artists, such as Albert Maltz, were being forced to defend themselves against accusations of un-American activities.[90] Contemporary America was being seen as an enemy. The journal's claim to present a balanced view of both East and West became increasingly difficult to justify. A review of Hermann Kasack's book, *Die Stadt hinter dem Strom*, reveals the underlying ideological development. To Kasack's description of the 'falschen Selbstbewußtsein des Abendlandes' as something which 'einmal tödlich zu Fall kommen müßte', the reviewer imputed Spenglerian error and lack of political insight: 'Kasack sieht nicht die Möglichkeit einer Erneuerung durch das sozialistische Proletariat, das den Begriff des "Abendlandes" in einer neuen und reineren Form verwirklichen könnte.'[91] In their condemnation of capitalism, the editors even referred to the Sermon on the Mount to vilify the rich as the evil of society.[92] The imbalance increased. In the preface of January 1949 we read: 'Hinter dem Nebel der tückischen Propaganda gegen die Sowjetunion wird zielbewußt die alte verrottete Ungeistigkeit konserviert und mit der lockenden, aber unehrlichen Jahrmarktsparole des "Abendlandes" übertüncht.'[93] The Western powers were condemned as persistent persecutors of the USSR: 'Die Gegner der Sowjetunion haben aus den Erfahrungen nichts gelernt.'[94] Identifying Arthur Koestler specifically, Kantorowicz referred to an anti-Bolshevist campaign of words which outdid Hitler, and, what was worse, 'das wird dann präsentiert unter der Kennmarke des Kampfes gegen den "Totalitarismus". Und niemand scheint es

---

89 Henry Wallace, 'Die Stimme des anderen Amerika', *Ost und West*, 2 (1948), H.9, 46-50 (p.47).

90 Scheer, 'Das Beispiel Albert Maltz', (p.5).

91 Cwojdrak, 'Hermann Kasack: "Die Stadt hinter dem Strom"', (p.87).

92 'Weihnachten', *Ost und West*, 2 (1948), H.12.

93 'Der Falsche Weg', *Ost und West*, 3 (1949), H.1.

94 'Spatzen und Menschen', *Ost und West*, 3 (1949), H.3.

zu merken.'[95] The most illiberal, fascist and aggressive forces were identified as western-based. Two months later the West was blamed outright for the division of Berlin and of Germany.[96]

This partisan approach was now in direct conflict with *Ost und West*'s original aspirations. The inevitable dichotomy that would result from the journal's approach had been evident all along. A preface in 1949 re-echoed Kantorowicz's original assessment of the situation: 'erst, wenn nicht alle Fragen in unserem Land von internationalen Auseinandersetzungen überschattet sind, erst dann kann der unbelastete Kampf für ein progressives, humanes Deutschland beginnen.'[97] An earlier editorial had also recalled the concern expressed in the opening issue that global polarisation would mean German division, and stated that they had been right — Germany was now divided.[98] Faced with the reality of division, the editors incorporated it into their plea for 'Besinnung' and insisted 'es ist nie zu spät, sich zu verständigen'.[99] The journal intended to remain loyal to the aims it had set itself at the beginning.[100] *Ost und West* even turned to American political figures Cordell Hull and Thomas Jefferson in an attempt to demonstrate 'die sinnvolle Fruchtbarkeit geistiger Auseinandersetzung'.[101] The most significant example of the journal's continuing attention to its initial aims came from Ulrich Noack. He proposed the expeditious withdrawal of occupation troops and urged that any Atlantic pact should ensure the neutrality of Germany between East and West. He argued for 'Regierung des Volkes durch das Volk und für das Volk' and provided detailed proposals for the future of a neutral independent Germany. Noack

---

95 Alfred Kantorowicz, 'Fortsetzung des Briefes an Herrn v. F.', *Ost und West*, 3 (1949), H.2, 81-86 (p.85).
96 'Spatzen und Menschen'.
97 'Zwei Jahre', *Ost und West*, 3 (1949), H.6.
98 'Besinnung!'.
99 ibid.
100 'Nach zwölf Monaten', *Ost und West*, 2 (1948), H.7, 101.
101 'Zu unseren Beiträgen', *Ost und West*, 2 (1948), H.6.

recommended economic re-unification in the interests of European recovery and European peace. He rejected both a 'Westeuropa-Union' and the undemocratic adoption of communism.[102] This express concern for the larger issue, Europe, is reminiscent of Kantorowicz's first article of *Ost und West*, where he espoused a unified European culture:

Die Sphäre und Einflußsphäre der "westlichen" Kultur hört nicht am Rhein oder an der Elbe auf, die "östliche" ist nicht begrenzt durch die Weichsel oder die Oder. Die Anführungszeichen, zwischen die "westlich" und "östlich" gesetzt sind, haben keinen polemischen Charakter; eher einen fragenden: wie denn etwa der Begriff "westliche Kultur" heute zu definieren wäre? Es ist fraglich geworden, ob wir noch wie bislang den Begriff der "westlichen Kultur" mit der europäischen gleichsetzen dürfen.[103]

Ost und West in general conveyed a positive, albeit muted, attitude to Europe. Heinrich Mann advocated that Germans become European patriots.[104] There was, however, a slant to this topic too. Kantorowicz argued that a pragmatic attitude to Europe was an essential lesson to be learnt from the past and blamed Europe as a whole rather than Germany alone for the fate of Czechoslovakia in 1938.[105] This opinion was repeated by a Czech writer in an article on the Munich agreement. He objected to the renewed efforts to keep the Soviet Union out of European politics, in particular the rebuilding of Germany. The development, peace, and democracy of Europe, he argued, were endangered by the campaign to exclude Russia.[106]

Literature

The deteriorating relationship between East and West had a marked effect on the journal's literary output. There was a rapid trend during the two years of its

---

[102] 'Entwurf zu einem Neutralisierungsvertrag', *Ost und West*, 3 (1949), H.5, 82-85.
[103] 'Einführung', (p.3).
[104] Letter from Heinrich Mann to Kantorowicz (27 August 1947), *Ost und West*, 1 (1947), H.3, 3.
[105] 'Zu unseren Beiträgen', *Ost und West*, 1 (1947), H.3.
[106] Jan Sládek, 'Nie wieder München', *Ost und West*, 2 (1948), H.9, 5-10 (p.10).

existence towards overtly anti-capitalist literature and to subject literature to biased political comment. Even the inevitable harkening back to the Classical Age, particularly to Goethe, revealed this. The socialist appreciation of Goethe dominated. Walther Victor referred to 'die Linie Goethe-Hegel-Marx', now extending to Lenin and Stalin, and Richard Drews evoked the idea of a 'Volks-Goethe'.[107] An advertisement for a new book proclaimed 'Eine neue Generation ist aufgerufen, das Erbe Goethes zu verwalten: die arbeitenden Menschen'. The August 1949 issue was largely devoted to the bicentenary of Goethe's birth. Here there were pieces by Arnold Zweig and Romain Rolland, and titles such as 'Goethe und Beethoven' and 'Goethe und die Demokratie'. Other past heroes of literature included the Grimm brothers, and Georg Herwegh, the revolutionary poet of 1848.[108] One article revived a forgotten German writer, Carl Schnauffer, as 'der erste proletarische Dichter der Deutschen'.[109]

A range of international writers was presented, selected to acquaint the German reader with 'den besten fortschrittlichen Kräften Amerikas, der Sowjetunion, Frankreichs, Englands, Spaniens, der Tschechoslowakischen Republik u.a.m.' and forming 'das geöffnete Fenster zur Welt'.[110] Some literary extracts were published for the first time in the German language, including a dramatic scene by Strindberg and speeches given by Thomas Mann in America during the war.[111] Similarly, the novelle *Das Telegramm* by the Russian writer Konstantin Paustowski was published in June 1948 following its appearance in Aufbau-Verlag, and a chapter from the memoirs of Martin Andersen-Nexö

---

[107] *Ost und West*, 3 (1949), H.8, (pp.93 and 96).

[108] Gertrud Meyer-Hepner, 'Die Berufung der Gebrüder Grimm nach Berlin', *Ost und West*, 3 (1949), H.6, 90-93.

[109] Hans Erman, 'Der ganz vergessene Dichter', *Ost und West*, 2 (1948), H.4, 82-84 (pp.82-83).

[110] AKN, 83: 'Ltz.', 'Weltverbindender Kulturwille: Ein Jahr Monatsschrift "Ost und West"', *Tägliche Rundschau*, 8 June 1948.

[111] August Strindberg, 'Walpurgisnacht auf Heiterbucht: Fragment aus dem Nachlaß', *Ost und West*, 1 (1947), H.3, 59-66; Thomas Mann, 'Welt-Zivilisation', *Ost und West*, 1 (1947), H.2, 3-6.

appeared in the January issue of the same year.[112] Contemporary literature included poetry by Brecht, Huchel, Friedrich Wolf, and Günther Weisenborn.[113] The great names of the Eastern Zone (Zweig, Renn, Niekisch, Nexö) were celebrated as well as Kantorowicz's own friends (Scheer, Feuchtwanger, Leonhard). The journal's approach to inner émigrés was favourable. Kantorowicz referred to the writers and scientists of both inner and outer emigration as equals in the task ahead.[114] In his address to the 1947 Berlin Writers' Congress, Kantorowicz made the same plea for cooperation between 'beiden geistig miteinander verbundenen, physisch für Jahre voneinander getrennten Gruppierungen'.[115] At that congress, his talk on exile literature had been accompanied by Elizabeth Langgässer's on inner emigration, both reproduced in the journal. In line with the sentiments of this first post-war Writers' Congress, literary theory in *Ost und West* reflected the search for objectivity. It advocated realism, rather than any self-absorption or indulgence in mysticism. Wolfgang Weyrauch argued that a writer should aim at precision and a clear moral stance: 'Er hat die Funktion, das Gute als gut zu bezeichnen, das Böse als böse. Auch darin muß er genau sein. Erst wenn er derart genau ist, kann er auch schön schreiben.'[116] Rejection of individualism implied a positive attitude to the collective. Citing Hermlin and Brecht, Gerhard Weidenmüller wrote, 'Die Ausdrucksformen einer kollektivistischen Epoche sind notwendig geworden, wenn die Lyrik nicht im faden Subjektivismus stecken bleiben soll.'[117] Peter Huchel's

---

[112] Konstantin Paustowsky, 'Das Telegramm', *Ost und West*, 2 (1948), H.6, 55-65; Martin Andersen-Nexö, 'Dichter des Alltags', *Ost und West*, 2 (1948), H.1, 52-61.
[113] See, for example, Günther Weisenborn, 'Gedichte', *Ost und West*, 3 (1949), H.3, 41-44.
[114] 'Einführung', (p.5).
[115] Alfred Kantorowicz, 'Deutsche Schriftsteller im Exil', *Ost und West*, 1 (1947), H.4, 42-51 (p.43).
[116] Wolfgang Weyrauch, 'Von der Beschaffenheit unserer Prosa', *Ost und West*, 2 (1948), H.7, 77-78 (p.78).
[117] Gerhard Weidenmüller, 'Lyrik zwischen Gestern und Heute', *Ost und West*, 3 (1949), H.3, 88-90 (p.90).

new poetry was commended for its reflection of social reality — according to the reviewer, Huchel's 1949 *Gedichte* 'sind eingebettet in den großen Strom der humanistischen deutschen Dichtung'.[118] The most definitive socialist line in literary theory was provided by Stephan Hermlin in a talk to young activists and writers in Leipzig. He challenged them to combat the barbarism which was still presented as 'culture' in the contemporary world: 'Eine neue Klasse ist berufen, Trägerin des großen Kulturerbes zu werden.'[119] Responding to Hermlin's famous question, 'Wo bleibt die junge deutsche Dichtung?', Kantorowicz commented that youth always had to forge a way against the conservatism, prejudice and misunderstanding of the older generation.[120] He attempted to support young writers by encouraging publishers to seize the opportunities which would come from a rebirth of young work.[121]

New publications reviewed often dealt with anti-fascist activities. Harald Hauser's autobiographical *Wo Deutschland lag* provided an example of a German anti-fascist hero who could stand alongside members of the French Macquis, exemplified by Aragon's *L'homme communiste*. The reviewer underlined the educational value of the text: 'Nach der Lektüre weiß jeder, wer sein Vaterland wirklich geliebt hat.'[122] Aragon was considered to be a progressive socialist thinker.[123] Another French writer, Paul Eluard, was introduced as providing 'das Beispiel souveräner westeuropäischer Geisteshaltung'.[124] Other foreign writers published included the Chilean anti-fascist writer, Pablo Neruda, and the Spaniard, Federico Garcia Lorca. Soviet writers in particular were presented as role-models: 'Der sowjetische Schriftsteller lebt und schafft immer aus seinem Volk [...]. Der

---

118 Herbert Roch, 'Peter Huchel: Gedichte', *Ost und West*, 3 (1949), H.5, 91-92 (p.92).
119 Stephan Hermlin, 'Ja und Nein', *Ost und West*, 2 (1948), H.11, 91-96 (p.96).
120 A. K., 'Wo bleibt die junge deutsche Dichtung?', *Ost und West*, 1 (1947), H.4, 88-91.
121 A. K., 'Die große Chance der deutschen Verleger', *Ost und West*, 1 (1947), H.2, 92-96.
122 Hans Günther Cwojdrak, 'Harald Hauser', *Ost und West*, 2 (1948), H.7, 80-81 (p.81).
123 See Louis Aragon, 'Die junge Leute', *Ost und West*, 3 (1949), H.4, 23-44.
124 'Zu unseren Beiträgen', *Ost und West*, 2 (1948), H.6.

sowjetische Künstler lernt von seinem Volk. Er ist dankbar für gerechte Kritik, mag sie auch manchmal bitter schmecken.'[125] Extracts from Maxim Gorky, Valentin Katajew, Alexander Blok and Wera Panowa, who received the second Stalin prize in April 1948, were published alongside many lesser-known Russian writers.[126] Two poems by Friedrich Wolf, 'Dein Volk' and 'Ost und West', celebrated his love for a Russian woman, whom he saw as a personification of the whole Russian people.[127] Wolf's idea of 'Ost und West' was of a Russian and a German. In April 1949, there was a report on a Moscow literary meeting attended by representatives of the Eastern Zone, Anna Seghers, Jürgen Kuczynski, Günther Weisenborn and the author of the report, Michael Hell. It celebrated the atmosphere of literary, political and personal friendship at this meeting.[128] A report on the 'discoveries' of German literature (Freiligrath, Herwegh and Weerth) in Moscow allowed Russia to be presented as the refuge of past liberal — and censored — German literature.[129] In 1949, the journal published a speech delivered by the Russian writer, Fadajew, at the international peace conference in New York. Not for the first time, it was suggested that Russians made the greatest contribution to such global events.[130] Political messages were clearly emerging in attitudes to literature and reports of literary events.

In the effort to remain or appear even-handed, American writers also featured frequently. But the selection betrayed ideological bias. The liberal writer Carson McCullers was a favourite of Kantorowicz; Agnes Smedley's profile of Mao Tse Tung was published; and Langston Hughes could provide witness to the conflicts which had affected him 'als Neger und als fortschrittlich denkenden

---

[125] Veronica Ensslen, 'Diskussion um einen Sowjetroman', *Ost und West*, 2 (1948), H.6, 85-88 (pp.86 and 88).
[126] For example, Vissarion Belinski, 'Brief an Gogol', *Ost und West*, 2 (1948), H.5, 45-49.
[127] 'Gedichte', *Ost und West*, 2 (1948), H.8, 29-32.
[128] Michael Hell, 'Unter Prominenten', *Ost und West*, 3 (1949), H.5, 54-59.
[129] Bruno Kaiser, 'Moskau entdeckt deutsche Gedichte', *Ost und West*, 3 (1949), H.3, 5.
[130] 'Es lebe die Freundschaft der Völker!', *Ost und West*, 3 (1949), H.6, 85-89.

Menschen'.[131] Another American, Albert Maltz, expressed his dismay at the persecution of communist sympathisers and the connected censorship in the United States:

Sind wir bestürzt, wenn wir im Jahre 1947 lesen, daß "Citizen Tom Paine", ein herrlicher und glühender Roman von Howard Fast aus den Bibliotheken der öffentlichen Schulen New Yorks und Detroits verbannt wurde? Ekelt es uns? Sind wir alarmiert? Erheben wir unsere Stimme?[132]

Maltz's call upon fellow American writers to preserve 'freies Denken' was reminiscent of Eastern slogans for literary creativity: 'Das ist unser Erbe. Unsere Verpflichtung ist, zu verteidigen, was wir ererbten, es zu bereichern und weiterzugeben.'[133] Kantorowicz, in the next issue, published his translation of an extract from Fast's controversial biography of Tom Paine, and compared the charge of un-American activities brought against Fast to the accusations of anti-German activities or attitudes trumpeted by the Nazis Streicher and Himmler.[134]

The ideological message continued in Heinrich Mann's essay 'Widerstehe dem Übel', which drew together two groups of people who had resisted Nazism: the young (the Weiße Rose) and the working class. They should both be remembered for their commitment: 'Arbeiter und Student, beide sind gleich überzeugt, [...] daß sie berufen sind, ohne sie geht es nicht, der Mehrheit fehlt der moralische Mut.'[135] Walther Pollatschek wrote about the republication of Brecht's *Dreigroschenroman*. Published in 1934 in Amsterdam, but banned in Nazi Germany, it was described as the most significant satirical novel in German literature. He underlined its message: 'Diese Welt ist eine Räuberhöhle, solange

---

131 See *Ost und West*, 1 (1947), H.1, 58-63; and 3 (1949), H.2, 4-5 and 15-26 (p.15) respectively.

132 Albert Maltz, 'Das Gewissen des Volkes', *Ost und West*, 2 (1948), H.8, 6-14 (p.13).

133 ibid., (p.14).

134 Howard Fast, 'Tom Paine geht an die Front', *Ost und West*, 3 (1948), H.9, 56-65; and A. K., 'Howard Fast', 51-55 (p.53).

135 Mann, 'Widerstehe dem Übel', (p.21).

wir den Kapitalismus dulden.'[136] Again, the anti-capitalist message of could not be clearer. One contributor agreed with the condemnation of literature in western Germany; it was effete and revealed 'Gespenster der Vergangenheit'.[137]

The handling of drama also showed marked political awareness. Scheer savagely dismissed Sartre's play *Les Mains Sales* as particularly dangerous to German audiences: 'Sartre reaktiviert in ihnen die Elemente des Nazismus.'[138] Sartre's objections that New York productions of his play were too anti-communist were dismissed by Kantorowicz as insincere.[139] In a wider debate on Existentialism, Roland Schacht defended the movement, countering accusations that it was subjective, led to isolation as opposed to human solidarity and induced passive quietism. Cécile Angrand, on the other hand, attacked it as 'eine Mode', which was both anti-Marxist and anti-democratic.[140] In May 1948, a considerable part of the journal was devoted to the theme 'Theater Gestern und Heute'. In his article, 'Theaterdilemma im deutschen Westen', Pollatschek lamented the loss of the vibrant German theatrical scene that had existed before 1933. A renaissance in the German theatre was now being prevented by the political division. Consultation between different theatre companies was being prevented, and western companies were prejudiced: 'Sie möchten als Förderer der neuen deutschen Dramatik erscheinen, möchten aber auf der anderen Seite alles ausschließen, was weltanschaulich fortschrittlich ist.'[141] Only foreign plays had been performed in western Germany in the previous year, and the pattern was of French plays in the French Zone, American plays in the American Zone, and

---

136 Walther Pollatschek, 'Bert Brechts Dreigroschenroman', *Ost und West*, 2 (1948), H.7, 79-80 (p.80).
137 Richard Drews, 'Neue Vernebelung', *Ost und West*, 3 (1949), H.2, 44-48 (p.44).
138 Scheer, 'Mord', (p.39).
139 Kantorowicz, 'Fortsetzung des Briefes an Herrn v. F.', (p.81).
140 'Existentialismus: Für und Wider', *Ost und West*, 2 (1948), H.2, 37-49.
141 Walther Pollatschek, 'Theaterdilemma im deutschen Westen', *Ost und West*, 2 (1948), H.5, 33-36 (p.34).

modern Russian drama nowhere to be seen. New German drama was only just beginning to appear, and first performances of plays by Bruckner and Nowak did not alter the basic tendency of the West to censor and control. In addition, American and British sponsorship of Zuckmayer's *Des Teufels General* was only due to the reactionary nature of the play. There was in the West an atmosphere of permanent 'Theaterkrise'.[142] Max Schröder, in his assessment of Berlin theatre, was more optimistic. Pointing out that the writers of *Tomorrow the World* had shown 'das tiefste Verständnis für Deutschland', he believed that 'das politisch-zeitkritische Theater Amerikas' had a place on the Berlin stage.[143] Theatre in Berlin, particularly the Berliner Theater, was, he said, thriving: 'Ihr Theater ist wieder eine Tribüne deutscher Kultur geworden.'[144] In the same issue, Fritz Erpenbeck also regretted the fact the national trend to stage plays which were classics, or were written in exile, or were foreign, and quoted a British source in his criticism: 'Die Intellektuellen und Schriftsteller verstecken sich hinter den vier Flaggen, die über der Stadt wehen. War das nicht immer eine deutsche Charaktereigenschaft, seine Verantwortung zu verneinen?'[145] In other words, German theatre was failing its people. The revelation that Goethe's *Faust*, subject to censorship in the Third Reich, was now again censored, was the final blow for Scheer — 'Doch ist es nicht mehr die Zensur der Bigotterie und der offenen Reaktion. Es ist die verschleierte Angst-Zensur gegen die zündende Wirkung des größten dramatischen Gedichts der deutschen Sprache.'[146]

---

[142] ibid., (pp.34-35).

[143] 'Die Berliner Bühnen 1948', *Ost und West*, 2 (1948), H.5, 18-28 (p.28).

[144] ibid., (p.27).

[145] ibid., (p.20).

[146] Maximilian Scheer, 'Hochverräter Goethe 1943', *Ost und West*, 2 (1948), H.5, 14-17, (p.17).

The last issue

Ost und West ceased publication in December 1949 for reasons Kantorowicz described to readers as financial. In its final issue, the journal continued its attack on the western German 'cultural crisis'.[147] Pollatschek argued that the very language used in East and West Germany was different. He commended *Ost und West*'s efforts to combat East-West division on the cultural level: 'Man braucht wohl nicht zu erläutern, daß und weshalb gerade die Zeitschrift OST UND WEST die Tribüne ist, von der aus über diese Tatsache gesprochen werden muß.'[148] The threat to culture in western Germany by American 'Kulturersatz' demanded further action.[149] Stalin was lauded by Kantorowicz as the 'Lehrmeister der nationalen Selbstbestimmung'. Kantorowicz's final article in *Ost und West*, however, was autobiographical. Twenty-five-pages long, it condemned the fascist lies of the American 'Hearst-Presse' and its defamation of Kantorowicz himself as a 'red' spy.[150]

Comment

In a letter to Kantorowicz in February 1950 Thomas Mann wrote, 'Ich bedauere dies Verschwinden aufrichtig, denn *Ost und West* hat mir persönlich oft Schönes und Bedeutendes geboten, und ich betrachte den Hingang des Blattes als einen entschiedenen Verlust.'[151] His regret was widely shared; the disappearance of *Ost und West* was seen as a loss to German intellectual discussion. As early as 1 November 1949 Walther Pollatschek too had written to Kantorowicz, expressing his 'extraordinarily deeply felt' disappointment. He particularly regretted that *Ost*

---

[147] 'Die westdeutsche Kulturkrise', *Ost und West*, 3 (1949), H.12 ('Das letzte Heft'), 58-67.
[148] Walther Pollatschek, 'Die Bedrohung der Kultur im Westen Deutschlands', *Ost und West*, 3 (1949), H.12, 61-65 (p.62).
[149] ibid., (p.65).
[150] Der Herausgeber, 'Abschied', *Ost und West*, 3 (1949), H.12, 77-101.
[151] IfZ, Hammer, ED 106, Band 33, (11 February 1950).

und West's influence would no longer prevail against the reactionary view that 'Sowjetisch lizenzierter Verlag = russische Propaganda = kommunistisch = undeutsch = Lüge'.[152] The interest of these letters is appropriate given the importance that *Ost und West* placed on dialogue with its readership. In the last issue, Kantorowicz explained the journal's disappearance as financially motivated. He was, however, later to write that the journal had been suppressed by the central committee of the SED.[153] It seems probable that both were true. Kantorowicz's own bequest throws light on events immediately leading up to the journal's demise. He had written to the SED in October 1949 to tell them that, without financial support, the journal would be in danger of collapsing.[154] He offered several solutions. One was a direct monthly subvention; the second was a guaranteed purchase of issues for public libraries (his own preference); the third was the take-over of the journal by one or other of the cultural or political institutions of the GDR, such as the ministry of education or of foreign affairs; and the fourth was the adoption of the journal by a newspaper, ideally the *Berliner Zeitung*. Justifying at some length the contribution which the journal had made, Kantorowicz stated that he was putting its fate into the hands of the political authorities. In reply, Stefan Heymann of the cultural section of the SED rejected Kantorowicz's pleas. Support on the grounds of its links between East and West was dismissed.[155] Heymann argued that these were due not to the journal itself, but to particular contributors. They could equally well write for *Aufbau*, and journalists would be free to work for the *Feuilleton* sections of the zone's newspapers. In view of this and its own financial restraints, the SED could not back *Ost und West*'s continuation. In any case, he contended, the journal's 1947 aims were no longer appropriate. Kantorowicz's expectations of financial support may well have been unreasonable.

---

152 AKN, 72, copy of letter (1 November 1949).

153 Kantorowicz, *Deutsches Tagebuch: Zweiter Teil*, p.51 (6 January 1950).

154 AKN, 92, letter from Kantorowicz to SED *Zentralsekretariat* (21 October 1949).

155 AKN, 92, letter from Stefan Heymann to Kantorowicz (1 November 1949).

A somewhat oblique reference by Heymann to certain comrades' poor opinion of the journal suggests that *Ost und West* might have had powerful political opponents. This is borne out in an entry in Kantorowicz's diary which displays his bitterness at the victimisation of his journal:

Um die Jahreswende 1948/49 führte ohne mein Wissen das SED-Politbüro einen Beschluß herbei, daß die Zeitschrift sofort einzustellen sei. Die Russen sagten: "Nein, die Zeitschrift bleibt bestehen." Das Unerhörte geschah: Der Beschluß des Politbüros mußte zurückgenommen werden. Nicht für lange Zeit. Gleich nach der Gründung der "Deutschen Republik" wurde als erste die Zeitschrift [...] abgewürgt.[156]

A letter written to Walter Hammer in 1960 emphasizes the contrast between Kantorowicz's bitterness towards the SED and his admiration of the Russian authorities: 'Besonders freut mich, daß auch Sie Dymschitz und andere russische Kulturoffiziere höher schätzen als die Rabaukenclique um Ulbricht.'[157] Newspaper accounts of the time support Kantorowicz's story. Western press articles anticipated the plan to reduce press effort to a tight body of pro-Eastern publications.[158] The Russian-backed *Tägliche Rundschau* gave clear support. It lamented the journal's departure from the scene and, recognising that such an event usually went unnoticed, pointed to the journal's unique contribution:

Tatsächlich aber verliert die fortschrittliche deutsche Öffentlichkeit mit der Liquidation dieser Zeitschrift eines der frischesten und lebendigsten Publikationsorgane von internationalem Rang. Niemand, der sich verantwortlich für die Wiederherstellung der deutschen Einheit fühlt, kann übersehen, daß "Ost und West" (sein Name schon war ein Programm) ein wichtiger und überparteilicher und interzonaler Mittler innerhalb der deutschen Länder war und daß in dieser Zeitschrift das Ost-West-Gespräch nie abriß.[159]

---

[156] Kantorowicz, *Deutsches Tagebuch: Zweiter Teil*, p.11.

[157] IfZ, Hammer, ED 106, Band 33, letter from Kantorowicz to Walter Hammer (22 January 1960).

[158] See, for example, 'SED-Politbüro will Zeitungen eingehen lassen', *Neue Zeitung*, 24 November 1949, (AKN, 83).

[159] AKN, 83, 'Ltz', 'Abschied von einer Zeitschrift', *Tägliche Rundschau*, 5 January 1950.

The fact that Kantorowicz was a regular contributor to the newspaper may account in part for this sympathetic treatment, but the statement implies support for *Ost und West*'s line.[160] They could perhaps afford to be generous given that the dirty work was already being done. In February 1950, Stefan Heymann, writing in *Sonntag*, condemned Kantorowicz's 'Mangel an politischer Erkenntnis'. The title of his journal made this clear. Kantorowicz did not appreciate that the question was not one of East and West, but of 'Fortschritt' and 'Reaktion'.[161] Heymann's vituperative dismissal of Kantorowicz and *Ost und West* confirmed that the German political élite disapproved of the journal.

Alfred Kantorowicz was variously described as one of the most evil enemies of the Nazi Reich, one of the most evil enemies of the GDR, and a 'red' or Stasi spy.[162] The product of early persecution, fleeing first to France and then to America, he returned home full of idealistic hope in a new future for Germany. It would be independent and respected as a mediator in the centre of Europe. He tried to fulfil in his journal both his feelings for the West and for freedom and his sense of social justice and socialism. Even at the journal's inception, however, it was probably too late for these ideals to be achieved. At the time of the first issue in July 1947, the gravity of the overall political situation must have been clear. This was the very month of the failure of the Munich Ministerpräsidentenkonferenz, an event that signalled serious East-West division within the ranks of German political leadership. Because of its 'Mittellage', Germany would find itself split in any division between East and West. The distance between the major powers, and Germany's involvement in it, were no longer matters of conjecture. Kantorowicz was aware of the situation: 'Die

---

[160] For Kantorowicz's contributions to the *Tägliche Rundschau*, see, AKN, 102.

[161] AKN, 92, Stefan Heymann, 'Ein schlechter Abgesang', *Sonntag*, 5 February 1950.

[162] See ZPA, SED ZK, Konferenzen und Beratungen des ZK der SED, IV2/1.01/407, 26 (Abusch's remarks); IfZ, Hammer, ED 106, Band 33; and 'Professor Kantorowicz: Rechenschaft'.

Spaltung vertieft sich. Die östlichen und die westlichen Teile Deutschlands beginnen, sich voneinander zu entfernen.'[163] Still he pursued his ambition that Germany should play a 'Vermittlerrolle' and that his journal should be 'zwischen den Fronten'.[164] Kantorowicz's claim to represent all fair-minded people throughout the country shows a certain naiveté: 'Männer und Frauen guten Willens in allen vier Zonen haben dem Wunsche Ausdruck gegeben, daß Deutschland, anstatt der Zankapfel zwischen den Mächten zu werden, die friedliche Brücke zwischen ihnen werden möge.'[165] This idea was first voiced in a radio broadcast in January 1947, in which he stated that Germany could be important once more, if its people of good will followed the example of Goethe, Marx, Beethoven and Lessing: 'Welch eine Aufgabe für alle, die guten Willens sind.'[166] As well as being idealistic, he could also be hard-headed, for example with regard to his publishing interests, his publicizing of his particular group of friends, and debatably his flight to the West in 1957. Nevertheless, his description of his friend Rudolf Leonhard is one of genuine admiration, and even aspiration:

Er sagt uns, daß er sein Leben zwischen Berlin und Paris teilen möchte, ein Vermittler zwischen Menschen guten Willens auf beiden Seiten, wohlbekannt und geachtet hier wie dort; keinen besseren Mann könnte man finden zum neuen Brückenschlag, zur Versöhnung der Menschen und der Kulturen, zu einem echten, nicht von machtpolitischen Erwägungen abhängig gemachten, sondern aus innerer Notwendigkeit kommenden deutsch-französischen Rapprochement.[167]

The journal undoubtedly made real attempts towards 'Verständigung', and, although it contained anti-American sentiments, its criticism of the West could not be interpreted as a dismissal of Western culture as a whole. Until the end attempts by the journal at mediation continued. In the penultimate issue, there were several

---

[163] 'Einführung', (p.7).
[164] Baerns, *Ost und West: Eine Zeitschrift zwischen den Fronten*.
[165] 'Einführung', (p.4).
[166] 'Vom moralischen Gewinn der Niederlage', Radio Bremen, January 1947, in Kantorowicz, *Vom moralischen Gewinn*, p.342.
[167] A. K., 'Rudolf Leonhard', *Ost und West*, 1 (1947), H.2, 70-75 (p.75).

features on American literature. They ran to six pages, but there were thirty pages of addresses welcoming the GDR. The imbalance was patent. What is undoubted is that the journal's alignment with the East became dominant, its neutrality compromised.

Ost und West succeeded remarkably in another of its aims — that of achieving dialogue with its readers. Although the authenticity of many of the readers' letters cannot be verified, there is no reason to doubt them, and they convey not just a vivid sense of the whole German tragedy, but genuine political criticism. This is evident in one reader's reaction to Scheer's commentary 'An Rhein und Ruhr', condemned by the reader as 'einseitig östlich gesehen'. This charge of partiality was directed not just at Scheer, but at the journal itself. The letter brings a rare example of criticism directed at the East: 'Wenn ich richtig vermute, so sollen Ihre "Beiträge" Ost und West verbinden und die leidige Trennung wenigstens auf geistigem Gebiet beseitigen helfen, wenn schon die politische Einheit zur Zeit ein frommer Wunsch zu bleiben scheint. [...] Wozu von "Schwarz ist Trumpf" entnazifizierter Gestapo-Beamten etc. sprechen, die durch Leumundszeugnisse der Geistlichkeit reingewaschen werden, wenn in der Ostzone der Beitritt zu einer Blockpartei zu demselben Resultat führt?' [168] For cases of Nazi involvement identified in the West, the reader gave equivalents in the Eastern Zone, together with positive aspects of the West which he accused Scheer of ignoring. He asserted that Scheer 'glauben machen will, als sei es in der Ostzone anders'. His conclusion effectively branded *Ost und West* as contributing to the general misinformation of the population: 'so glaube ich, daß das geteilte Deutschland eine völlig schiefe Anschauung der meisten Teile bekommt.' His dry closing sentence was a scathing indictment of the journal's failure to implement its own editorial policy: 'Statt Polemik eine Synthese zwischen Ost und West zu

---

168 'Drei Briefe', (p.90).

suchen, wäre schöner, meiner unmaßgeblichen Meinung nach.'[169] Maximilian Scheer's response was dismissive: 'Ich ergreife gern die Gelegenheit, die mir sein Brief bietet, mit ihm zu besprechen, ob seine Denkrichtung zu einer realen Synthese führen kann oder zu einem Knusperhäuschen im Niemandsland führen muß.'[170] Whether Scheer truly participated in Kantorowicz's philosophy for the journal is debatable. Although he expressed hope for a positive sense of national identity ('Wir sollten Deutschsein verstehen als eine Verantwortung vor dem geistigen Erbe, der gemeinsamen Sprache'), his unsubstantiated accusations against the West and the implicit message in his dismissal of any collaboration with former Nazis, contradict this:

> Mit ihnen eine Synthese zu finden, ist unmöglich. Sie sind die Kräfte von gestern. Wir wollen einen Akkord mit den Kräften von heute und morgen. Wir wollen die Synthese des Menschen diesseits und jenseits des Ozeans, aller Menschen, die nicht ihre Mitmenschen verbrannten oder verbrennen wollen — sei es im Vernichtungsofen oder im Atominferno.[171]

Another reader, who 'in den Westzonen leben muß', agreed with Scheer's perception of developments in the West, and identified *Ost und West* as the kind of publication needed to counteract them:

> Auf tönernen Füßen marschierend, bedürfen wir notwendig derartiger Zeitschriften wie der Ihrigen, um nicht allen Mut und alle Hoffnung zu verlieren, die wahrhaftig in der Aussichtslosigkeit der KZs größer waren als sie es heute sind, wenn man klarsichtig genug ist, zu sehen, wohin wir wieder einmal steuern oder, besser gesagt, gesteuert werden.[172]

These examples not only demonstrate readers' participation, they also show *Ost und West*'s willingness to publish criticism from both sides. It is hardly surprising then that it was attacked by both sides. Kantorowicz described this as *Ost und*

---

169 ibid.

170 Maximilian Scheer, 'Nachwort', *Ost und West*, 2 (1948), H.7, 91-95 (p.91).

171 ibid., (p.95).

172 'Ost- und West-Leser schreiben', *Ost und West*, 2 (1948), H.4, 92-95 (pp.94-95).

West's 'Zweifrontenkampf'.[173] By 1949, with growing hostility towards him and his journalism in the East, there were also obstacles to his voice being heard in the West; *Neues Deutschland* and *Tribüne* both record the arrest in April 1949, in Wilmersdorf in the British sector of Berlin, of 'Gerda W.' for carrying several copies of *Ost und West*.[174]

Ost und West's contribution to the literary scene was clearly politically orientated. Contributors were in the main chosen because they came from the same background of freedom fighting as the editors. Literary works selected contributed to the left-wing slant and were frequently preceded by commentary on the author, his writing or his political life. Even authors not in themselves political were used to make political points, as instanced by the adoption of Goethe's works as education for the working class. The most useful comment on *Ost und West* could be said to be provided by its readers. The voices of ordinary Germans ring out. It was levelled too high; it contained too many foreign words: 'Hier vertreten Sie den üblichen, kleinbürgerlichen, überheblichen, von Bildungsdünkel strotzenden Literatenstandpunkt. Unbewußt entfernen Sie sich von der Sprache des Volkes.'[175] It was unfair to the West; it was what was needed in the West. The overall impression, however, is that it provided comfort and inspiration: 'ich finde es gut und richtig, daran zu arbeiten, selbst wenn diese Brücke nur die Konsistenz eines Regenbogens hätte.'[176]

In his opening editorial Kantorowicz had expressed his hopes that *Ost und West* would be a catalyst in the rebuilding of Germany as a mature, independent and neutral state of its own devising. Germany was to occupy the middle ground,

---

173 Alfred Kantorowicz, *Deutschland-Ost und Deutschland-West: Kulturpolitische Einigungsversuche und geistige Spaltung in Deutschland seit 1945*, Sylter Beiträge (Münsterdorf: Hansen and Hansen, 1971), p.10.

174 *Neues Deutschland*, 24 April 1949, and *Tribüne*, 25 April 1949, (AKN, 83).

175 'Ost- und West-Leser schreiben', *Ost und West*, 2 (1948), H.2, 92-95 (p.92).

176 'Für und Wider aus West und Ost', *Ost und West*, 1 (1947), H.6, 95-96 (p.95).

where it could act as a mediator, a bridge between East and West, and *Ost und West* was to be its literary manifestation. Involvement of ordinary Germans in the intellectual debate would be a means towards this end. It is the tragedy of this journal that, just as it appeared to have provoked political discussion, particularly amongst German youth, it was silenced most probably by German politicians.

In his pursuit of independence and neutrality, Kantorowicz had approached all four occupation powers for a licence to publish. No specific statement of alignment was made. It is nevertheless clear that the socialist ethics held by the editors and repeatedly expressed in the journal were more in line with the aims of the USSR than with those of the other occupying powers. The East welcomed the journal as an ambassador of socialism which would not only facilitate Soviet policies of re-education but also reach an audience in western Germany. The formation of two diametrically opposed camps within Germany dashed its hopes for the establishment of a united independent Germany and with them the potential for mediation between East and West. Increasing co-operation with the authorities in East Berlin was necessary for survival. Its ideological sympathies became increasingly harnessed to the growing Sovietization. It was inevitably drawn deeper into the entrenchment symptomatic of Cold War Germany. *Ost und West*, despite these compromises, strove to maintain its neutral stance, and it is significant that it did not survive. Rudolf Majut's judgement that it saw East and West as a German-Russian axis 'which may become the nucleus of a politically and culturally integrated Europe' was misguided.[177] To categorize *Ost und West* as a journal of the East is to misrepresent it. It remained a journal of East and West.

---

[177] Rudolf Majut, 'The Cultural Periodicals of Post-War Germany' *GLL*, 7 (1953/4), 17-27 (p.23).

Conclusions

Ost und West was first published in 1947 and continued for two years, its demise coinciding with the establishment of the GDR. Although licensed by the Russians, it had no official connection with any Eastern Zone institution, but was the creation of one individual, Alfred Kantorowicz. It reflected his ideas, his aims, and his friends, and relied on his financial backing. The journal's aim was to look both to East and to West for inspiration in the cultural progress towards a new Germany. Germany rebuilt was to be the product of German thinking and decision-making, and not a copy of either East or West. The journal was thus a protagonist of the 'Third Way'. With the Cold War already advanced at the time of its inception, however, the 'Third Way' was a forlorn hope. The journal finally alienated vested interests and its fate was sealed by its own countrymen in the SED.

CHAPTER FOUR
DER MONAT

Der Monat was launched in Berlin in 1948 under the editorship of Melvin J. Lasky. It was licensed by the American military authorities and owed its existence in part to the events of the Berlin writers' conference in 1947. This conference had exposed, in a dramatic fashion, the extent to which the Cold War in Germany had taken root. Attended by writers from all four zones, in the presence of mainly Eastern military officers, the initially hopeful gathering became a statement of East-West division. According to reports, Western journalists, and particularly Lasky, took umbrage at scarcely veiled insults directed against the 'imperialist' West. Günther Weisenborn invited Lasky to prepare a response, and this response precipitated uproar. He began with some approving remarks about general cultural recovery which drew applause from communist delegates, but then turned to deliver a forthright condemnation of the suppression of writers in the Soviet Union. Colonel Dymschitz, the Soviet cultural officer, walked out in disgust, and Eastern Zone newspapers subsequently condemned Lasky as a Western warmonger.[1] Press response to the affair rang alarm bells, not only about the political situation, but about the dearth of Western journals which could effectively counter Eastern propaganda.[2] Criticizing the existing American journals, *Amerikanische Rundschau* and *Neue Auslese*, as 'canned foods', Lasky argued that what was required was 'fresh vegetables' and proposed the establishment of a new cultural journal.[3] Despite doubts in some quarters about his suitability, General Lucius

---

[1] See in particular Boris Schub, 'An Incident in Berlin (October, 1947)', in *Melvin J. Lasky: Encounter with a 60th Birthday*, ed. by Helga Hegewisch (*Encounter* Special edition, 1980), pp.26-30; and *Der erste Gesamtdeutsche Schriftstellerkongress*, ed. by Wende-Hohenberger.

[2] Elmer Plischke and Henry P. Pilgert, *U.S. Information Programs in Berlin* (HICOG: 1953) p.18.

[3] Interview with Lasky.

Clay, head of OMGUS, approved Lasky's appointment as editor, and with his support and that of Ernst Reuter, *Der Monat* appeared the following year.[4]

Melvin J. Lasky, born in America in 1920, was of Polish Jewish extraction. Having studied history at the universities of Michigan and Columbia, he started work as a journalist on the magazine, *The New Leader*. This journal was published by Sol Levitas, a Menshevik who had been persecuted by the Bolsheviks and who now used his journal in his anti-Stalinist campaign.[5] At that time in the late 1930s an 'unaffiliated anti-Stalinist socialist', Lasky soon became fervently opposed to communism — an attitude which subsequently dominated his political philosophy.[6] From 1943 to 1946 he served as a war historian with the 7th US Army, arriving in Germany for the first time in 1945.[7] Before assuming his editorship of *Der Monat*, Lasky was required to become a member of OMGUS, giving him official status as an American cultural officer. To offset this, *Der Monat* declared that the opinions it expressed were not to be taken as those of the editors.

The subtitle of *Der Monat* — *Eine internationale Zeitschrift für Politik und geistiges Leben* — announced the journal's intention to be a forum for discussion of political or intellectual matters. Each month's edition of *Der Monat* was devoted to a single theme examined from different points of view. To fulfil its claims to be international it recruited a constellation of writers who were famous world-wide. They had a certain solidarity of approach; many subsequently became members of the Congress for Cultural Freedom which opposed communist totalitarianism. *Der Monat*'s average circulation is a matter of some disagreement. Lucius D. Clay claimed that the circulation was 60,000, while Harold Zink

---

[4] ibid.

[5] Coleman, pp.16-17; and Daniel Bell, 'Our New York Days', in Hegewisch, pp.3-7 (p.7).

[6] Nathan Glick, 'In the Bronx, and After...', in Hegewisch, pp.2-3 (p.2).

[7] Melvin J. Lasky, *Wortmeldung zu einer Revolution: Der Zusammenbruch der kommunistischen Herrschaft in Ostdeutschland* (Frankfurt a. M.: Ullstein, 1991); and Melvin J. Lasky, 'Ein Amerikaner in Berlin (im Jahre 0)', unpub. Ms.

estimated it to be 30,000.[8] A figure of 50,000 for the initial circulation was produced by yet a third analysis.[9] When Lasky left in 1958 to edit *Encounter* in London, *Der Monat*'s sales were certainly over 25,000, making it the 'largest review of its kind in Europe'.[10] This last figure included 'underground' sales in East Germany. According to Lasky, they 'overprinted' when financially possible to support their secret circulation in the East, which ranged between two and ten thousand copies.[11] After Lasky's departure, *Der Monat* remained in publication until 1971. Its passing, after 23 years and 270 editions, was widely mourned; 'Keine Tageszeitung, kein Kulturkommentar im Funk ohne Nekrolog', according to one commentator, even if, as may be supposed, anti-American feeling in Europe may have reduced coverage of its demise.[12] That its impact was considerable is largely explained by the panoply of prominent thinkers published in its pages. This strength was established at the very beginning. *Der Monat* burst onto the Cold War scene with an impressive array of intellectual names, producing an intellectual forum that was itself an event. As a result, the dynamism of the project undoubtedly exacerbated the antagonism the journal and its editor attracted in official circles in the East. Among the writers published were Arthur Koestler, Benedetto Croce, Friedrich Hayek, Wilhelm Röpke, Hannah Arendt, Bertrand Russell and A.J.P. Taylor.

---

[8] Lucius D. Clay, *Decision in Germany* (London: Heinemann, 1950), p.287; and Harold Zink, *The United States in Germany 1944-1955* (Princeton, NJ: van Nostrand, 1957), p.240.

[9] Hans Borchers, and Klaus W. Vowe, *Die zarte Pflanze Demokratie: Amerikanische Re-education in Deutschland im Spiegel ausgewählter politischer und literarischer Zeitschriften (1945-1949)* (Tübingen: Narr, 1979), p.43.

[10] Coleman, p.95.

[11] Interview with Lasky.

[12] Hans Bender, 'Reflexionen über Zeitschriften', in *Literaturbetrieb in Deutschland*, ed. by Heinz Ludwig Arnold (München: Richard Boorberg, 1971), pp.224-33 (p.230); and Hermann Glaser, *Kulturgeschichte der Bundesrepublik Deutschland* (München: Hanser, 1985), I: *Zwischen Kapitulation und Währungsreform, 1945-1948*, p.196.

Setting the tone

The first issue of *Der Monat* appeared in October 1948. Its theme, 'Das Schicksal des Abendlandes', was explored individually by Bertrand Russell, Franz Borkenau and Arnold Toynbee. Other contributors to the first issue were Jean-Paul Sartre and Stephen Spender, the British Labour politician, Richard Crossman, the prominent anti-communist Arthur Koestler, and the American journalists, Rebecca West and James Agee. On the inside cover appeared the following statement of the journal's position:

DER MONAT ist eine internationale Zeitschrift für Politik und geistiges Leben. Die in seinen Spalten wiedergegebenen Gedanken entsprechen weder in jedem Fall der Ansicht der Redaktion, noch sind die Beiträge einzelner Autoren Ausdruck irgendeiner offiziösen Haltung.
DER MONAT soll als Forum einer offenen Aussprache und Auseinandersetzung auf der Grundlage freier Meinungsäußerung dienen und beabsichtigt, einer möglichst großen Zahl verschiedener Stimmen aus Deutschland und allen Teilen der Welt Gehör zu verschaffen.

There was to be free expression of opinion over a broad range of topics and from as wide a range of contributors as possible. Its chosen themes would, it was hoped, attract authors whose views might be 'weit auseinandergehend'.[13] Open and balanced argument would exemplify the West and Western democracy. The first debate was introduced by an editorial posing the question 'Wird die westliche Zivilisation, die uns als das Erbteil der letzten zweieinhalb Jahrtausende überliefert worden ist, dem Ansturm ungeheuerlichen Ausmaßes gewachsen sein, der ihr ganz augenscheinlich heute droht?'.[14] Alluding to precedent in historical theory, the journal warned its readers about the growth of communism and cautioned them against superficially attractive slogans. It commended its contributors as men of wisdom qualified to explore the issue. In the section 'Die Autoren des Monats', Bertrand Russell was introduced as 'eine Art demokratischer, freisinniger Sozialist,

---

[13] 'Das Schicksal des Abendlandes: Drei Perspektiven', *Der Monat*, 1 (1948/9), H.1, 3.
[14] ibid.

ohne je mit dem Marxismus gemeinsame Sache zu machen' and Franz Borkenau as a revisionist Marxist.[15] In the first of the three essays Bertrand Russell argued that the repression of Poland was a clear indication of what Russian supremacy would bring. Exploring the hypothetical situation of world dominance by one or other superpower, he warned against Russian hegemony and described American victory as 'wünschenswert'.[16] What distinguished West from East was freedom. Franz Borkenau rejected 'das alte Märchen, daß der imperialistische Kapitalismus unvermeidlich dem Krieg zusteuere'.[17] It now symbolized active hostility. As a defence measure, the build-up of arms against Russia was justifiable. Arnold Toynbee, in the third essay, speculated about the state of contemporary Western civilisation in an anthropological study.

Also in the first issue of *Der Monat* was an account of a trip to the Soviet Union by Drew Middleton. Its title, 'Sowjet-Rußland ohne Propaganda', underlined the idea of giving the true story, of enlightening the German reader as a matter of urgency. There was an article on the craft of writing by Sartre, a series of contributions on the American writer Thomas Wolfe and, in its main literature section, a review of Goebbels's diaries by Richard Crossman. Separate sections covered film, fine art, theatre and poetry. The section on film deplored the persecution until his recent death of the Russian film-director, Sergei Eisenstein, after his film *Ivan the Terrible* was denounced for drawing parallels between Ivan and Stalin.[18] Coverage of fine art included a review of an exhibition from Berlin collections which was touring the United States.[19] In the poetry section, C.M. Bowra profiled the Italian poet, Salvatore Quasimodo. An accompanying

---

[15] 'Die Autoren des Monats', *Der Monat*, 1 (1948/9), H.1, 111-12 (p.111).
[16] Bertrand Russell, 'Der Weg zum Weltstaat', *Der Monat*, 1 (1948/9), H.1, 4-8 (p.6).
[17] Franz Borkenau, 'Nach der Atombombe', *Der Monat*, 1 (1948/9), H.1, 9-16 (p.9).
[18] James Agee, 'Eisensteins letztes Werk', *Der Monat*, 1 (1948/9), H.1, 98-99.
[19] Clement Greenberg, 'Berliner Kunstschätze', *Der Monat*, 1 (1948/9), H.1, 102-04.

comment regretted the damage inflicted on Italian art by fascism.[20] Finally, correspondents' letters from Tel Aviv, Helsinki and Mexico City were included in an effort to fill the gap in foreign news reaching the German public.[21]

In every respect this first issue pointed to the patterns to be followed in structure, points of emphasis and personalities. Over the next fourteen months until the end of 1949, there was a further issue devoted to the East-West conflict, an issue on Europe, one on the definition and nature of socialism, a double issue on German nationalism, and three on the future of the world. These titles indicate clearly the emphasis on political discussion.

History and ideology

In December 1948 in the journal's third issue, which was entitled 'Hoffnung auf eine bessere Welt?', an editorial posed the almost inevitable questions about the disasters which had beset the twentieth century. Did their origins lie in the 'Mißbrauch der Technik, im Versagen der Religion, in einem allgemeinen Niedergang der Kultur, in der Bürokratisierung der Politik — oder worin sonst?'?[22] Benedetto Croce, in his article 'Der Antichrist in uns', asked whether the reasons lay in the presence of the 'Antichrist' in the human spirit, 'eine Tendenz unserer Seele'.[23] For him, fascism, racism and Bolshevism were all manifestations of the Antichrist.[24] Croce, who was described as a democratic liberal, perceived totalitarianism not just as a political system, with its phenomena of 'Einheitspartei' and 'Parteigehorsam', but also as a human tragedy: 'die Menschen gehen wie verzaubert der eigenen Knechtschaft und Erniedrigung, dem Tode und der

---

[20] C. M. Bowra, 'Ein italienischer Lyriker: Salvatore Quasimodo', *Der Monat*, 1 (1948/9), H.1, 107-10 (p.107).

[21] 'Autoren des Monats', *Der Monat*, 1 (1948/9), H.1, 111-12 (p.112).

[22] 'Hoffnung auf eine bessere Welt?', *Der Monat*, 1 (1948/9), H.3, 3.

[23] Benedetto Croce, 'Der Antichrist in uns', *Der Monat*, 1 (1948/9), H.3, 3-7, (p.3).

[24] ibid., (p.6).

Vernichtung entgegen, als erwarte sie darin die Seligkeit.'[25] An editorial comment accompanying this suggested that the remedy for Western Europe was one of 'eines sozialen Aufbaus auf internationaler Grundlage', a clear vindication of the journal's own international approach.[26] Hans Kohn believed that progress from the eighteenth century to the twentieth century had been characterized by a change from the struggle against the tyranny of one person to the struggle against the tyranny of the masses. This brought the threat of war on a much larger scale, endangering whole civilisations, not just individuals.[27] The similarity between Marxism and National Socialism had already been mentioned by Boris Schub in the second issue. He argued that it had been apparent in the revolutionary developments of 1933.[28] Acknowledging that most Germans associated the Weimar Republic with national disgrace, Schub nevertheless defended it. He argued that the revolution of 1918 had brought about political and cultural freedom: both Remarque and Goebbels were able to air their views. Opposites had been accommodated: 'Pazifismus und Militarismus, Weltbürgertum und Chauvinismus, Toleranz und Bigotterie, Reichsbanner und SA, den *Zauberberg* und *Mein Kampf*, freie Gewerkschaften und die Krupp-Werke'.[29] The phenomenon of German fascism was thus examined within the wider context of anti-totalitarianism and the continuing ideological conflict.

The question of collective guilt did not feature prominently. In a review of Robert d'Harcourt's *Les Allemands d'Aujourd'hui*, which suggested that the Germans felt no remorse, Alfred Kellner asserted that the question of German guilt could only be addressed in the context of the historical dilemmas in which the German people had found itself:

---

[25] ibid., (p.5); see also 'Die Autoren des Monats' in the same issue, 124-26 (p.124).
[26] 'Hoffnung auf eine bessere Welt?'.
[27] Hans Kohn, 'Das Jahrhundert des Verrats', *Der Monat*, 1 (1948/9), H.3, 7-14 (pp.7-9).
[28] Boris Schub, 'Revolution im November', *Der Monat*, 1 (1948/9), H.2, 87-90 (p.90).
[29] ibid., (p.89).

Der Vorwurf, die Deutschen seien drei Jahre nach Beendigung des Krieges verstockter und "unbußfertiger" als bei Kriegsende, sie weigerten sich, das *mea culpa* auszusprechen, mag richtig sein, doch darf der Beobachter seine Konsequenzen nicht allein aus den nüchternsten greifbaren Tatsachen ziehen, sondern muß tiefer in die Niederungen des deutschen Dilemmas hinabsteigen.[30]

Kellner particularly objected to the sentence 'die deutsche Schuld ist die moralische Bastion der Alliierten' and suggested that d'Harcourt was less interested in historical fact than in 'eine Sicherung der eigenen nationalen Position gegen alle Eventualitäten'.[31] Despite this largely dismissive review of the French academician's analysis, Kellner insisted that his compatriots had to accept their guilt:

Diejenigen aber, die sich vor alledem immer wieder hinter die bornierte Ausflucht: "Die anderen sind ja noch schlimmer als wir" zurückziehen, sollten ihr Gewissen an der Frage des katholischen Schriftstellers Reinhold Schneider prüfen, den d'Harcourt zitiert: "Wie würde ich mich verhalten haben, wenn Hitler den Krieg gewonnen hätte?[32]

The victims of Nazism were mentioned only infrequently. The Jewish people were complimented by Arthur Koestler, in his 'Brief aus Tel Aviv', on their civilized approach to balancing different interests within their new state. Koestler suggested that the ghetto-isation of Jews in Europe before the French Revolution had confined them to roles as merchants and middle men not integrated in the indigenous social culture. In their own newly established state of Israel, there was by necessity a 'working class', but, because these workers were in control of the capital, there was no class struggle in the traditional sense.[33] In addition, Zionist ideology was manifesting itself in a return to the land and to the ideals of craftsmanship. Koestler held up the creation of this 'freiwillige Proletariat' as a

---

30 Alfred Kellner, 'Bericht über die Deutschen', *Der Monat*, 1 (1948/9), H.3, 111-13 (p.112).
31 ibid., (p.112-13).
32 ibid., (p.113).
33 Arthur Koestler, 'Brief aus Tel Aviv: Die umgestülpte Pyramide', *Der Monat*, 1 (1948/9), H.1, 24-26 (p.25).

contrast to the forced revolution of communism.[34] Israel had neither a new form of socialism, nor capitalism, nor communism, but a unique form of society. Hannah Arendt was introduced as one of the most important writers on German guilt. Although Jewish herself, she was later to be severely criticized for her theory of the 'banality' of evil, which was regarded by many Jews as excusing the Holocaust.

Even when articles were not so announced, attention to recent historical events was a recurring theme. Eastern Zone writer Arnold Zweig's book, *Das Beil von Wandsbeck*, was praised for its portrayal of how the German people became 'schuldlos schuldig' — it was, the reviewer claimed, 'die erste große Darstellung jener deutschen Tragödie'.[35] Inevitably Crossman's review of Goebbels's diaries concentrated on the lies of the 'Third Reich' and their subsequent exposure. Crossman emphasized the inherent inconsistency of propaganda ('Göring hätte das Recht, britische Städte zu coventrieren; wenn "Bomber-Harris" Gleiches mit Gleichem vergalt, war er ein Schlächter') and argued that downfall was unavoidable once Goebbels had begun to believe the lies himself: 'Aus diesem Tagebuch kann man erkennen, wie der Übermensch sich selbst zerstört. Sich selbst "jenseits von Gut und Böse" zu stellen, bedeutet letztlich, auch die Möglichkeit zu verlieren, Wahrheit und Lüge auseinanderzuhalten.'[36] Hitler, meanwhile, was described by Barbara Ward as 'ein geisteskranker Hysteriker' in her essay on the future possibility of war with Russia.[37]

The history of Germany's relationship with Russia was of supreme importance, and the discovery of documents in Potsdam occasioned a series of

---

[34] ibid., (p.24).

[35] Herbert Pfeiffer, 'Die verborgenen Möglichkeiten', *Der Monat*, 1 (1948/9), H.2, 93-95 (pp.94-95).

[36] R. H. S. Crossman, 'Dr. Goebbels privat', *Der Monat*, 1 (1948/9), H.1, 90-93 (p.93).

[37] Barbara Ward, 'Ist der Krieg mit Russland unvermeidlich?', *Der Monat*, 1 (1948/9), H.2, 3-7 (p.4).

articles in *Der Monat*.[38] New details of efforts towards Russo-German rapprochement had come to light in the papers of General von Seeckt who, in 1922, had stated, 'In späterer Zeit mag ein deutscher Politiker vor der Wahl zwischen Ost und West, Rußland und England, wieder stehen.'[39] This material revealed details of secret cooperation between the Russian and German armies in the twenties, including proposals to divide Poland between Germany and Russia, and would be of value to future historians, Julius Epstein argued, in understanding subsequent developments in both Germany and Russia. Eugen Fischer-Baling, also inspired by the Seeckt find, wondered whether, in the wake of the Nürnberg Trials, there would be even more unpleasant discoveries about Germany's history.[40] Epstein's discussion of the Potsdam documents contained a reference to a document 'von einiger staatsmännischer Klugheit', a memo in which Graf Brockdorff-Rantzau warned of the consequences of Seeckt's proposals.[41] Lasky regarded the Seeckt plan and its pre-1940 implementation as a double absurdity. The Germans had collaborated with the Russian military only to be defeated and then occupied by them. And the Russians had cooperated with the Germans only to see European Russia destroyed.[42] A direct consequence of this German-Russian collaboration was the destruction of almost the whole of Europe. Europe's recovery, then, depended on the avoidance in future of any such distortion of the principles of international co-operation.[43] This series of articles provoked a response from readers. One letter expressed the wish that the journal would continue to publish material uncovering historical lies.[44] A second letter was

---

38 'Der Seeckt-Plan', *Der Monat*, 1 (1948/9), H.2, 42-58.

39 Julius Epstein, 'Aus unveröffentlichten Dokumenten', *Der Monat*, 1 (1948/9), H.2, 42-50, (p.45).

40 Eugen Fischer-Baling, 'Politik und Kriegsromantik', *Der Monat*, 1 (1948/9), H.2, 50-55, (p.50).

41 Epstein, 'Aus unveröffentlichten Dokumenten', (p.42).

42 M. J. L., 'Seeckt, Stalin und Europa', *Der Monat*, 1 (1948/9), H.2, 55-58 (p.58).

43 ibid.

44 'Briefe des Monats: Seeckt, Stalin — und Churchill?', *Der Monat*, 1 (1948/9), H.3, 127-28.

introduced rather ambiguously in the following way: 'Zum Thema "General v. Seeckts Geheimplan" [...] erhielten wir von dem Kenner der neueren deutschen Militärgeschichte, dem die *Neue Zeitung* das Pseudonym Horst Falkenhagen verliehen hat, eine ausführliche Stellungnahme.' This letter was a most outspoken attack on Bolshevist ideology and its importation into Germany by Germans. The writer saw a connection between the Seeckt spirit of Russian co-operation and communism in 1930s Germany and pointed to the phenomenon of 'Nationalbolschewismus', which had connections in both Russia and China. The influence of this interconnection was such that, he concluded, the East German unity party, the SED, was the product of German National Bolshevism. To support his argument, he pointed out that the insignia of the National Bolshevist movement — the Prussian eagle, with hammer, sickle and sword, could be a direct link between the 'black' army and the 'red' army.[45] He also noted that this insignia had been used by the journal *Widerstand*, that its 'Programm des deutschen Widerstandes' was interchangeable with the Communist Manifesto, and that its editor, Ernst Niekisch, now taught at the Humboldt-Universität in East Berlin.[46] He even drew a parallel in accusing the Slavs of pursuing 'Volksraum' and claimed that East Germany was an example of this. He attacked the 'Partei-Bonzokratie der SED, diesen korrupten, an bourgeoises Parasitendasein hingegebenen Haufen bezahlter Funktionäre!'. He denounced what was being inculcated there:

Volksraumträumereien, Ordensmythos vom "harten Leben", Hoffnung, den Dritten Weltkrieg im Sinne des "Und ihr habt doch gesiegt!" durch Raumgewinn im Westen zu beenden, konspirative Tätigkeit im Stil der "Fünften Kolonne", Anwerbung der noch politisch unaufgeklärten alten Kameraden in den Westzonen, fanatische Besessenheit von einer durch und durch diesseitigen Idee, diesseitiger noch als die Sippen- und Rassenidee der Waffen-SS.[47]

---

45 'Briefe des Monats: Von der Schwarzen zur Roten Reichswehr', *Der Monat*, 1 (1948/9), H.4, 122-25 (p.122-23).

46 ibid.

47 ibid., (p.125).

A third letter on the subject was signed by Fritz Tschunke, an economist who had been mentioned in the Seeckt papers. He accused *Der Monat* of failing to distinguish between Russia and Bolshevism, claiming that it had let itself be drawn into anti-Russian propaganda which would only destroy the possibility of understanding between East and West.[48] Lasky regarded such misunderstandings as sufficiently important to reply himself. He pointed to the tragic 'anti-Russian' attitude of the Soviet dictatorship itself. Agreeing that Russia and Bolshevism were not synonymous, he stated that no-one had the right to sit in judgement over a whole people. Differentiation between a dictatorship and the people suffering under it was a basic 'moral' principle of democracy, and one which the new European society had to honour. Lasky insisted that there was no question of an orchestrated bias against any people:

Der Monat ist kein freiwilliger oder unfreiwilliger Bestandteil einer "Anti-Rußland-Propaganda" und beabsichtigt auch in Zukunft nicht, sich für einen solchen Feldzug anwerben zu lassen. Die Zeitschrift vertritt die Grundsätze eines demokratischen Humanismus auf internationaler Basis und würde sich ebensowenig dazu herbeilassen, anti-russischen wie anti-französischen, anti-englischen oder anti-deutschen Propaganda-Unsinn abzudrucken.[49]

The question arose again when the journal published an extraordinary squabble between Lasky and the West Berlin newspaper *Tagesspiegel*.[50] Lasky had objected to the condemnatory stance which the newspaper was adopting on Russia.[51] It had argued that, although there had been resistance efforts in Germany, there had been none in Russia, and that no-one could rely on the Stalinist dictatorship being overthrown from within.[52] Lasky protested that the West did not know whether there had been resistance in Russia or not. He reminded *Tagesspiegel* that, even when the very fact of Stauffenberg's plan to assassinate

---

48 'Briefe des Monats: Rußland und der Bolschewismus', *Der Monat*, 1 (1948/9), H.4, 125-26.
49 ibid.
50 'Ein Briefwechsel mit dem Berliner "Tagesspiegel"', *Der Monat*, 1 (1948/9), H.6, 107-11.
51 Melvin J. Lasky, 'Anti-sowjetisch oder anti-russisch', *Der Monat*, 1 (1948/9), H.6, 107-08.
52 'Die Antwort', *Der Monat*, 1 (1948/9), H.6, 108-09.

Hitler in July 1944 had been known, the outside world had ignored it and withheld support. They had been reluctant to believe in two Germanies. Lasky asserted 'Es gibt auch ein anderes Rußland.'[53] In this reply, in early 1949, Lasky posed the question 'was ist heute wichtiger als ein Verständnis der "Russischen Frage"?'.[54] For him, the 'German Question' had already been superseded.

Despite this sympathy with the Russian people, *Der Monat*, with its anti-totalitarian stance, necessarily became anti-Soviet, a bias which was evident in the majority of articles, some of them extremely unrestrained. The nature of communism itself was particularly vilified. James Burnham presented a damning account of the Communist Party as an organisation of 'Verschwörung'. He argued that communists were essentially criminals, describing 'die legale Arbeit der Kommunisten' as 'ein Deckmantel für ihre im wesentlichen illegale Betätigung'.[55] His main condemnation centred, however, on the terror which resulted from the system:

Jedes politische Regime beruht auf Macht und Mythos, auf Polizei, Soldaten, Gefängnissen und auf einer Ideologie, die wenigstens teilweise von der Wirklichkeit abweicht. Den Kommunismus unterscheidet von allen anderen, daß er sich auf den Terror stützt und der Inhalt seines Mythos vorsätzlicher Betrug ist.[56]

He attacked those in the West whom he described as vulnerable to communist thought as representing the greatest problem — 'die Zehntausende von Mitläufern der Kommunisten in den westlichen Demokratien und die Hunderttausende von Ahnungslosen, die dem Kommunismus dienen'.[57] His use here of the term 'Mitläufer' must have struck an uneasy chord with German readers. Norbert Mühlen, in an article describing communist activities in America, also referred to 'Mitlaüfer'. He blamed these 'fellow-travellers' for providing a smoke-screen

---

53 M. J. L., 'Politik oder Polemik', *Der Monat*, 1 (1948/9), H.6, 109-11, (p.110).
54 ibid., (p.109).
55 James Burnham, 'Vom Wesen des Kommunismus', *Der Monat*, 1 (1948/9), H.2, 18-29, (pp.21-22).
56 ibid., (p.23).
57 ibid., (p.24).

behind which a network of communists was undermining American democracy.[58] The mundane façade of communist infiltration was emphasized by Burnham:

Gute Staatsbürger hegen keinerlei Bedenken, sich mit Kommunisten zu Komitees für alle möglichen verdienstlichen Zwecke zusammenzuschließen oder mit Kommunisten in der Redaktion von Zeitschriften zusammenzuarbeiten. Liberale reagieren mit Empörung, sobald sich Kommunisten beklagen, daß sie in ihren staatsbürgerlichen Rechten beeinträchtigt werden.[59]

Mühlen identified the Soviet Union as 'das sowjetische System der Konzentrationslager, der Sklavenarbeit, der abgeschafften Gedankenfreiheit, der vergewaltigten Glaubensfreiheit, der gesetzlosen Parteidiktatur'.[60] Barbara Ward pointed out the resemblance of the Soviet Union's activities in Czechoslovakia to National Socialist practices.[61] Yet the danger she saw was not that the Soviet Union was seeking 'Volksraum', but that it was a dictatorship and in pursuit of yet more power.[62] Ward warned that the 'Ostfrage' required a clear indication from the West that further Soviet action would invite a military response. She advocated containment, calling for a defensive alliance to protect the West and halt the tide of communism.[63] Continuing her condemnation of communism, she described its basic denial of the worth of the individual, something which was enshrined in Western civilization, and particularly in Christianity. She argued that renewed commitment to the beliefs of the West was necessary: 'Die Zivilisation des Abendlandes wurde auf gewaltige Glaubensakte gegründet — auf den Glauben, daß die Menschen als Kinder Gottes frei und gleichberechtigt geboren seien und das einzelne Menschen-leben unendlichen Wert besitze.'[64] Drew Middleton identified the Soviet Union as the originator of Cold War antagonism: 'Von 1945

---

58 Norbert Mühlen, 'Brief aus Amerika: Eine Demokratie verteidigt sich', *Der Monat*, 1 (1948/9), H.2, 71-77 (p.75).
59 Burnham, 'Vom Wesen des Kommunismus', (p.19).
60 Mühlen, 'Brief aus Amerika', (p.71).
61 Ward, 'Ist der Krieg mit Russland unvermeidlich?', (p.3).
62 ibid., (pp.4-5).
63 ibid., (p.5).
64 ibid., (p.7).

an verhielten sich die Vertreter der Sowjetunion feindselig gegenüber den Vereinigten Staaten, und zeitweise sogar beleidigend.'[65] He depicted the Soviets as habitually aggressive: 'Einen Feind muß es für sie immer geben.'[66] Franz Borkenau's article on the creation of the Kominform in 1947 provided a deeper analysis of the objections to global communism.[67] He described the Kominform as different to its predecessor, the Komintern, only in the fact that Stalin ruthlessly eliminated any dissent. He referred to the power Moscow exerted on communist parties throughout the world, and the duplicity with which it had exercised its foreign policy. He held the Soviet Union responsible for the defeat of the Spanish social revolution. He spoke of the Hitler-Stalin pact and claimed that German and Russian despotism had been in league. He reminded readers that the KPD had not been exempt from Moscow's manipulation. As early as the twenties, its leadership had been interfered with, with Ruth Fischer among others being removed. It had not resisted Hitler's seizure of power, being itself intrinsically anti-democratic.[68] Borkenau claimed that even German resistance efforts had been undermined by the betrayal by communists of non-communist resistance fighters to the Gestapo.[69] For Borkenau, new communism was 'nichts weiter als des Machtinstrument der Moskauer Herrenschicht'. As for its methods, 'Betrug ist sein innerster Kern.'[70] Communism was now the embodiment of Soviet imperialism. The depiction of Stalin as a ruthless despot and murderer was nowhere more dramatic than in Bertram Wolfe's review of Trotsky's biography; it was as if, Wolfe said, 'der Satan über den Erzengel Michael geschrieben hätte'.[71] Described by the journal as 'einer der besten Historiographen der sozialistischen Ideologie', Sidney Hook presented a

---

[65] Drew Middleton, 'Sowjet-Rußland ohne Propaganda', *Der Monat*, 1 (1948/9), H.2, 61-70 (p.69).
[66] ibid.
[67] Franz Borkenau, 'Die Neue Komintern', *Der Monat*, 1 (1948/9), H.4, 50-60.
[68] ibid., (pp.53-55).
[69] ibid., (p.58).
[70] ibid., (p.57).
[71] Bertram D. Wolfe, 'Trotzki über Stalin', *Der Monat*, 1 (1948/9), H.3, 106-11 (p.106).

treatise on the shortcomings of communist thinking and the horror of its consequences; his was a clear attempt to convince the reader that communism was a dangerous totalitarian system.[72] He identified the three fundamentals of Western thinking, embodied in Western institutions, which he argued were under attack: the principle of free consent; the experimental and empirical approach to knowledge; and the recognition of the value of variety. He was enraged that the Atlantic democracies on the one hand and Russia on the other were both being presented as democratic. This he regarded as 'eine Vergewaltigung unserer Sprache'.[73] As far as Hook was concerned, the campaign for Western democracy should be led above all by 'Erzieher und Publizisten'.[74] The participation of Germans in this as equals was essential — leaders were to regard themselves 'nicht mehr als Engländer oder Franzosen, Deutsche oder Amerikaner [...], sondern als Mitglieder einer übernationalen Gemeinschaft'.[75]

The anti-communist, anti-Soviet stance of these contributors was patent. The Soviet Union was portrayed as a dangerous occupying power. Lasky referred to the Eastern Zone as 'annexed' rather than occupied.[76] The SED was a front for a ruthless secret police acting for the Moscow power-base.[77] The cynical short-term toleration of other parties was an example of insidious perfidy.[78] Moreover, as the East's policies themselves excluded any co-operation with the West, the breakdown of Allied co-operation was inevitable.[79]

Since any route which led to Stalinist communism was to be avoided at all costs, a redefinition of socialism was urgently needed. *Der Monat*'s theme of

---

[72] See 'Die Autoren des Monats', *Der Monat*, 1 (1948/9), H.2, 109-11 (p.109); and Sidney Hook, 'Drei Grundzüge westlichen Denkens', *Der Monat*, 1 (1948/9), H.2, 8-17 (pp.8-9).

[73] ibid., (p.12).

[74] ibid, (p.17).

[75] ibid.

[76] M. J. L., 'Seeckt, Stalin und Europa', (p.58).

[77] Borkenau, 'Die Neue Kominten', (p.58).

[78] ibid.

[79] Middleton, 'Sowjet-Rußland ohne Propaganda', (p.70).

February 1949, 'Der Streit um den Sozialismus', centred on the search for a practical system of social responsibility and welfare provision accompanied by freedom of ownership and of political activity. The aim was to explore the relationships between communism and socialism, and between socialism and democracy.[80] The theme was addressed by Wilhelm Röpke, Ernst Tillich, Sidney Hook, Friedrich Hayek, Joseph Schumpeter and Willy Brandt. Hayek expounded the theories advanced in his recent work, *The Road to Serfdom*, identifying socialism as a denial of personal freedom and therefore politically indefensible. He referred to earlier warnings by liberals against the dangers of collectives. Despite this, 'thinkers' had rejected these liberal ideas in favour of the very socialism which limited the freedom of the individual. Hayek argued that the fascism now being attacked in Stalin's Russia was the product of the socialist system.[81] He argued that democratic socialism was the great contemporary delusion, that it could not be realized, and that any attempt to implement it would result in something quite different and undesirable.[82] Hook, identifying himself as a socialist and a democrat, argued that the 'die Zukunft der demokratischen Linken' lay in the coalition of all democratic elements — from the non-fascist Right to the non-communist Left.[83] Röpke warned democratic socialists of the danger that 'Sozialtechnik' would produce political extremism.[84] Willy Brandt, however, contended that socialist democracy was the only alternative to totalitarian communism.[85] Brandt was particularly welcomed by the journal as a member of the young generation who hoped to adapt socialist values to the modern age.[86] Another contributor reminded readers that problems with regard to the relative positions of socialism and

---

[80] 'Der Streit um den Sozialismus: Sechs Stellungnahmen', *Der Monat*, 1 (1948/9), H.5, 3.
[81] Friedrich A. Hayek, 'Die große Illusion', *Der Monat*, 1 (1948/9), H.5, 17-21 (p.19).
[82] ibid., (p.21).
[83] Sidney Hook, 'Die Zukunft der demokratischen Linken', *Der Monat*, 1 (1948/9), H.5, 13-17 (p.17).
[84] Wilhelm Röpke, 'Die bedrohte Freiheit', *Der Monat*, 1 (1948/9), H.5, 4-8.
[85] Willy Brandt, 'Weitergeführte Demokratie', *Der Monat*, 1 (1948/9), H.5, 29-33 (p.33).
[86] Editorial note, 29.

communism had earlier been elaborated by Ignazio Silone. Silone had argued in 1942 that the conflict between fascism and socialism would not be resolved by the war, but that there would be an extension of this conflict with the appearance of 'red fascism', a new variety of fascism with a façade of democracy or socialism.[87] This Italian journalist, himself a communist, had worked for a number of left-wing newspapers, but had finally given up editorship of *Avanti* in 1947, when he perceived the party to be becoming increasingly totalitarian.[88] Silone's description of the situation, 'Sozialismus am Kreuzweg', was apt, and his percipience lent scale and depth to this ongoing debate in *Der Monat*.[89]

In June 1949 *Der Monat* introduced a double issue on the theme of German nationalism. The was entitled 'Erwacht Deutschland schon wieder?: Von der Gefahr des Nationalismus'. Both Allied and German contributors agreed that there was increasing evidence of the national idea in Germany. Raymond Aron argued that the occupying powers were partly responsible: 'Die Wiedererweckung des nationalen Bewußtseins ist also durch die Fehler der Besatzungsmächte beschleunigt worden.'[90] No-one could foresee, however, how this would turn out: 'wird dieses Nationalbewußtsein wieder einmal in einen aggressiven Nationalismus ausarten oder wird es zum Geist einer friedlichen Gemeinschaft werden?'[91] A.J.P. Taylor complained of the false notion that the Germans had suffered more than any other European people, and had consequently become 'das christlichste, das friedlichste, das bewunderungswürdigste Volk'.[92] He described this as the work of manipulative 'Humanitätsapostel', but pointed to the danger of Germans feeling so

---

87 George Woodcock, 'Ignazio Silone: Persönlichkeit und Werk', *Der Monat*, 1 (1948/9), H.10, 49-57 (p.57).
88 ibid., (p.56).
89 Ignazio Silone, 'Der Sozialismus am Kreuzweg: Ein politisches Bekenntnis', *Der Monat*, 1 (1948/9), H.10, 84-89.
90 Raymond Aron, 'Für ein europäisches Deutschland', *Der Monat*, 1 (1948/9), H.8/9, 11-15 (p.12).
91 ibid.
92 A. J. P. Taylor, 'Einigkeit!', *Der Monat*, 1 (1948/9), H.8/9, 42-45 (p.43).

victimised that they were again vulnerable to nationalist thought. As strategies to combat these dangerous inclinations, Richard Crossman argued for Germany's membership of an Atlantic community, Taylor argued for its unity, and Aron for it to become European. To put the German point of view, Erik Reger, Eugen Kogon, Franz Borkenau and Dolf Sternberger were invited to contribute, and were subsequently praised by a reader for their 'selbstkritischen Ton'.[93] Reger, introduced by the journal with his nickname in the East, 'Öffentlicher Feind Nr. 1!', described past manifestations of German nationalism as compensations for a 'minority complex'.[94] He advocated 'ein gesundes Nationalbewußtsein' as distinct from nationalism.[95] Although this proper national consciousness might be expected to lead to unity, there was now a readiness among West Germans to write off Berlin and the East. For some people, however, a 'healthy national consciousness' in some way involved dispensing with ideas of Germany's significance. Such people sought a role for Germany as 'Vermittler', a global role, regardless of whether it brought victory or defeat. His scathing reference to this as 'eine mystische Mission' was effectively a denunciation of 'Third Way' politics as irrational and irresponsible.[96] Reger attacked the SPD for what he saw as nationalistic tendencies. In an attempt to defend itself against accusations of collusion with Soviet communism, it had aligned itself with the CDU, despite inherent disagreement on the national interest. Reger asserted that the fears abroad of a return to Hitlerism ignored other, subtler, forms of 'Restauration'.[97] The sweeping away of the rubble would not reveal 'ein neues Menschengeschlecht im Glanze europäischen Denkens'.[98] Denazification would not abolish all National Socialist tendencies, and, what was more, the 'new' voices of democracy were the

---

[93] Briefe des Monats: Die Kunst des Vergessens', *Der Monat*, 2 (1949/50), H.14, 220.
[94] Erik Reger, 'Anfangs- oder Enderscheinung?', *Der Monat*, 1 (1948/9), H.8/9, 53-57 (p.54).
[95] ibid., (p.55).
[96] ibid.
[97] ibid.
[98] ibid., (p.56).

same as those of the theoreticians of the Weimar Republic. Above all, what Germany needed was 'gute Vorbilder der Demokratie'.[99] These would also combat the threat of 'nationalism' in the East, which he described as an 'auf Geheiß Moskaus "gepflegte" Nationalismus' and 'eine vorübergehende Groteske'.[100] Eugen Kogon (of *Frankfurter Hefte*) saw only one possible source of a resurgent, militant German nationalism: 'Nationalbolschewismus' in the East.[101] 'Neutrality' and 'unity' he described as seductive slogans which might win over idealists. But since Prussia no longer existed, he felt that nationalism was less likely than after the First World War. What Germany needed now was 'Normalisierung' and a positive outcome in the new Federal Republic elections. He called for rapprochement between European nations to be 'übernational' rather than 'zwischennational'. The future, he suggested, lay in a united Europe, allied with the United States.[102] Borkenau alleged that Soviet pressure had split people in Western Germany. There was both bitter nationalistic feeling against the East, but also a certain readiness to succumb, both viewed by him as a lack of faith in the strength of the democratic process.[103] Claiming that the West had not made the German struggle to attain democracy any easier, Borkenau insisted that it was up to the Germans to make the right decision between 'hell' or becoming the vanguard in a world-wide battle for freedom.[104] Only a decision to join the Western community would answer the problem.

Europe

Europe as a solution to the problems of Germany was dealt with by *Der Monat* in its January 1949 issue, 'Wege zu einem neuen Europa'. The journal published

---

99 ibid., (p.57).
100 ibid., (p.56).
101 Eugen Kogon, 'Der Nationalismus als Gegner', *Der Monat*, 1 (1948/9), H.8/9, 58-60 (p.60).
102 ibid., (pp.59-60).
103 Franz Borkenau, 'Mut am rechten Ort', *Der Monat*, 1 (1948/9), H.8/9, 60-64, (p.63).
104 ibid., (p.64).

contributions from two Americans and four western Europeans. In 'Die Deutschen in Europa', Walter Maria Guggenheimer, a journalist in the American Zone, argued for the re-establishment of 'Gemeinsamkeit' and 'Zusammengehörigkeitsgefühl'.[105] Stating that smaller economic units might hinder the creation of a European Union, he argued that supranational economic institutions had to be devised. He further warned that these economic institutions should not be managed solely by politicians. It was important to develop a new sense of European identity: 'eine neue Zentrierung, die Schaffung eines neuen politischen Ich, der Glaube an ein neues politisches *Wir*: an das *Wir* der Europäer'.[106] Guggenheimer concluded that a redefinition of this European identity would depend on the recognition and acceptance of eastern cultures.[107] The editorial staff disagreed with this article, distancing themselves from the primacy given to the larger European view over smaller-scale cooperation, for example between the German zones.[108] The economic background in this early European debate was also the main theme of Arthur Schlesinger's article. Praising the OEEC as the greatest achievement of the Marshall Plan, he welcomed the interest within Europe in the extension of this co-operation to the political sphere.[109] In the absence of military security, however, he warned that a European union could not offer sufficient protection to its members. The Berlin blockade and Czechoslovakia provided examples of the threat to 'free Europe'. Even if the British example of remilitarisation was followed by others, Western Europe could not defend itself. Military support from America was essential for two reasons: firstly, the success of a European union depended on it being able to protect its members in times of crisis. Secondly, it

---

[105] Walter Maria Guggenheimer, 'Die Deutschen in Europa', *Der Monat*, 1 (1948/9), H.4, 26-29 (p.26).
[106] ibid., (p.29).
[107] ibid.
[108] Editorial note to 'Wege zu einem neuen Europa', *Der Monat*, 1 (1948/9), H.4, 3.
[109] Arthur M. Schlesinger Jun., 'Brief aus Washington: Die transatlantische Gemeinschaft', *Der Monat*, 1 (1948/9), H.4, 11-19.

would protect European Recovery Programme funds from being diverted for military purposes.[110] He looked to his own country, the United States, to provide the economic and military support which would help 'den bürgerlichen Mittelparteien und der nichtkommunistischen Linken' to rebuild Europe. He suggested a return to the reciprocal Lend-Lease agreements and supported the creation of a 'West-Union' as a defensive response to the 'bösartigen kommunistischen Feldzug gegen die Gesundung Europas'.[111] Karl von Schumacher described the Marshall plan as a 'Dokument amerikanischer Großmut und Großzügigkeit'. He suggested, however, that the plan, as a form of charity, was not an ideal basis for the new Europe.[112] He feared that it would bring world-wide inflation. Despite these misgivings, he supported the 'cold' economic war, in which Europe was being 'immunised' against communism. It had to be matched, however, by the 'Ausbau einer echten europäischen Zusammenarbeit'.[113] European recovery depended on 'europäischem gutem Willen und [...] amerikanischer Kredithilfe'. The Frenchman, Bertrand de Jouvenel, suggested that any economic contraction would bring about a European neurosis, similar to the anti-Semitism which had resulted from the recession of the Weimar years. The belief that Europe was surrounded by hostile forces had to be overcome. These forces were mostly peoples' own 'Spukgesichte und morbiden Ängste'.[114] De Jouvenel's interpretation of political history as prima facie the result of economic forces was disputed by the editorial staff, who expressed the conviction that history was dominated by ideology.[115] Barbara Ward pointed to the success of the Marshall Plan, comparing the position of Europe before and after.[116] She urged

---

[110] ibid., (p.16).
[111] ibid., (p.19).
[112] Karl von Schumacher, 'Kann der Marshall-Plan Europa retten?', *Der Monat*, 1 (1948/9), H.4, 19-22 (p.21).
[113] ibid.
[114] Bertrand de Jouvenel, 'Expansion und Kontraktion', *Der Monat*, 1 (1948/9), H.4, 3-5, (p.5).
[115] Editorial note to 'Wege zu einem neuen Europa', *Der Monat*, 1 (1948/9), H.4, 3.
[116] Barbara Ward, 'Die Initiative liegt bei uns', *Der Monat*, 1 (1948/9), H.4, 6-11 (pp.8-9).

that the Germans join a wider community to fight Soviet oppression.[117] She detailed the aggressive actions of the Soviet Union during 1947 and pointed out the dangers to Western Europe: 'Wo die Sowjets gefahrlos mit bewaffneter Gewalt vorgehen können, machen sie davon Gebrauch. Die Rote Armee deckte die gewaltsame Einführung des Kommunismus in ganz Osteuropa.'[118] She was confident, however, that the West was in a better position to dictate global politics.[119] 'Sicherheit anstatt Chaos' was how Drew Middleton described the effect of the Marshall Plan.[120] Applauding the European Recovery Programme as contributing to the stability of western Europe, Middleton, however, spoke in Cold War terms. 'Bridging' the gap was inappropriate — there was a 'kulturelle Kluft' between Russia and Germany.[121] Russia was not European.

Culture and politics

Middleton's dismissal of the Soviet system extended to the cultural sphere. He alleged that it 'degraded' art to a propaganda tool.[122] On this question of propaganda, James Farrell insisted that the writer had to follow his own inclinations, not the values of another, for otherwise, it would mean 'seinen künstlerischen Tod' — according to Farrell, 'Die Zukunft der Literatur gehört [...] dem Unabhängigen.'[123] He called for an outburst of new energy, telling writers not to wait for a new and better world to be created.[124] *Der Monat*'s series on 'Intellektuellen in der Krise der Gegenwart' focussed on these questions of the production of new thought and literature and coming to terms with the immediate past. Commenting on the 'German Question', Max Frisch stated that it had

---

117 ibid., (p.11).
118 ibid., (p.7).
119 ibid., (pp.8-9).
120 Middleton, 'Sowjet-Rußland ohne Propaganda', (p.70).
121 ibid., (p.65).
122 ibid., (p.63).
123 James T. Farrell, 'Was braucht die Literatur?', *Der Monat*, 1 (1948/9), H.4, 66-71 (p.71).
124 ibid.

become a distraction. The Germans were not an ignorant, primitive and useless people, but a nation of major cultural achievement. This Swiss writer admitted to the fear that, if 'Unmenschen' had emerged among people who spoke his language, the same potential existed within him. Frisch regarded with horror the use of culture as an 'alibi' for barbarism.[125]

In general, Lasky saw *Der Monat*'s role as lying in cultural development and particularly the provision of literature. He was inspired by T.S. Eliot and accordingly, the December issue of 1948 was largely devoted to Eliot on his being awarded the Nobel prize. Extracts from his 'Death in the Cathedral' and other works were reproduced in both English and German. *Der Monat* was praised for publishing writers such as Kafka at a time when books were still scarce. Its literary policy, however, was not always popular.[126] The amount of material devoted to one writer, an American at that, annoyed one reader: 'Das erste Heft umreißt Rahmen und Richtung einer Zeitschrift wie das Anfangskapitel den Roman, wie die Eröffnungsvorstellung den Spielplan. Es verspricht also viel, daß *Der Monat* seinen literarischen Teil mit 26 Seiten von und über Thomas Wolfe einleitet.'[127] W.H. Auden, as a member of the younger generation of poets, paid tribute to the Irish writer, W.B. Yeats, in an analysis of his work.[128] The French anti-communist writer, André Gide, figured prominently in one issue. In January 1949 the impending publication of George Orwell's *Animal Farm* was advertised on the inside cover of the journal. Its importance was underlined by the comment that this 1945 text had 'finally' appeared in Germany and Austria. Orwell's *1984* was also

---

[125] Max Frisch, 'Kultur als Alibi. Die Intellektuellen in der Krise der Gegenwart', *Der Monat*, 1 (1948/9), H.7, 82.

[126] For praise see Zeller, p.306.

[127] 'Briefe des Monats: Enthusiasmus und Kritik', *Der Monat*, 1 (1948/9), H.2, 111-12 (p.112).

[128] W. H. Auden, 'W.B. Yeats als Vorbild', *Der Monat*, 1 (1948/9), H.4, 113-19.

featured by *Der Monat*. Lasky was an admirer of Orwell, whose warning, he stated, had come 'too early'.[129]

Political discussion was never far from literary criticism. Lasky himself addressed a major debate on Sartre's new play, *Les Mains Sales*. He dismissed Sartre's own claim that the work was unpolitical: 'wenn [...] *Die schmutzigen Hände* unpolitisch sein sollen, dann ist *Der Monat* ein Modejournal.'[130] Alluding to Sartre's left-wing 'orthodoxy', Lasky used Sartre's depiction of a militant communist cell in Eastern Europe as a springboard to discuss the workings of the Communist Party in general. For him, the two main characters, Hoederer and Hugo, were the opposite of reality. Real communist leaders were not kind, idealistic and generous, and ruthless acts of destruction were not committed by the young. On the contrary, young idealists were betrayed by the cynical manipulation of older party leaders. This was why so many had turned from communism — Malraux, Koestler, Silone, and Sartre himself. Malraux and Koestler had exposed the reality in their works. *La Condition Humaine*, *Darkness at Noon* and Hemingway's *For whom the Bell Tolls* were all, for Lasky, examples of literature which exposed the truth about communist activism.[131] Lasky appeared mystified: why did Sartre give such an inaccurate picture when he was better informed. The real-life leaders — including Ulbricht — were condemned by Lasky as 'meistens krankhafte, neurotische Fanatiker, die seit langem ihren persönlichen Ehrgeiz und ihre opportunistische Feigheit mit dem "Bedürfnis der Massen" und dem "Wohl der Menschheit" verquickt haben'.[132] Günther Birkenfeld claimed that the young generation of writers were basing their 'temporary nihilism' on Koestler as much as on Sartre. He claimed that wider knowledge of Koestler's work was due to its

---

[129] Melvin Lasky, opening address at 'A Last Encounter with the Cold War: Lessons of the Past, Problems of the Future', conference in Berlin, 9-11 October 1992.

[130] Melvin J. Lasky, 'Die vertauschten Hände', *Der Monat*, 1 (1948/9), H.4, 102-04 (p.103).

[131] ibid., (p.104).

[132] ibid.

appearance in German journals since 1945.[133] Another important member of the anti-Stalinist literary community, Ignazio Silone, was recognized in a mini-anthology of his work.[134]

True to the journal's aspirations, most contributors were from the international community, and there was little emphasis on German literature. The August issue of 1949, however, marked the Goethe anniversary with major contributions on Goethe's humanity by Karl Jaspers and on the 'German miracle' by Thomas Mann. In a highly political article, Mühlen used Goethe's *Wilhelm Meister* to emphasize the freedom enjoyed in the United States and the threat which communism posed to this.[135] Thomas Mann himself was featured in an article written by the sub-editor, Hellmut Jaesrich, on *Doktor Faustus*.[136] A lengthy extract from this work, which had been published in America in 1948, was reproduced in this issue. Jaesrich, agreeing with one American critic's description of Mann's text as a kind of spiritual homecoming, described the 'geistige Heimkehr des *praeceptor Germaniae*, dem die physische Heimkehr heute nur unter Zögern gelingen will'. In the same vein, Jaesrich applauded Mann's examination of 'die bisher vergessene Dimension der göttlich-teuflischen Musik' and presented him as the patriotic German, cut off from his homeland and nostalgic for its spiritual and intellectual depth.[137] Both the novel and Thomas Mann himself had a mixed reception in Germany. This was highlighted in Arnold Bauer's essay in his defence.[138] Bauer tackled two particular articles which were critical. The first had appeared in *Frankfurter Hefte* and suggested that Mann's work was tainted by Nazism. Bauer contended that this criticism smacked of the attitude which led to

---

[133] Günther Birkenfeld, 'Die Deutschen und Arthur Koestler', *Der Monat*, 1 (1948/9), H.4, 99-101 (p.99).
[134] *Der Monat*, 1 (1948/9), H.10.
[135] Mühlen, 'Brief aus Amerika', (p.77).
[136] Hellmut Jaesrich, 'Dr. Faustus in Amerika', *Der Monat*, 1 (1948/9), H.4, 92-94.
[137] ibid., (p.94).
[138] Arnold Bauer, 'Thomas Mann und seine Widersacher', *Der Monat*, 1 (1948/9), H.6, 68-75.

the book burnings of 1933. He reminded its author that such people as Heine had experienced similar attacks. In the second criticism referred to, published in *Merkur*, a writer of the young generation had criticized Mann's novel as 'undeutsch', with nothing left of the original but an infection. Bauer explained that the 'infection' was a symbol of the 'vom Satan besessene Deutschland' of Hitler and formed the 'am ehesten entsprechende Gleichnis des deutschen Unheils'.[139] Bauer stated that Thomas Mann's rejection was due to a failure to understand his writing, and that his exile was a sign of the times. Bauer's article stimulated an unexpected response from Eastern journal *Aufbau*. Bauer's reference to 'falschen Freunden' was used against *Der Monat*. *Aufbau* claimed Mann as its own, quoting his positive response to their publication of Georg Lukács's analysis of *Doktor Faustus*. Lasky in turn quoted a positive response to the journal from Thomas Mann. He took exception to the East's efforts to score political points from a work of art and repudiated any suggestion that Mann would support a system where literary and artistic activity was dominated by party politics. These politics had forced a terrible choice — 'für Ost oder West, für das Falsche oder das Wahrhafte'.[140] In response to a reader's letter which referred to Mann's praise of other Marxist literary critics, *Der Monat* concluded that he had been his own worst 'friend' in recent months.[141]

Der Monat and *Aufbau* had already had a confrontation over literary criticism. In the second issue of *Der Monat*, a recent collection of 'Negro' poetry by Stephan Hermlin was dismissed as 'eine tendenziöse Anthologie'. The reviewer saw it as an attack on the West: 'Man möchte [...] annehmen, daß Stephan Hermlin bei der Zusammenstellung seiner Anthologie sich mehr von seiner Animosität gegen amerikanische Ideen und die amerikanische Politik leiten ließ als von dem

---

139 ibid., (p.73).

140 M. J. L., 'Briefe des Monats: Falsche Freunde und unechte Polemik', *Der Monat*, 1 (1948/9), H.8/9, 157-58 (p.158).

141 'Briefe des Monats: Der angestrengte gute Wille', *Der Monat*, 2 (1949/50), H.14, 219-20 (p.220).

Wert der ausgewählten Gedichte.'[142] Edouard Roditi rejected Hermlin's accusations against the United States for its treatment of black Americans by challenging Hermlin to look closer to home.[143] Hermlin defended himself in *Aufbau*, and the whole exchange became symbolic of the different perceptions of freedom, East and West.

By late 1949, the political divide was resonant in the pages of *Der Monat*'s cultural coverage. The launch of the Eastern literary journal *Sinn und Form* was greeted with scathing remarks. Under the heading 'Form ohne Sinn?', Terence Boylan cynically observed that the journal 'wird [...] von recht strengen politischen Vorurteilen beherrscht, die vielleicht weniger aus der Zusammenstellung der Beiträge als in der Auswahl der Autoren deutlich werden'.[144] Inferring that writers for *Sinn und Form* would have prove their "Salonfähigkeit", Boylan pointed out that many prominent literary figures would be excluded.[145] He even described the leading figures of the Kulturbund as 'Wölfe'.[146]

1949

This review by Boylan typifies the Cold War response to Eastern developments. Included with it in the issue of November 1949 was an instalment of George Orwell's *1984*, and the opening pages gave full vent to Orwell's satirical view of totalitarianism: 'Der grosse Bruder sieht dich an!' Franz Borkenau wrote a lengthy book review under the title 'Stalin im Schafspelz', and Hugh Trevor-Roper, another contributor who was to join the Congress for Cultural Freedom, contributed an account of Hitler as general. This issue, on the journal's first anniversary, is also demonstrative of *Der Monat*'s openness to discussion. It devoted some space to an extended article on the controversial writer Ernst Jünger

---

[142] Edouard Roditi, 'Gibt es eine Neger-Lyrik?', *Der Monat* 1 (1948/9), H.2, 102-07 (p.103).
[143] ibid.
[144] Terence Boylan, 'Form ohne Sinn?', *Der Monat*, 2 (1949/50), H.14, 213-14 (p.213).
[145] ibid.
[146] ibid., (p.214).

and his elusive work, *Strahlungen*, published that year. More noticeable, however, was the apparent openness to criticism in *Der Monat*. Accused of approaching ideological and political questions in too rational and intransigent a way, *Der Monat* stated that it proposed to open up the debate.[147] Christianity was to be explored as a solution to contemporary dilemmas by three observers. The first was Erwin Reisner, a German evangelical theologian, responsible with the Russian philosopher, Berdjajew, for the journal, *Orient und Okzident*. The second was the French Catholic theologian, Jacques Maritain, and the third the prominent German sociologist, Alfred Weber. In this issue, 'Der Mensch im Zwiespalt', the journal reaffirmed its intention to accommodate a variety of ideas, as it had promised a reader in an earlier issue: 'Wir wollen in unsern Spalten jedoch weder einen allgemeinen Kulturpessimismus noch einen verstandesmäßigen Materialismus die Überhand gewinnen lassen.'[148]

Comment

Der Monat was the product of its time and place. Its first issues were delivered from the *Neue Zeitung* plant in Munich in the planes of the Berlin air lift.[149] Editorial staff took part in the mass demonstrations at the Reichstag in protest against the blockade, and major figures such as Sidney Hook and Bertrand Russell flew in to lend support.[150] It was in this atmosphere of crisis that *Der Monat* published its first year's issues. The tone of its articles must be judged in this context. They included a vivid account of the Air Lift by a prominent member of

---

[147] 'Der Mensch im Zwiespalt', *Der Monat*, 2 (1949), H.14, 138.

[148] Die Redaktion, 'Briefe des Monats: Der Mensch ist nicht das Maß', *Der Monat*, 1 (1948/9), H.3, 126-27 (p.126).

[149] Lasky, address, 'A Last Encounter'.

[150] 'Die Autoren des Monats', *Der Monat*, 1 (1948/9), H.2, 109-11 (p.109-10).

the staff of *Time*, Charles J.V. Murphy. He described it as an effort to secure 'den Vorposten des Westens und der Freiheit' in Berlin.[151]

Der Monat was not just born in conflict, but was born out of conflict. The circumstances in which its editor and prime mover, Melvin J. Lasky, was appointed were controversial. He had gained instant notoriety as a result of his appearance at the Berlin writers' conference in 1947, and not only was there opposition to his editorship, there had even been a suggestion within the American camp that he be removed from the Berlin scene altogether. While some had dismissed him as too junior initially, for others he was perhaps too provocative. Lasky himself had ambitions for his journal which outweighed even these major events. His interest was in world affairs, and in working for the common good and for freedom by the sharing of a common cultural inheritance amongst all peoples. In these rather lofty aims, he was inspired above all by T.S. Eliot, as he was later to acknowledge in the journal, *Encounter*:

> We had, in the early post-war years, listened to his words recalling his own efforts in the 'twenties and 'thirties (as editor of *The Criterion*) at "bringing together the best in new thinking and new writing in its time, from all the countries [...] that had anything to contribute to the common good".[152]

Eliot had contacted editors of periodicals in virtually every European capital and appealed to their sense of common purpose. His hope was that they could disperse knowledge of literary trends in different cultures and thus achieve more general understanding amongst peoples.[153] Eliot's idea of a community of editors came to be reflected not only in *Der Monat*, but in the Congress for Cultural Freedom. In August 1949 Melvin Lasky met Ruth Fischer and Franz Borkenau in Frankfurt to

---

151 Charles J. V. Murphy, 'Die Konstruktion der Luftbrücke', *Der Monat*, 1 (1948/9), H.4, 41-49, (p.41).

152 Melvin J. Lasky, 'Preface', in *Encounters*, p.xii.

153 See T. S. Eliot, 'The Unity of European Culture', first broadcast by the BBC to Germany in the spring of 1946, reprinted in T. S. Eliot, *Notes Towards the Definition of Culture* (London: Faber and Faber, 1948).

plan an international conference of 'anti-Communist Leftists'.[154] This Congress for Cultural Freedom eventually took place in June 1950 in Berlin. It was sponsored by *Der Monat* and funded by the newly established and relatively unknown CIA. Arthur Koestler produced its manifesto — 'The citizen of the totalitarian state is expected [...] to conform in all his thoughts and actions to a prescribed pattern. Citizens are persecuted [...] as "enemies of the people" or "socially unreliable elements".'[155] Declaring that there was a 'positive obligation' to defend 'intellectual liberty', the document concluded 'we address this manifesto to all men who are determined to regain those liberties which they have lost and to preserve and extend those which they enjoy'.[156] The common ground of the members lay in their opposition to totalitarian ideology. Active members of the Congress, in addition to Lasky himself, included Denis de Rougemont, Sidney Hook, Benedetto Croce and Bertrand Russell — all major contributors to *Der Monat.* Many had themselves been involved with communism or with Marxism and had now turned to reject its centralized Stalinist version. The three at that first meeting in Frankfurt were typical: Ruth Fischer had been a leader of the German KPD in the twenties; Borkenau had been a Marxist; and Lasky was a socialist. Although the Congress had the reputation of being a right-wing organisation, Peter Coleman, its biographer, has pointed out that 'the basic hallmark [...] of the Congress's anti-Communism was that it felt itself to be of the Left and on the Left'.[157] The opposing views of the Congress's political ideology also affected *Der Monat* because of the close links between the two. Its reputation as a journal of the Right conflicts with the identity of its contributors who were mostly of the Left. This is to oversimplify. Lasky himself expressed his pride in the wide range of contributors to *Der Monat,* from Röpke and Hayek on the conservative right, to

---

[154] Coleman, p.15.
[155] ibid., p.251.
[156] ibid.
[157] ibid., p.12.

Schumacher and Brandt, who were Social Democrats.[158] His own early membership of the League for Cultural Freedom and Socialism is indicative of his own stance.[159] *Der Monat*'s image was further affected by the connection with the CIA. Although the journal was later to be the recipient of CCF funding, which in turn was financially backed by the CIA, the cost of the early issues was borne privately, with some assistance from local organisations and the American Ford Foundation.[160]

Given the conflicts of the time, the anti-Soviet stance of the journal was inevitable. An overtly militant line was taken by many of its contributors. The sentiments expressed were often extremely immoderate. The equation of Hitlerism and Stalinism induced expressions which were often frankly belligerent. Burnham's description of communists as criminals and Mühlen's fear of American 'Mitläufer' have to be regarded now as extreme. One analysis identified these as harbingers of McCarthyism, and concluded that the journal's anti-communism represented crude prejudice.[161] There were vitriolic references to the Eastern Zone and to the Soviet Union, and some articles are easily recognisable as 'skirmishes in the Cold War'.[162] The response in the Eastern Zone was predictable. Lasky himself was branded a 'Zeitungsranzer', 'Westentaschentrotsky' and a 'Neo-Nazi'.[163] What was more significant was that the journal was banned in the East and readers faced internment.[164] Even within West Germany there were accusations of Americanization. One reader described the journal as 'ein wenig wie eine amerikanische Insel'.[165]

---

[158] Interview with Lasky.

[159] See *Partisan Review*, Summer 1939, 125-27; and Coleman, p.16.

[160] Interview with Lasky; and Hellmut Jaesrich, 'An American in Berlin', in Hegewisch, pp.9-12 (p.11).

[161] Borchers and Vowe, p.44.

[162] Bark and Gress, p.419.

[163] Lasky, address, 'A Last Encounter'; see also Dieter Borkovsky, 'A Tale from the Underground', in Hegewisch, pp.31-33 (p.31).

[164] Interview with Lasky; and Borkovsky, 'A Tale from the Underground'.

[165] 'Briefe des Monats: Zärtliche Inkonsequenz', *Der Monat*, 1 (1948/9), H.5, 110.

Lasky, however, was not a puppet of the American military authorities, nor of any covert Western operation. His own writings show this. In a significant article, published in the *New Leader* and then in *Der Sozialdemokrat*, he criticized the military approach which was in marked contrast to Eisenhower's initial humane plan for the occupation. For Lasky, this meant that the mission in Germany was 'schizophrenic'. In his eyes, the real aim was 'die kulturelle Freiheit wiederherzustellen'. Such an important task was not achieved through divided and harsh policies. Lasky stated: 'Der Amerikaner in Deutschland war ein Wesen mit zwei Köpfen. Kein Wunder, daß unsere Politik zwei Gesichter hatte.'[166] What is surprising given East-West conflict is that any of Lasky's original aims shine through at all. Yet, while the world at large was grappling with the phenomenon of communism for the first time, Der *Monat* was providing a vehicle for the discussion of alternative post-communist philosophies. As the contents show, the possibilities were not confined to conservative capitalism. Certainly, the writers who were to join the CCF rejected the label of capitalist. The journal's major commitment to the redefinition of the contours of socialism led to its publication of a variety of stances embracing liberalism, socialism, neo-conservatism, and social democracy. Whatever the brand of socialism, it seemed to aspire to a political middle ground in Europe. As Silone stated: 'Die internationale Funktion der sozialistischen Bewegung ist heute eine unmittelbare und dringende Notwendigkeit für Europa.'[167] Alfred Weber, defining the two power blocs as two social religions, allocated a third social religion of sorts to Europe — democratic socialism.[168] Lasky was certainly highly encouraging about Germany's place in Europe: 'Ich habe immer geglaubt [...], daß Deutschland zu Europa gehört und daß die Deutschen nach der Befreiung vom Nationalsozialismus wieder ihren Platz in

---

[166] Melvin J. Lasky, 'Von Hitler zum Chaos', *Der Sozialdemokrat*, 8 October 1947, p.2, (AKN, 65).

[167] Silone, 'Der Sozialismus am Kreuzweg', (p.88).

[168] Alfred Weber, 'Geschichte und Gegenwart', *Der Monat*, 2 (1949/50), H.14, 145-48 (p.145).

der Völkerfamilie einnehmen würden.'[169] Although there were many allusions in *Der Monat* to an Atlantic pact between Europe and America, in the main, its proponents in the journal were Europeans.

In many of the discussions, whether about the Cold War, about socialism, or about Europe, echoes of a 'Middle Way' were discernible. Boris Schub proposed a 'Mittelweg' for both Germany and Russia. It would not be socialism, but a means to achieve political and social stability. Otherwise, Schub argued, Germany and Russia could pose a threat to world peace: 'Solange [...] Russen und Deutsche nicht jede für sich den erlösenden Mittelweg gefunden haben, werden diese beiden großen Völker sich immer weiter quälen und die ganze Welt beunruhigen.'[170] The idea that Europe could be a 'Dritte Macht' between the United States and the USSR was dismissed by Manuel Gasser as a delusion. He cited the Benelux experience as a warning that reconciling individual national interests within a larger community was highly problematic.[171] Burnham pointed to the East's scathing dismissal of any 'Third Way' theory. There could be no other way than socialism or bourgeoisie: 'Es gibt keinen Mittelweg. (Denn die Menschheit hat keine dritte Ideologie geschaffen [...]).'[172] For Lasky and most of the contributors, any 'Middle Way' was to be found would lie between capitalism and socialism. Curiously, the journal has been accused of impeding the search for a 'Third Way' through its anti-communism. Western commentators claimed that it espoused the 'Middle Way' only to discredit it.[173] While Erik Reger's condemnation of 'Third Way' idealism in Germany was a particularly eloquent protest at this phenomenon, the discussions about socialism in particular in the journal clearly left room for 'Middle Way' conclusions.

---

[169] M. J. L., 'Politik oder Polemik', (p.111).
[170] Schub, 'Revolution im November', (p.90).
[171] Manuel Gasser, 'Brief aus Brüssel: Benelux als Beispiel', *Der Monat*, 1 (1948/9), H.4, 22-26.
[172] Burnham, 'Vom Wesen des Kommunismus', (p.27).
[173] Borchers and Vowe, p.59.

Der Monat's international ambitions necessarily restricted its coverage of German writers. Sidney Hook was, however, clear that German writers should be accorded the respect given to equals.[174] Yet Lasky regarded the German character as having a fatal flaw. It was, he stated, in tolerance. Lasky stated that, to foster greater tolerance, he was willing to 'polemicize where necessary'.[175] This seeming contradiction reveals much of Lasky's character and approach. He was prepared to be dogmatic about cultural liberty and democratic behaviour, an approach which in itself risked being identified as ideological manipulation. In response to criticisms that the journal represented American political one-sidedness, Lasky countered that, if the journal advocated 'American pluralism', that was only to be welcomed.[176]

In 1963 Lasky wrote in a preface to a selection from *Encounter*, that

> a review is a way of looking at the world, a record of glimpses and perspectives, concerned with the colour of things and not only with their meaning, with the visible surface of life as well as its hidden patterns. A review is also a way of talking with the world, and, if worth listening to at all, alive with a sense of conversation, a feeling for the continuous dialogue which alone, in our days of agitated pictures and violent excitements, can sustain an imaginative interest in words and texts.[177]

This way of looking at the world was embodied in the campaign for cultural freedom, and was reflected throughout the first year of *Der Monat* in its selection of art, film and literature. The international focus was evident in the mainly foreign prose and poetry. There was also already perhaps tired topic of inner emigration and exile. Yet the quest for cultural freedom rested on political issues and, with many important contributors, Orwell, Koestler, Sartre, Huxley, Gide, Malraux, Hemingway, Silone, Eliot, known opponents of Stalinism, the political slant was evident. Even discussions of art were symptomatic of this. Edouard Roditi,

---

174 Hook, 'Drei Grundzüge', (p.17).

175 Interview with Lasky.

176 ibid.

177 Lasky, 'Preface', in *Encounters*, p.xiii.

writing in June 1949 about the state of Berlin's art galleries and museums, accused the Russians both of destruction and of theft.[178]

Inevitably, scholars aiming to assess the imposition of cultural norms by the occupying powers generally judge *Der Monat* as an agent of this cultural enforcement. For the cultural historian Hermann Glaser, the journal is an important example of occupation culture.[179] His judgement of its influence on the literary life of Germany underlines the criticism of post-war cultural importation. Another recent German study implicates the journal as an agent of cultural colonialisation.[180] Generally, *Der Monat* is regarded as a CIA-backed arm of the Cold War offensive (a later association which colours judgement of the early years of the journal), and as a symbol of the Americanization of Europe.[181] The value of *Der Monat*'s contribution is difficult to judge. Whether it was of benefit to Germans to be exposed to the breadth of international literature, or whether this was more of an unwelcome imposition is difficult to say. Lasky himself denies any propagandistic motives: 'wir waren uns keiner propagandistischen Sendung bewußt'.[182] He dismisses the tendency to dramatize the political circumstances and argues that many have exaggerated the political nature of the journal.[183] Lasky's hope was that *Der Monat* should address the political and cultural events of the time and combat Germany's cultural vulnerability. As Lasky himself said in 1948, 'Never in modern history, I think, has a nation and a people revealed itself to be so exhausted, so bereft of inspiration or even talent.'[184] To achieve his aim, he employed the cream of the international intelligentsia. The political tenor was

---

178 Edouard Roditi, 'Bildende Kunst: Der Leidensweg der Berliner Museen', *Der Monat*, 1 (1948/9), H.8/9, 141-46.

179 Glaser, *Kulturgeschichte*.

180 Borchers and Vowe.

181 See, for example, King, p.29; and Borchers and Vowe.

182 Hermann Rudolph, 'Die Intellektuelle Front im Kalten Krieg', *Der Tagesspiegel*, (Feuilleton), 9 October 1992.

183 Interview with Lasky.

184 M. J. L., 'Berlin Letter', *Partisan Review*, 1 (1948), quoted by Coleman, p.18.

determined by the anti-totalitarianism of these contributors, some of whose tones were strident. Yet it was truly international, unmatched, according to Max Frisch, in the German-speaking world.[185] And Sidney Hook claimed that *Der Monat* was 'vielleicht die beste kulturpolitische Zeitschrift auf der ganzen Welt'.[186] It strove to produce creative contact between nations, a commitment appreciated by West German politician Carlo Schmid, and George Santayana praised its attempts to inspire 'moral' relationships between different peoples.[187] The political edge was undoubted, but perhaps the most telling comment was given by the Nordwestdeutscher Rundfunk, which described the journal as 'ein Protest gegen jede Form der Despotie und der Verletzung der Menschenrechte'.[188] The journal was undoubtedly a 'Cold Warrior', but its categorization as a tool of the American capitalist West is unfair.

Conclusions

Der Monat was the last of the five journals to appear. Its first issue was printed in October 1948, and it was then published continuously until 1971. For the purposes of this study, only the first year of its life — fourteen issues — have been considered. The journal's reputation is one of being a tool of the capitalist West, and particularly the Americans, through its editor, Melvin J. Lasky, himself an American. *Der Monat* is best regarded, however, as the combined effort of a group of cosmopolitan intellectuals, most of whom were to become members of the Congress for Cultural Freedom. Their combined approach was anti-totalitarian and mainly left-wing. The journal's achievement was that encouraged discussion of the political and cultural topics of the day at the very highest level. Although its anti-Soviet bias was apparent, it fostered the ideals of freedom, culture, and the

---

[185] ibid.
[186] 'Der Monat nach einem Jahr', *Der Monat*, 2 (1949/50), H.14, inside cover.
[187] ibid.
[188] ibid.

'middle way'. As a child of its time, the time of the Berlin airlift, *Der Monat* was truly the voice of the Cold War. It was, however, a successful international journal, and because it was more international, it was not a German voice, but not an American one either.

CHAPTER FIVE
DER RUF

Der Ruf was first published in a German prisoner-of-war camp in Van Etten, New York State in March 1945. It formed part of the American initiative towards the re-education of the German nation. Writers and journalists of known anti-Nazi sympathies were recruited from among the German prisoners-of-war. Among them were Hans Werner Richter, Walter Kolbenhoff, Walter Mannzen, Gustav René Hocke, Franz Wischnewski, Alfred Andersch, and the publisher Curt Vinz.[1] Their participation frequently led their fellow prisoners to regard them as collaborators.[2] Production of this American *Der Ruf* was eventually transferred to the headquarters of the post-war cultural planning group at Fort Kearney, Rhode Island — clearly it was thought important in the re-education programme. It was now one of an elite of 'überregionale Zeitungen, die von der Gewahrsamsmacht gegründet und gesteuert, aber von Kriegsgefangenen gemacht werden [...] Ihr Auftrag hieß politische Umerziehung'.[3] *Der Ruf*'s purpose was to be a tool of US psychological warfare against the Germans.[4]

In April 1946, production of the journal in America ceased. It resumed several months later in Germany, when Alfred Andersch and Hans Werner Richter were granted a licence by the American occupation authorities. In addition to the Van Etten staff, others to join included Friedrich Minssen, Horst Lange and Walter Maria Guggenheimer, Nikolaus Sombart, Karl Krolow, and Heinz Friedrich. *Der Ruf* was now expected to pass on 'American' values to a wider German readership. As the subtitle changed from 'Zeitung der deutschen Kriegsgefangenen' in the American version, to 'Unabhängige Blätter der jungen

---

1 Volker Christian Wehdeking, *Der Nullpunkt: Über die Konstituierung der deutschen Nachkriegsliteratur 1945-1948 in den amerikanischen Kriegsgefangenenlagern* (Stuttgart: Metzler, 1971), pp.17-18.

2 Interview with Caspar.

3 Kurt W. Böhme, *Geist und Kultur der deutschen Kriegsgefangenen im Westen*, Zur Geschichte der deutschen Kriegsgefangenen des zweiten Weltkrieges, 14 (Bielefeld: Gieseking, 1968), p.1.

4 For a detailed account of the American *Ruf*, see Wehdeking, *Der Nullpunkt*, pp.6-11 and 17-20.

Generation' in the German, the journal signalled its intention to pursue these ideas of democracy in an independent manner. *Der Ruf* attracted considerable interest among the German population, and was soon much in demand. The peak of its popularity was in the winter of 1946/47. The circulation figure then would have been dramatically high, had it not been for the paper shortage. Starting from about 35,000, the figure rose to at least 70,000 in early 1947, with other estimates putting it higher at 100,000 and 120,000.[5] In March of the same year, after only fourteen editions, a limit of 50,000 was imposed by OMGUS.[6] Whether this was a warning which its editors ignored, or whether it was the initial step towards complete suppression, *Der Ruf*'s relationship with the American authorities continued to worsen, and barely one year after its appearance, Hans Werner Richter and Alfred Andersch had their licence withdrawn.

The first issue

The first issue, published in Munich on 15 August 1946, was the most exciting journalistic launch of the period. A photograph of a German soldier silhouetted against the sky with his arms raised in surrender dominated the front cover. This dramatic image of capitulation, entitled 'Bedingungslose Übergabe', was juxtaposed with a compassionate quotation from Roosevelt. His belief that capitulation was vital for Germany's new beginning, and his conviction that there existed in all peoples, 'ohne Ausnahme, ein Sinn für die Wahrheit, ein Streben nach Gerechtigkeit und eine Sehnsucht nach Frieden' provided comfort to counter the realism of the photograph. This became symptomatic of *Der Ruf*'s whole approach: the defeat and shame of National Socialism were bitter realities and had to be accepted, but the future had to be approached with hope and faith. Pessimism was directly challenged in the main headline of the first issue — 'Das

---

[5] Bark and Gress claim that circulation reached 100,000, although they do not specify any dates (p.163), while Pross suggests a level of 120,000 for the first year (*Literatur und Politik: Geschichte und Programme der politisch-literarischen Zeitschriften im deutschen Sprachgebiet seit 1870* (Olten: Walter, 1963), p.141), and Vaillant suggests 70,000 as the maximum level (*Der Ruf*, p.146).

[6] Vaillant, *Der Ruf*, p.146.

junge Europa formt sein Gesicht'. By focusing on 'das junge Europa', the journal evoked a new innocence, to be found in Germany, yet free from the shackles of its past, a bringer of change. In this, his opening article, Alfred Andersch expanded his ideas and concerns for German youth, significantly within the European context, and proposed that socialism should be its guiding force.[7] Also in this first edition, the editors made what they described as an essential statement on the Nürnberg trials, and in it, accused the leaders of the Third Reich of betrayal. An article by Arthur Koestler described the prevailing mood of pessimism, and Hans Werner Richter gave an account of a visit to the Eastern Zone. Other articles reported on German prisoners-of-war in America, on students, and on the press. The literature section featured in particular, an extract from a novel by Walter Kolbenhoff about two young soldiers, one of them in the *Werwolf* group, entitled 'Der Streit mit dem Einbeinigen Soldaten'. One whole page was occupied by a poem by Hans Sahl. This poem, 'Der verlorene Sohn', described the plight of young soldiers returning home to find their families and homes lost or changed for ever. The imperative used in the last lines of the poem encapsulates the overall mood of *Der Ruf*:

Es ist Zeit, zu vergessen,
was wir verloren haben.
Laßt uns Brote backen
und den Toten eine Messe lesen.

Youth, Europe, socialism, and social concern were to remain the keywords of *Der Ruf*.

Guilt and the young

Germany's recent past received immediate attention. *Der Ruf* voiced resentment at the destruction of German honour. It vilified the Nazis' criminal abuse of Germany's 'besten Eigenschaften'. *Der Ruf*'s lament for these qualities, 'seine Treue, seine Tapferkeit, seine mystische Inbrunst', can be seen not just a reminder

---

[7] (DR) (Die Redaktion), 'Das junge Europa formt sein Gesicht', *Der Ruf*, 1, H.1 (15 August 1946), 1-2.

of what had been but also of what might be again.[8] At this, the time of the Nürnberg Trials, Andersch identified the chief culprits as those who held power, 'diejenigen, die mit den roten Streifen der Generalsuniform und mit allen Orden und Insignien angetan sind, die Macht verleihen kann'. In his condemnation of them he argued that 'ihnen gilt der Haß der Jugend doppelt und dreifach'. Their crime had been 'die Nation in die Ehrlosigkeit zu führen' in contrast with those who had been merely weak. Calling them the 'Wissenden', he compared them with other, lesser, criminals of the Third Reich, 'die Verbrecher aus Instinkt und Anlage oder die Narren oder die berauschten Kleinbürger'.[9] *Der Ruf* emphasized that guilt for the horrors of fascism was attributable to the top politicians and military alone. The German population at large could not be tarred with the same brush. This, it maintained, was particularly true of the young, whose resentment should be directed towards the real villains.[10] That Baldur von Schirach, the bard of National Socialism, was now expressing at his Nürnberg trial a desire to undo the damage he had done to the nation's young, was considered crass hypocrisy.[11]

Germany's disastrous past was blamed on previous generations: 'Wir haben es [...] schwer, weil die Generation nach dem ersten Weltkrieg erst aus Romantik und dann von Staats wegen alle Brücken abgebrochen hat.'[12] The rise of fascism in Germany was attributable to industrial magnates and to the betrayal of the German working classes.[13] The Weimar Republic, the scene of both of these developments, had functioned as 'die Mutter des Dritten Reiches'.[14] Determined that the whole of German youth should not be condemned as fascist, Andersch stressed the 'Nicht-Verantwortlichkeit' of his young compatriots, who

---

[8] (DR), 'Notwendige Aussage zum Nürnberger Prozeß', *Der Ruf* 1, H.1 (15 August 1946), 2.
[9] ibid.
[10] ibid.
[11] C. H. Ebbinghaus, 'Statt einer Verteidigung', *Der Ruf*, 1, H.2 (1 September 1946), 8.
[12] (Sbt.), 'Bemerkungen', *Der Ruf*, 1, H.1 (15 August 1946), 8.
[13] Walter Heist, 'Das deutsche Volk und die Demokratie', *Der Ruf*, 1, H.16 (1 April 1947), 1-2 (p.1).
[14] Alexander Parlach, 'In unserem eigenen Saft', *Der Ruf*, 1, H.1 (15 August 1946), 7.

clearly had had no say in Hitler's coming to power.[15] *Der Ruf* categorically rejected the theory of collective guilt.

As its subtitle indicates, *Der Ruf*'s target and inspiration was the young generation. Widely dismissed as 'verloren', the young were not only the most vulnerable sector of society, but also the hope for the nation's future. *Der Ruf* wanted to protect them and to encourage their intellectual development. In this way, they could be freed from 'dem üblen Klischee' of the 'lost' generation and provided with inspiration for the future.[16] While actively promoting this cause, *Der Ruf*'s editors mourned the loss of youthful freedom suffered by this generation: 'Sie kommen nicht aus der Stille von Studierzimmern [...], sondern unmittelbar aus dem bewaffneten Kampf um Europa, aus der Aktion.'[17] Their dreadful experiences and bewilderment cut them off from their elders and left them isolated and alienated. There was a 'geistige Kluft' between the two generations, so that they were now involved in a 'Kampf zwischen Jung und Alt'.[18] By referring to them as the 'Zwischengeneration', *Der Ruf* implied that thought should be given to their separation from the generation younger still.[19] Defining this 'Zwischengeneration', Richter defined them as those between the ages of twenty and forty years.[20] They, he argued, could still be called 'young', because they had not yet occupied positions of influence in public life. They did not include teenagers, who would now be schooled in democracy, but they were the generation of the future. They were better described as the 'Front-Generation', and they now stood in their tattered uniforms, faced with endless bureaucracy. *Der Ruf* was for them — 'von und zu dieser Generation sprechen wir'.[21] It declared that the silence of this generation could be explained by both their

---

[15] (DR), 'Das junge Europa formt sein Gesicht', (p.2).

[16] ibid.

[17] ibid., (p.1).

[18] (DR), 'Warum schweigt die junge Generation?'; and 'Bemerkungen', both *Der Ruf*, 1, H.2 (1 September 1946), 1-2 (p.1); and 8 respectively.

[19] Alfred Andersch, 'Das Unbehagen in der Politik: Eine Generation unter sich', *Frankfurter Hefte*, 2 (1947), 912-25.

[20] Hans Werner Richter, 'Jugend und junge Generation', *Der Ruf*, 1, H.6 (1 November 1946), 7.

[21] ibid.

confusion and others' lack of understanding: 'Sie schweigt, weil man sie nicht verstehen will; sie schweigt, weil sie nicht verstehen kann.'[22] The journal's defence of the young against these charges of mutism found an echo in its readership. One young reader who graphically described his situation as one of 'lockjaw', wrote: 'Der "Ruf" ist für mich der erste ernste Wiederbelebungsversuch an einer Generation, die sich im Starrkrampf zu befinden scheint.'[23] Andersch also rejected the charges of nihilism levelled against the young:

Die Negation, in der heute die jungen Deutschen leben, ist nicht das Zeichen eines endgültigen Triumphs des Nihilismus, sondern sein Gegenteil. Die negierende Haltung aller "Belehrung" gegenüber beweist, daß man das *Erlebnis* der Freiheit sucht, daß man den radikalen Neubau will.[24]

What was perceived as negative and destructive, he alleged, was proof of the will for a more open and radical approach. Arthur Koestler emphasized that pessimism had a certain short-term value: 'Was wir nötig haben, ist eine handelnde Gemeinschaft von Pessimisten (kurzfristige!).' Such pessimism was, he said, a realistic reaction in the circumstances, but it still left room for rational optimism about Germany's future: 'Wer im Grunde seines Wesens Optimist ist, wird Tatsachen ins Auge sehen können; in seinen kurzfristigen Voraussetzungen wird er pessimistisch sein.'[25]

Europe, democracy and socialism

Der Ruf's vision of the future lay in a united socialist Europe. It encouraged the 'Front-Generation' to unite in 'einer einzigen politischen Elite' and to lead the nation towards this goal.[26] In its self-appointed role as spokesman for young Germans, the journal stated that they saw themselves not just as German, but as European, and that they were eager to be part of a united Europe. *Der Ruf* also

---

22 (DR), 'Warum schweigt die junge Generation?', (p.1).
23 'Rufe an den "Ruf"', *Der Ruf*, 1, H.4 (1 October 1946), 4.
24 (DR), 'Das junge Europa', (p.2) (Andersch's emphasis).
25 Arthur Koestler, 'Die Gemeinschaft der Pessimisten', *Der Ruf*, 1, H.1 (15 August 1946), 3-4 (p.4).
26 (DR), 'Der grüne Tisch', *Der Ruf*, 1, H.3 (15 September 1946), 1-2 (p.2).

believed that, as a result of its experiences of fascism, not just German, but all European youth, had to be socialist in outlook. In addition, it argued that within the European community Germany was seen to fill a tragic, not an evil role :

Ein Blick nach Frankreich oder nach Italien, nach Spanien oder nach Polen lehrt uns aber, daß wir in enger Solidarität mit den anderen Erben des Abendlandes über das Schicksal Europas zu entscheiden haben werden. Uns ist das Gefühl, in diesem Kreise nur ein besonders drastisches Exempel zu statuieren, der stolzeste Trost.[27]

Andersch stated that there was no obstacle to co-operation since 'das junge Europa ohne das junge Deutschland nicht existieren kann'. He urged positive commitment to the unification process, describing it as a 'Gesetz'.[28] Within a year the dream of European unity had to some extent faded. Churchill's protestations of support for a European parliament were inconsistent with the now emerging trend to particularisation.[29] Abhorring the idea of a 'Westblock' set against the East and bolstered by the atom bomb, *Der Ruf* called for renewed attention to the larger European question. Unless this could be tackled, there was the risk that aggression could recur. It promulgated the idea of a union of equal states within Europe, which it called a 'Staatenbund', and repeated its belief in a socialist Europe, arguing that a united Europe could only be a socialist Europe.[30]

The journal drew attention to the governments in France, Britain and America, which could be used as models. This confirmed the journalists' perception of a general move towards the Left. Britain's Labour government, in particular, was frequently admired in the discussions about socialism.[31] *Der Ruf* distanced itself from more extreme brands of left-wing politics, specifically from 'jenes alten orthodoxen Marxismus, der die Determiniertheit des Menschen von seiner Wirtschaft postuliert und die menschliche Willensfreiheit leugnet'.[32] Richter

---

[27] (Sbt.), 'Bemerkungen'.
[28] (DR), 'Das junge Europa', (pp.2 and 1 respectively).
[29] (DR), 'Churchill und die europäische Einheit', *Der Ruf*, 1, H.14 (1 March 1947), 1-2.
[30] ibid.
[31] See, for example, (DR), 'Das junge Europa'; and Alfred Andersch, 'Die sozialistische Situation', *Der Ruf*, 1, H.15 (15 March 1947), 4-6.
[32] (DR), 'Das junge Europa', (p.1).

pointed out that true democracy and communist dictatorship were incompatible.[33] The attraction of the Westminster system as a parliamentary model rested on its flexibility. Its 'politische Elastizität' provided a direct contrast to the rigidity so feared by *Der Ruf*: 'Weder die Sozialisten noch die Konservativen in England sind Weltanschauungsparteien. Für sie kommt zuerst das Interesse ihres Landes.'[34] This was what *Der Ruf* desired for Germany. Within this kind of political framework a sense of nationhood, 'die Liebe zu unserem Land und zu unserer Nation', was legitimate.[35] While nationalism had proved it could be destructive, this did not mean 'daß wir nicht mehr vaterländisch denken dürfen'.[36] On the contrary, Heinz Friedrich argued, the Germans could become 'völkisch frei'.[37] The establishment of a parliamentary system similar to that of the Westminster model required 'die Konstituierung einer großen Gemeinschaft sozialistischer Praktiker, die sich in einem Klima geistiger Toleranz zusammenfinden'.[38] Tolerance and pluralism were to be sought; 'Weltanschauung' at all costs avoided.[39]

A prerequisite of the peaceful, socialist Europe envisaged by *Der Ruf* was German unity. Thus, the threat posed to this unity by the division of Germany into East and West, was anathema. This would lead to instability and the risk of another war. The journal was vigorous in its opposition to this division. As to the most suitable form of government for Germany, *Der Ruf* acknowledged that both political systems, East and West, had potential, but that neither was sufficient in itself. It preferred something in between: 'Die Entwicklungstendenz in den großen Demokratien des Westens zeigt den Weg zum Sozialismus an, der Wille zur Demokratisierung des öffentlichen Lebens in der Sowjetunion den Weg zur

---

33 Richter, 'Jugend und junge Generation'.
34 'Parteipolitik und Weltanschauung', *Der Ruf*, 1, H.7 (15 November 1946), 1-2 (p.2).
35 (DR), 'Notwendige Aussage'.
36 Heinz Friedrich, 'Nationalismus und Nationalismus', *Der Ruf*, 1, H.14 (1 March 1947), 8.
37 ibid.
38 (DR), 'Die Chance der SPD', *Der Ruf*, 1, H.7 (15 November 1946), 3.
39 ibid.; and 'Parteipolitik und Weltanschauung'.

Demokratie.'[40] An appropriate compromise was suggested in a synthesis, 'in der die sozialistische Planung sich mit der Freiheit des Menschen verbinden kann'.[41] In the article 'Die sozialistische Situation', Andersch discussed the difficulties of defining socialism at this time. He agreed that it was at a 'Wegkreuzung'. The success or failure of Labour control in Britain, he suggested, would determine how socialism and democracy might successfully be implemented in Germany.[42] In the editorial, 'Die Wandlung des Sozialismus — und die junge Generation', the objectives for Germany were defined. What was sought was a balance of socio-economic planning and individual freedom. *Der Ruf* referred to the international discussion already under way involving Koestler, Silone, Malraux and Spender. Persuaded of the necessity of socialist structures, the journal aligned itself with these socialist thinkers. It appeared comfortable with this 'rebellion' of socialists and confident in the outcome. The journal concluded by restating its belief that the young generation needed socialism, and socialism needed the young generation.[43]

Several writers rejected proportional representation as an option for contemporary Germany. Regarding it as one of the causes of Weimar Germany's fall, *Der Ruf* aligned itself with the campaign initiated against this option by the Heidelberg publication *Die Wandlung*.[44] Criticism of political parties was at times abrasive. In one expression of disappointment at how the parties were representing the German people, it was alleged that not one of them regularly pressed for the release of prisoners-of-war. A further scathing comment was that the politicians were more intent on squabbling amongst themselves.[45] The political

---

[40] (DR), 'Deutschland — Brücke zwischen Ost und West', *Der Ruf*, 1, H.4 (1 October 1946), 1-2 (p.1).

[41] (DR), 'Die Wandlung des Sozialismus — und die junge Generation', *Der Ruf*, 1, H.6 (1 November 1946), 1-2 (p.2).

[42] Alfred Andersch, 'Die sozialistische Situation', *Der Ruf*, 1, H.15 (15 March 1947), 4-6 (pp.5-6).

[43] (DR), 'Die Wandlung des Sozialismus', (p.2).

[44] See Friedrich Minssen, 'Verfassungen — kritisch beleuchtet', *Der Ruf*, 1, H.6 (1 November 1946), 3-4; and (DR), 'Eine Kardinalfrage — und eine Forderung', *Der Ruf*, 1, H.8 (1 December 1946), 3.

[45] Alfred Andersch, 'Die Kriegsgefangenen / Licht und Schatten', *Der Ruf*, 1, H.5 (15 October 1946), 6-8 (p.8).

party closest to *Der Ruf*'s thinking was the SPD. It had expressed its intention to resist any ideological fixation. Nevertheless, the journal advised wariness towards political parties in general, and itself stopped short of overt approval.[46] As for the CSU, Richter doubted whether any party which claimed a monopoly on Christianity could actually be socialist at all.[47] *Der Ruf* was highly critical of politicians themselves and regarded much political representation as emasculated.[48] The allegation was made that the politicians were no different from those of the past. As Friedrich Minssen argued: 'Die Arbeitsweise der Verfassungsgebenden Versammlung entsprach nicht ganz dem Bilde, das man sich vom Neubeginn deutschen politischen Lebens machen möchte.'[49] Criticism was also levelled at the failure to communicate with the ordinary people. Siegfried Heldwein expressed frustration that the term socialism was misunderstood, and Christian socialism even more so. Arguing that such confusion was dangerous, he pleaded for clarity: 'Dankbarer als für Propaganda wären wir für klare Definitionen.'[50] It was feared that the confusion was obstructing the establishment of a healthy political life, a situation on which Richter elaborated: 'Wir leben in einer Zeit geistiger Verwirrung. [...] Die Kommunisten nennen sich Demokraten, die Sozialisten Christen, die Christen Sozialisten, die Marxisten Humanisten und die Humanisten Marxisten.'[51] His concern was that the confusion particularly affected the young. Hans Joachim von Goertzke suggested that they should be trained in political discussion. In order to achieve this the political parties would have to pursue 'uneigennützige politische Erziehung der Nation'.[52]

---

46 (DR), 'Die Chance der SPD'.

47 Richter, 'Jugend und junge Generation', (p.7).

48 See Minssen, 'Verfassungen'; and (DR), 'Eine Kardinalfrage'.

49 Friedrich Minssen, 'Von der Würde des Volksvertreters', *Der Ruf*, 1, H.5 (15 October 1946), 8.

50 Siegfried Heldwein, 'Um Klarheit', *Der Ruf*, 1, H.6 (1 November 1946), 8.

51 Richter, 'Jugend und junge Generation', (p.7).

52 Hans Joachim von Goertzke,'An dem ganz unbedeutenden Nesenbach', *Der Ruf*, 1, H.6 (1 November 1946), 8.

Criticising Allies and Germans

Along with its criticism of political parties and politicians, the journal was also outspoken against much political reporting. Contemporary political and social comment was condemned by *Der Ruf* as inadequate:

Was an den zahlreichen neuerstehenden Zeitschriften Deutschlands ebenso peinlich berührt wie an den neuerstandenen Parteien, ist der Mangel an Unterschiedlichkeit, der Mangel an bewußter Individualität. Wie die meisten politischen, und vor allem die meisten sozialen Programmpunkte sich bei allen Parteien wiederfinden lassen, so sagen auch alle Zeitschriften im Grunde dasselbe aus. Die geringen Ausnahmen lassen die Regel nur um so deutlicher hervortreten.[53]

Der Ruf was convinced that the journals in general were insufficiently independent in approach, and that the shortcoming was all the more serious as the political parties also fell short of their duty to engage in free and wide discussion. *Der Ruf* had specific ideas about the responsibility of the press in post-war Germany:

Es gibt zwei Arten journalistischen Schreibens. Die eine will den Leser mit aller Macht überreden. Sie geht auf den Zweck aus. Die andere will berichten und klären, dabei aber die Urteilskraft des Lesers stärken. Sie ist um der Sache und um des Menschen willen da. [...] Aus dem Zusammenwirken von verantwortungsbewußter Presse und kritischen Lesern erwächst politische Bildung. Und was wäre nötiger heute?[54]

In September 1946 the journal's critical attitude to political reporting in general culminated in the allegation that the continual reference to the status quo in Germany as democracy was wrong. According to *Der Ruf*: 'Wir leben noch nicht in einer Demokratie. Wir haben eine Militärregierung, die befiehlt. Und insofern lebt ihr tatsächlich noch immer "unter" einer Regierungsform.'[55] The criticism took on a note of bitterness when, speaking out against the retention in Britain of three hundred and ninety thousand German prisoners-of-war, *Der Ruf* openly accused the German press of being less interested in their welfare than was the British press. Referring to the British authorities' excuse that there might be no employment for them in Germany, *Der Ruf* came close to accusing the German

---

[53] (DR), 'Idee und Equipe: Französische Zeitschriften als Gemeinschaftswerk', *Der Ruf*, 1, H.5 (15 August 1946), 3-4 (p.3).

[54] (DR), 'Zeitungen lesen...', *Der Ruf*, 1, H.1 (15 August 1946), 8.

[55] (DR), 'Der grüne Tisch', (p.1).

press of connivance: 'Die Behauptung, die Heimkehrer bildeten für Deutschland eine unerträgliche wirtschaftliche Belastung, darf nicht durch ein Stillschweigen auf deutscher Seite heimlich sanktioniert werden.' While sympathising with the difficulties of the 'deutschen Regierungsvertreter' in this matter, it indignantly reminded its journalistic colleagues that there was no censorship prohibiting calls for the return of prisoners-of-war.[56] *Der Ruf* itself was actively campaigning for their return and publishing lists of distressed inquiries about lost relatives.

Its critical approach also extended to the Allies, and particularly to their policy of re-education. The very term was deemed 'kein schönes Wort. Jedenfalls nicht sehr viel schöner als das nationalsozialistische Wort von der "Umschulung"'.[57] Andersch pointed out its impracticality: 'Können junge Menschen, die sechs Jahre lang fast ununterbrochen dem Tod gegenüberstanden, noch einmal zu Objekten eines Erziehungsprozesses gemacht werden?'[58] The programme in practice he described as a 'Tragikomödie', citing the decision not to allow the showing of Charlie Chaplin's 'The Great Dictator'.[59] *Der Ruf* in fact criticized the whole philosophy underlying the re-education programme. It argued that Germany be responsible for her own re-education, advocating 'Die Wandlung als eigene Leistung'.[60] Andersch described this as 'der andere Weg', and one which Germany's young had to navigate alone.[61] Stephen Spender's sympathetic view that not only Germany, but other nations also required to be re-orientated ('Es ist nicht allein nur Deutschland, sondern ganz Europa und die ganze Welt, die umerzogen werden müssen') was used to support *Der Ruf*'s position.[62]

The journal's stance on other issues also clashed with Allied policy. There was a proposal that military occupation should cease forthwith, so that a synthesis might be achieved between East and West, and Germany cease to be the irritant

---

[56] (DR), 'Die Vergessenen?', *Der Ruf*, 1, H.3 (15 September 1946), 2-3 (p.3).
[57] (DR), 'Das junge Europa', (p.2).
[58] ibid.
[59] Alfred Andersch, 'Chaplin und die Geistesfreiheit', *Der Ruf*, 1, H.7 (15 November 1946), 8.
[60] (DR), 'Das junge Europa', (p.2).
[61] ibid.
[62] Stephen Spender, 'Auf der Suche nach Europas Bestimmung', *Der Ruf*, 1, H.14, (1 March 1947), 5-6 (p.6).

between them.[63] On another serious issue, the journal complained that Germany was unrepresented at the negotiating table where its border with Poland was being decided. Even the loss of Pomerania and Silesia behind an 'Iron Curtain', as Churchill had described it, was not to be an issue for the German people themselves.[64] There were other protests — the journal argued that the Nürnberg trials should be held in a German court in front of Germans.[65] On the subject of denazification, it quoted the joke about the Thousand Year Reich: '12 Jahre waren die Nazis da und 988 Jahre dauert die Denazifizierung.'[66] It complained at the lack of press freedom, referring particularly to the prohibition of any criticism of Allied policies.[67] The British came under attack again for their approach to the prisoner-of-war issue; Walter Heist indignantly pointed out that Germany's 'moralische Erholung' was more urgent than Britain's 'wirtschaftliche Erholung'.[68] The Eastern Zone came in for censure in a report which alleged that SED's election tactics involved bribery and deplored the treacherous behaviour of SED members who were said to 'spitzeln und horchen wie die Nazis'.[69]

Der Ruf finally turned its pen against the traitors within the gate. It described two types of German, the 'Freiheitskämpfer', seeking synthesis between East and West, and the 'Nationalisten', self-seeking and maintaining the 'Un-Erziehbarkeit' of its own people. The latter group were described as 'entweder hemmungsloser Churchill-Anhänger oder Träger aller "rechten Abweichungen" innerhalb der SED'.[70] In the article 'Grundlagen einer deutschen Opposition', it was argued that this German nationalism was encouraged by the apparent inability of the Allies to draw up a proper peace treaty with Germany. *Der Ruf*'s solution

---

[63] (DR), 'Die Zonen und der Weltfriede', *Der Ruf*, 1, H.6 (1 November 1946), 3.
[64] (DR), 'Die östliche Grenzfrage', *Der Ruf*, 1, H.8 (1 December 1946), 3.
[65] (DR), 'Nürnberg 1946', *Der Ruf*, 1, H.6 (1 November 1946), 2.
[66] Hans J. v. Goertzke, 'Ein politisches Experiment', *Der Ruf*, 1, H.2 (1 September 1946), 7-8 (p.7).
[67] Erhard Rumpf, 'Kommentar oder Kritik', *Der Ruf*, 1, H.8 (1 December 1946), 4.
[68] Walter Heist, 'Nur eine Notiz...', *Der Ruf*, 1, H.14 (1 March 1947), 8.
[69] Ernst Brücher, 'Nördlich Landshut', *Der Ruf*, 1, H.14 (1 March 1947), 6-7 (p.6).
[70] (DR), 'Grundlagen einer deutschen Opposition', *Der Ruf*, 1, H.8 (1 December 1946), 1-2 (p.1).

was that of 'einer jungen demokratischen Opposition'. The word 'opposition' might be shocking, but the concept was central to the democratic process.[71]

Although much of *Der Ruf*'s comment might be construed as anti-Allied, publicity was also given to positive attitudes in both Britain and America. Fritz Woelcken drew attention to the 'Stimmen des Friedens' emanating from Britain.[72] They included the Bishop of Chichester's outspokenness against the bombardment of German cities, the committee 'Save Europe Now', and the BBC's broadcasting of prayers for former enemies. One editorial in particular praised the Americans' generous contribution to the economic reconstruction.[73] France above all was sympathetically portrayed. One entire issue was devoted to Franco-German rapprochement, again with the young generation well to the fore — 'Begegnung mit dem jungen Frankreich'.[74] *Der Ruf*, while acknowledging France's grievances against Germany, saw a distinct possibility of closer understanding with France than with other nations. It was the French after all who had distinguished between the 'boche' and the 'allemand'.[75]

Literature

Just as the young were to provide the main political thrust, so also were they to create the new German literature. It was not *Der Ruf*'s practice to conjure up literary heroes of the distant past. It nevertheless identified Nazi poetry as a 'Zwischenspiel' which had nothing to do with the true development of German poetry and condemned it as symptomatic of the 'geistigen Scheinexistenz'.[76] *Der Ruf* did not condemn outright all literature produced under the Nazis, but many writers of that time were considered to have fled from reality 'in das Idyll und in

---

71 ibid.

72 Fritz Woelcken, 'Die deutsche Schuld', *Der Ruf*, 1, H.6 (1 November 1946), 8.

73 (DR), 'Sorgen im Lager der erhobenen Zeigefinger', *Der Ruf*, 1, H.13 (15 February 1947), 3.

74 *Der Ruf*, 1, H.5 (15 October 1946).

75 Nikolaus Sombart, 'Junge Franzosen — Jeunes Allemands!', *Der Ruf*, 1, H.5 (15 October 1946), 1-2 (p.1).

76 Introduction to "'Es ist unmöglich, Herr — es ist vollbracht": Aus der Wandlung eines nationalsozialistischen Lyrikers', *Der Ruf*, 1, H.2 (1 September 1946), 12.

die entferntesten Winkel der Historie und Wissenschaft'.[77] They had been influenced by their instinct for self-preservation ('Gebot der Vorsicht') and by the pre-existing trend towards provincialism, the 'Neigung zu dem exemplarischen Provinzialismus, dem die deutsche Literatur seit lange vor Hitler hoffnungslos anheimgefallen ist'.[78] The literature of the Third Reich had been affected not only by Nazi censorship and propaganda but also by previous tradition.

Interest in inner émigré or Nazi literature was eclipsed by the stress on contemporary writing. Overwhelmingly, *Der Ruf*'s pages were given over to new young literature. Much of this had been produced in the prisoner-of-war camps. Indeed, Richter judged that artistic recovery began among German prisoners-of-war. In 'Lyrik der Kriegsgefangenen', he argued 'so entstand auch in den deutschen Gefangenenlagern in Amerika, in Frankreich und in Rußland ein neues künstlerisches Leben'.[79] Many of the titles published to illustrate his point evoke the suffering of the time. 'Totenklage' by Walter Krumbach, written at Camp Fort Devens in the US, revisits the battlegrounds of the Ukraine: 'Wir singen nicht mehr, unser Mund ist stumm, | Es modern unsre Gebeine'. 'Die Bäume daheim', written by 'M.M.' at Camp Bolbec in France, nostalgically recalls the garden of his home. 'Kriegsjunge', written by Adrian Russo at Camp Atlanta in the States, expresses the helplessness of the innocent young generation: 'Ich kann ja nicht dafür, daß ich hier sitze | und daß zerfallne Häuser mich umgeben | und daß ich jung bin'. Everywhere in these poems was the question 'why?'.[80] *Der Ruf*'s promotion of prisoner-of-war literature was underlined when it invited them to submit work for an anthology being prepared. Much of this literature has remained obscure, but *Der Ruf* did feature two major writers — Günter Eich and Wolfdietrich Schnurre. Eich's 'Kahlschlag' poem 'Latrine' was first published in

---

[77] Alexander Parlach, 'In unserem eigenen Saft', *Der Ruf*, 1, H.1 (15 August 1946), 7.
[78] ibid.
[79] Hans Werner Richter, 'Lyrik der Kriegsgefangenen', *Der Ruf*, 1, H.3 (15 September 1946), 9-12 (p.9).
[80] ibid., (pp.9-10).

November 1946 as one of three poems, 'Gedichte aus dem Lager', and a further series of prisoner-of-war poems in March 1947 included Schnurre alongside Eich.

Die Neue Zeitung's suggestion that young German writers were silent was rebutted by *Der Ruf*. The newspaper, arguing that the older people were too old and the younger too full of the lies they had been fed, concluded that Germany's literary recovery must wait. The journal, insisting that young people *were* writing, pointed out that they had the most powerful of inspirations: 'in Wahrheit und Gültigkeit vor ihren toten und lebenden Kameraden zu bestehen'.[81] In typically direct style, *Der Ruf* contrasted the independence of this literature with potential sources of literary dictatorship: 'Sie läßt sich weder ihre Form noch ihren Erscheinungstermin von den Bärten diktieren, die heute im deutschen Zeitungswald rascheln.' Moreover, in this literary and political context some degree of silence could be appropriate: 'fest steht, daß ihr das Verharren im Schweigen gegenwärtig noch als angemessene Haltung erscheint — im Angesicht der Blutopfer, die sie zu bringen hatte.'[82]

The literary section in *Der Ruf*, 'Studio', introduced Walter Kolbenhoff in the first issue as representative of the young generation. The extract from his unpublished novel, 'Von unserem Fleisch und Blut', was an exploration of 'die tiefe Problematik' of the time. It referred to the clandestine Werwolf movement and included an encounter between two friends, one a war invalid: 'Das ist eine verfluchte Zeit, in der wir leben. Statt sich zu freuen, wenn man einander sieht, fürchtet man sich.' It is a depressing picture of the mistrust symptomatic of Germany in the last days of the war. In subsequent issues, 'Studio' featured short stories by Schnurre, 'Die Tat' and 'Der Fremde', and extracts from writers such as Koestler and de Beauvoir. Critical and theoretical essays also appeared.

Which direction young writers should take was explored in several major articles. In one, 'Deutsche Kalligraphie oder Glanz und Elend der modernen Literatur', an exclusively aesthetic approach to writing was rejected; the balance

---

[81] Anon., 'Kassandra Distelbarth', *Der Ruf*, 1, H.1 (15 August 1946), 8.
[82] ibid.

should be shifted towards content. Aesthetically inclined inner émigrés had failed to address contemporary reality, thought Gustav René Hocke, and while possibly understandable during the Third Reich, that kind of approach was no longer valid.[83] Horst Lange agreed with this criticism of inner émigrés.[84] He complained that the expected catharsis following their experiences of the Third Reich had not occurred. The authors, he felt, were not solely to blame. Publishers and businessmen saw books as products, rather than objects of intellectual value — that did not encourage new departures in literature. Lange pleaded for an outburst of creative effort. Richter made the same point in his article, 'Literatur im Interregnum'. He also complained that inner émigrés had not changed with the times; since 1945 they had clung to their dated positions of 'Einsamkeit', and this had nothing more to offer. He was also critical of exile literature, which, because 'cut off from its roots', had became 'eine Literatur der Stagnation'. What remained for the future was an 'Experimentierfeld'. The experiences of the Nazizeit and the war called for new forms and new styles: 'Sie verlangen nach neuen Formen der Gestaltung und des Ausdrucks.' Richter called for objectivity, for realism, but not for the realism of the past, of Fontane, but rather one inspired by Wolfe, Hemingway and Faulkner, though not slavishly imitating them. Authors must be true to their own experience. There had to be a distinction between truth and others people's perception. He warned of the reappearance of 'Träumer' in German literature, stating that their 'Weg nach Innen' could only lead to catastrophe.[85] There was nothing to be gained by painting things in a rosy light — reality lay in the ruins of Germany, and this was what should be the basis of the new literature: 'Die Aufgabe einer neuen Literatur wird es sein, in der unmittelbaren realistischen Aussage dennoch hinter der Wirklichkeit das Unwirkliche, hinter der Realität das Irrationale, hinter dem großen

---

[83] (DR), 'Deutsche Kalligraphie oder Glanz und Elend der modernen Literatur', *Der Ruf*, 1, H.7 (15 November 1946), 9-10 (p.10).

[84] Horst Lange, 'Bücher nach dem Kriege: Eine kritische Betrachtung', *Der Ruf*, 1, H.10 (1 January 1947), 9-10.

[85] Hans Werner Richter, 'Literatur im Interregnum', *Der Ruf*, 1, H.15 (15 March 1947), 10-11 (p.10).

gesellschaftlichen Wandlungsprozeß die Wandlung des Menschen sichtbar werden zu lassen.'[86] Schnurre, one of the most important young writers of the time, seemed to accept these strictures, arguing that Rilke, Goethe and Hölderlin should be dispensed with as idols, and that the young should rely on their own experiences to sustain their writing. Warning that time was running out, he rallied young writers to venture into the new world: 'Taumeln wir nicht mit Scheuklappen, stolpern wir nicht, Strophen der Vergangenheit lallend, in sie hinein. Unsere Sprache, unser Denken sei ihr gemäß. Unsere Lieder seien neue Lieder. Finden wir die Ausdrucksform, finden wir die Klarheit, die sie bedingt.'[87] Hocke too, commending Balzac as a source of inspiration, exhorted young writers to describe their lives and times.[88] Berthold Spangenberg expressed the hope that the literary developments to come would draw from recent historical experience and, that, as a result, German literature would have significant messages for the whole world.[89] *Der Ruf*'s editorial on the subject ended on a note of optimism: 'Es mag der Beginn sein für den "schöngeschriebenen Inhalt" einer neuen realistischen Dichtung, die nach langen Jahren der Flucht und Furcht, der Lüge und Heuchelei oder des Irrtums und der Pseudo-Wirklichkeit eine neue Zeit unseres Schrifttums einleiten könnte'.[90]

With its focus on the young and the new, *Der Ruf* devoted less attention to more established German writers. It welcomed the writers who were returning from exile and regretted that in particular Thomas Mann had so far elected to stay in America. It lamented those writers who had taken their lives, and would never return:

Stefan Zweig, schied freiwillig aus dem Leben 1938 in Brasilien.
Kurt Tucholsky, schied freiwillig aus dem Leben 1934 in Paris.
Ernst Toller, schied freiwillig aus dem Leben 1943 in New York.[91]

---

[86] ibid., (p.11).
[87] Wolfdietrich Schnurre, 'Alte Brücken — Neue Ufer', *Der Ruf*, 1, H.16 (1 April 1947), 12.
[88] (DR), 'Deutsche Kalligraphie'.
[89] Berthold Spangenberg, 'Notizen aus Konstanz', *Der Ruf*, 1, H.1 (15 August 1946), 13-14 (p.13).
[90] (DR), 'Deutsche Kalligraphie', (p.10).
[91] Walter Kolbenhoff, 'Die Verjagten kommen heim', *Der Ruf*, 1, H.10 (1 January 1947), 5-6.

Exile literature which was published in *Der Ruf* included Bertolt Brecht's 'An die Nachgeborenen' with its plea to the next generation to regard his own with clemency. Also publicized was Anna Seghers's novel *Das Siebte Kreuz*, commended both as anti-fascist and as evidence of a new form of novel:

Als anti-faschistische Kampfschrift, als Gestalt schaffende Schilderung der seelischen und realen menschlichen Existenz des "Dritten Reichs", als Zeugnis einer neuen Romanform, hat "Das Siebte Kreuz" nicht seinesgleichen.[92]

Mannzen's appreciation of Seghers's rejection of bourgeois methods of characterization points to common ground between East and West in the question of how novel-writing should develop after the Third Reich. As ever, *Der Ruf* grasped unpleasant realities by commending Eugen Kogon's *Der SS-Staat* to its readers for their urgent attention. Books selected for review varied in subject from the Spanish Civil War to the psychological effects of prisoner-of-war camps. Through its book reviews it thus revealed its commitment to historical record and to addressing the harsh realities of post-war German life.

Foreign writers featured were mostly French. Gide, Camus, de Beauvoir and Sartre were all published. French socialist writers were particularly favoured and Malraux, Aragon and Elsa Triolet were included. Anouilh's *Antigone* was praised by Andersch as a 'Drama der Jugend'. Anouilh had shown that the uncompromising attitudes of youth were not something to be feared or dismissed as fascist, but were essential to society. Andersch applied Anouilh's dramatic ideas to the real-life situation: 'Ohne die Bereitschaft der Jugend zur Tragik, zum gefährlichen Leben, gibt es keinen Aufschwung.'[93] He alleged that contemporary German critics had failed to appreciate the full impact of this. In contrast, the young generation had recognized, in the sacrifice of Antigone, their own tragic fate. Andersch concluded by remarking on the magical quality of the ashes in which Antigone had perished, which, to him, conjured up ideas of a phoenix-like

---

[92] Walter Mannzen, 'Das Netz und das Gewebe', *Der Ruf*, 1, H.11 (15 January 1947), 15.
[93] Alfred Andersch, 'Jean Anouilh's Antigone', *Der Ruf*, 1, H.2 (1 September 1946), 13.

rebirth.[94] The following month, *Der Ruf* published a letter objecting to this use of a hysterical and obsessive Antigone as a model for the young. It rebuked Andersch for his misinterpretation of the applause the play had received from German forces of occupation in Paris. This reader's experience was of audience rejection rather than applause.[95] Carl August Weber's discussion of literary movements in France was part of the contemporary debate about Existentialism. The non-Christian nature, the 'Trostlosigkeit', of Sartre's philosophy forced a choice between Christianity or communism. Weber, exclaiming that the bourgeois and feudal image of western Christianity was indefensible, and therefore doomed, stated that Christianity could now survive only in the form of a personal creed. For society as a whole, the way forward could only be in socialism or humanism.[96] In this issue, devoted to France, Weber regretted that the Vichy system had produced the same type of realism in the art of the young generation as had National Socialism in Germany.[97] The French theme continued with the reproduction of drawings by Fernand Leger.

Andersch reported from a Swiss conference attended by European literary figures. Describing this enthusiastically as 'eine Konferenz des jungen Europa', he suggested it become an annual fixture, and that in time young German writers might take their rightful place.[98] Of interest is the list of participants — Stephen Spender, Ignazio Silone, Denis de Rougemont, Karl Jaspers, Georges Bernanos — all eventually to take part in the Congress for Cultural Freedom.

The last issue of *Der Ruf* to be edited by Andersch and Richter, that of April 1947, revealed the now familiar preoccupations. The editorial expressed alarm at restrictions on freedom in the East, and simultaneously at American

---

[94] ibid.

[95] Peter Recht, 'Diskussion um Anouilh's "Antigone"', *Der Ruf*, 1, H.5 (15 October 1946), 14-15.

[96] Carl August Weber, 'Die literarischen Strömungen in Frankreich und die junge Generation', *Der Ruf*, 1, H.5 (15 October 1946), 13.

[97] caw, 'Junge Kunst in Frankreich', *Der Ruf*, 1, H.5 (15 October 1946), 11-12 (p.11).

[98] Alfred Andersch, 'Eine Konferenz des jungen Europa', *Der Ruf*, 1, H.6 (1 November 1946), 13.

moves in Greece and Turkey.[99] It also continued to voice protest at the struggle against hunger and the plight of refugees. An article on music once more identified the young as the only ones who could change Germany from being simply 'ein Einfuhrland für Kulturgüter'; one on art insisted on involvement in contemporary European movements; and one on literature, by Schnurre, encouraged renewal.[100]

Comment

In all of its aims and methods, the *Der Ruf* of Andersch and Richter was provocative. As their colleague Heinz Friedrich was later to say, what distinguished Andersch and Richter's *Der Ruf* was 'die Entschiedenheit und Unbedingtheit, mit der Andersch und Richter ihre Sache verfochten, die nicht nur ihre, sondern die Sache ihrer Generation war'.[101] It is interesting to note here that 'Unbedingtheit' was exactly the word Andersch had used in his discussion of *Antigone* to define youth. The German version of *Der Ruf* was not intended to be the mouthpiece of the American occupying authorities. Nevertheless, as a 'made in the USA' product, it was expected, not just by the Americans, to have absorbed true American values and to be sympathetic to American rule. They assumed that it would introduce its German readership to the principles of democracy, and specifically to those of the free press, with objective comment, open debate and honest criticism. Perhaps it had learnt those principles too well.

Der Ruf had an additional agenda. In the telling opening article of the first issue, 'Das junge Europa formt sein Gesicht', Alfred Andersch spelt out the convictions which informed this agenda. He insisted that younger Germans had the right to freedom and to a radical new beginning. In defence of this 'Zwischengeneration', whom it saw as the real victims of Nazism, *Der Ruf* was

---

99 (DR), 'Jahrhundert der Furcht', *Der Ruf*, 1, H.16 (1 April 1947), 3.

100 Karl Wörner, 'Fragen um zeitgenössische Musik'; Schneider-Lengyel, 'Heilige Kunst'; and Schnurre, 'Alte Brücken — Neue Ufer', *Der Ruf*, 1, H.16 (1 April 1947),10-11 (p.11), 11, and 12 respectively.

101 Heinz Friedrich, 'Deutschland im Jahre Null: Die Zeitschrift "Der Ruf", nach 25 Jahren wiedergelesen', *Süddeutsche Zeitung*, (Feuilleton), 18/19 December 1971.

ready to take on all comers. In the first article of the first issue, the seeds of confrontation with the occupation authorities were already evident.

The principles which were to guide *Der Ruf*'s journalists were set out in a document entitled 'Redaktionelle Prinzipien des Ruf'. Here, the journal committed itself to political and confessional independence: 'Seinem Untertitel entsprechend, wird "Der Ruf" parteipolitisch und konfessionell völlig unabhängig sein'.[102] The emphatic 'völlig' and the inclusion of 'konfessionell' bear witness to *Der Ruf*'s commitment to inclusiveness. The journal aimed to encourage a new form of humanistic, democratic thinking among the German people through 'direkte Aussage, freie Diskussion, sorgfältige Analysenarbeit und lebendige Reportage'.[103]

For *Der Ruf*, free and committed journalism was fundamental both for the establishment of democratic thinking and for the liberation of the 'Front-Generation' from the shackles of the past. For *Der Ruf*, to pursue one, was to pursue the other. The journal tackled the task of representation with fervour, Richter later claiming that 'zweifellos war der "Ruf" in dieser Zeit das Blatt der jungen heimkehrenden Generation'.[104] It approached its task on two levels, firstly, by refuting the whole idea of collective guilt. Having stressed the 'Nicht-Verantwortlichkeit' of its young compatriots, *Der Ruf* regarded the theory of collective guilt as applied to this group as an abomination. Secondly, it provided a vision of the future, and set out the means by which it thought this could be achieved. The material needs and physical well-being of the population were addressed first. The journal campaigned vigorously for the return of prisoners-of-war and for their welfare once they had returned. In September 1946 it spoke out against the retention of German prisoners-of-war in Britain. Andersch had earlier written a report on the treatment of German prisoners-of-war, pointing out the 'nervenzerrüttenden Turnus' imposed on many who, after shipment from America,

---

[102] 'Redaktionelle Prinzipien des Ruf', quoted by Vaillant, *Der Ruf*, p.194.

[103] ibid.

[104] Hans Werner Richter, 'Beim Wiedersehen des >Ruf<', in *Der Ruf: Eine deutche Nachkriegszeitschrift*, ed. by Hans Schwab-Felisch (München: dtv, 1962), p.8.

were refused entry to French camps on medical grounds and returned to the United States, where the procedure began anew.[105]

In addition to the severe material problems of the population, its spiritual and moral welfare was addressed. Although the journal recognized the value of religious thought for the spiritual health of the people, it was not moralistic. Even the less desirable aspects of everyday behaviour in post-war Germany were treated with understanding: 'Man kommt aus dem Krieg, hat nichts anzuziehen und bekommt nur gesagt, daß alles, was man vorher dargestellt hat, von Grund auf falsch gewesen ist. [...] Korruption und Schwarzhandel sind die scheinbar einzigen Grundlagen eines auskömmlichen Lebens.'[106] In one article Catholics proposed that their religion equipped them best for the political challenges ahead.[107] *Der Ruf*, however, did not espouse Christianity, preferring humanism. It nonetheless saw religion as a necessary ingredient in the treatment of the contemporary existential crisis. Religion it saw as a matter of individual choice, but the search for truth and justice it equally viewed as a 'religious experience', something which had become fundamental to the young generation as a result of the war.[108] Ultimately, the goals of independence and freedom coincided with the religious search: 'Nichts beweist die Freiheit des Menschen mehr als seine freie Entscheidung für oder gegen Gott.'[109]

Within its aspirations for the spiritual and moral welfare of the population, particularly the young, it regarded education as of prime importance, especially university education. It argued for better educational facilities. There had been a ban on books during the Third Reich; now, there was a famine. They had a devalued currency, copyright arrangements were slow, and provision of books was dependent on such ventures as American libraries. In this situation, the re-

---

105 Andersch, 'Die Kriegsgefangenen', (p.7).
106 (Sbt.), 'Bemerkungen'.
107 Paul Bolkovac und Ernst Kessler, 'Sozialismus der Christen?', *Der Ruf*, 1, H.13 (15 February 1947), 5-6 (p.6).
108 (DR), 'Das junge Europa', (p.1).
109 ibid.

education process was necessarily inefficient.[110] The journal, however, continued to encourage the literary creativity of the young. Horst Lange demanded a loud response from them. In this most vulnerable of groups, it encouraged realism. It continued its advocacy of young writers and its achievement may be seen in its sponsorship of Schnurre and Eich.

Above all, the journal pursued a political vision, and the means by which to achieve it. The vision it saw in the larger context of a united Europe, and the means it saw in socialism or, if not socialism, then in something near to it. It rejected totalitarian systems outright and thus communism ('Es ist Hitlers historisches Verdienst, daß er uns gegen totalitäre Utopien immunisiert hat'), but neither did it accept capitalism.[111] It affirmed the need to redefine what was meant by socialism. What was to be desired was some form of socialist democracy, a 'Third Way'. Domination of Germany by one or other bloc was unacceptable. There was a possibility that Germany could be a bridge between East and West — this was 'Deutschlands politische Möglichkeit'.[112] Crucially, *Der Ruf* required that Germany and the Germans should help define these long-term aims. Germans should be represented in discussions of such matters as the East-West divide and its own eastern border. Most of all, it wanted to see the young generation actively involved in working towards solutions to these problems.

Der Ruf strove to engender hope for the future, and the tone was often lighthearted and humourous. Cartoons portrayed a laconic view of current affairs. One parodied bureaucracy, showing a man, faced with rebuilding an annihilated city, standing in front of a row of prosperous offices which provided for the bureacratic requirements of the new Germany.[113] Another, taken from the *Manchester Daily Dispatch*, satirized the Allies' aim of demolishing German militarism. Making a pun of the nuclear capability, it showed a caricature of a German militarist with large weapons aimed at him, the caption reading: 'Wir

---

110 (DR), 'Bücher, die wir nicht lesen dürfen', *Der Ruf*, 1, H.3 (15 September 1946), 13.
111 Koestler, 'Die Gemeinschaft', (p.4).
112 (DR), 'Deutschland — Brücke zwischen Ost und West', (p.2).
113 1, H.4 (1 October 1946), 5.

bombardieren den Kern mit demokratischen Prinzipien und spalten ihn in zwölf Teile.'[114] In all these ways, *Der Ruf* crusaded on behalf of the German people, and particularly the young.

The crusaders themselves, Andersch and Richter, had both been active in the Communist Party as far back as 1933. Richter had actually been expelled as a Trotskyite, on the occasion of the *Machtergreifung*. Andersch had been interned twice in Dachau on the grounds of his membership of the Communist Youth of Bavaria. He had subsequently deserted from the German army on the Italian front.[115] It was rumoured that both men had fallen foul of the American authorities during their days with the American *Der Ruf*. Andersch became main editor of the German journal and was responsible for the first issue and for its crucial opening article. He took a particular interest in French matters, and particularly in Existentialism. Richter, however, was described by one of their fellow journalists as 'sicherlich der politischeste Kopf unter ihnen', and he was the journal's spokesman in the rebuttal of any criticism.[116] Following the withdrawal of the licence, he founded the Gruppe 47, which became the dominant post-war literary movement of western Germany. Novelists and poets gathered at his invitation to discuss and read from their work, in a grouping which subsequently gained a reputation for left-wing criticism of the Federal Republic. Analyses of *Der Ruf* frequently suggest that the journal was merely the forerunner of the Gruppe 47. Although many of the personalities were the same, and many of the sentiments and beliefs common to both, this assessment tends to play down the significance of *Der Ruf*. Richter's attempts to start a second journal, *Der Skorpion*, were thwarted when the American authorities refused it a licence.[117] The reputation he had gained from *Der Ruf* had effectively blacklisted him.

---

114 1, H.8 (1 December 1946), 3.

115 See Alfred Andersch, *"...einmal wirklich leben". Ein Tagebuch in Briefen an Hedwig Andersch 1943 bis 1975*, ed. by Winfried Stephan (Zürich: Diogenes, 1986), p.233.

116 Walter Maria Guggenheimer, 'Keineswegs wie Donnerhall', *Frankfurter Hefte*, 18 (1963), 350.

117 *Der Skorpion* (August / September 1947), Wallstein-Verlag reprint 1992.

Given its ready criticism, *Der Ruf* was bound to attract opposition, even among Germans themselves. In distinguishing between an older guilty generation and a young innocent one, it inevitably attracted resentment. Helmut Müller has called such a distinction a 'political position'. The rejection of 'old' values represented a return to an older tradition still — most notably in the revolutionary nineteenth-century Junges Deutschland movement. Carl-Hermann Ebbinghaus used the metaphor of Germany as a ship, with the older generation in charge and happy to use the younger in the necessary repair work, while the younger make new plans.[118] As for the attack mounted by *Der Ruf* on its fellow journalists, a return of fire is hardly surprising. It had castigated their approach to democracy, to their compatriots in foreign captivity and to the silence of the young. There was bitter criticism of Manfred Hausmann for referring to the guilt of the young in an article in *Aufbau*.[119] After initially welcoming *Aufbau*, *Der Ruf* then used it as an example of the poor quality of organised left-wing journalism. It contrasted it with more successful liberal journalistic efforts, such as *Frankfurter Hefte*.[120] Especial censure was directed at the German political parties. They did not represent their people, and, moreover, they were made up of the same type of people, if not exactly the same, who had been there before. The politicians of Bavaria and Württemberg-Baden were singled out for particular criticism, for *Der Ruf* saw certain regressive tendencies in the constitutions which they had drawn up — 'die deutsche Krankheit der autoritätssüchtigen Hörigkeit'.[121] As for other states, they had shown insufficient distance from past models: 'Sie erscheinen in einem undeutlichen Zwielicht zwischen gestern und morgen.'[122] In one article, eastern politicians were even described as fraudsters. The Church did not escape criticism. *Der Ruf* described a dangerous narrow-mindedness in religious teaching, and

---

118 Carl-Hermann Ebbinghaus, 'Wir wollen raus!', *Der Ruf*, 1, H.6 (1 November 1946), 6-7 (p.6).
119 Friedrich Minssen, 'Auf zwei Schultern', *Der Ruf*, 1, H.8 (1 December 1946), 7-8.
120 an., '"Deutsche Beiträge"', *Der Ruf*, 1, H.10 (1 January 1946), 15.
121 Friedrich Minssen, 'Verfassungen — kritisch beleuchtet (II)', *Der Ruf*, 1, H.7 (15 November 1946), 3-4 (p.3).
122 ibid., (p.4).

proposed instead, in the spirit of Cavour, 'die freie Kirche im freien Staat'.[123] The most self-destructive criticism, however, was directed against the Allies. The editors were convinced that wrongs or inconsistencies should be pointed out, not ignored because of the subject status of the German population. The British government was criticized for placing its economic situation before Germany's moral well-being. The Russians are said to have been offended by an article on the French communist, Marcel Cachin. Both he and Lord Vansittart were accused of the same 'manische Besessenheit' against Germans as the Germans had manifested against Jews, Jesuits and Freemasons.[124] American officials were constantly disconcerted by articles criticizing the fate of German prisoners-of-war, soldiers, or refugees. They were annoyed by the constant references to the impossibility of Germans' living up to the challenge of democracy when they were contending with cold, hunger, and shortages. *Der Ruf* had embarked on a dangerous indictment of the occupying powers. They were presented as yet another form of imposed government, and the Allies as having suppressed true democratic development: 'Daß wir keine Demokraten seien, sei Schuld der Demokratien. Damals, im Mai 1945, wäre das deutsche Volk so bereit gewesen, die Demokratie anzunehmen.'[125]

In rejecting collective guilt, in rejecting imposed re-education, in rejecting denazification procedures, in deriding superpower politics overall, and finally in its proposition that young Germans should become an opposition, *Der Ruf* itself became an opposition.

That there was a backlash is hardly surprising. It came in April 1947 with the withdrawal of the licence awarded to Andersch and Richter. The circumstances, however, have attracted much comment, and *Der Ruf*'s fate was one of the most controversial events of the time. What is certainly puzzling is that Richter himself seemed unsure of the reason. The Americans' earlier reduction of their circulation may have been an indication of their displeasure. Correspondence

---

123 ibid.

124 'Politisches Notizbuch', *Der Ruf*, 1, H.13 (15 February 1947), 4.

125 Walter Mannzen, 'Klippschule der Demokratie', *Der Ruf*, 1, H.14 (1 March 1947), 4.

suggests that there were, in American circles, objections to a new version of nationalism reminiscent of the 'good old stab-in-the-back legend'.[126] According to Andersch and Richter, Hans Wallenberg, a member of OMGUS and editor of the *Neue Zeitung*, had been particularly annoyed by two articles in the fourteenth issue.[127] In one of these, Gerd Klaass described a station water pump with signs in both English and German, the English prohibiting, and the German allowing drinking of the water. Klaass suggested that this might be a kind of Werwolf monument, entitling the article 'Das patriotische Trinkwasser'.[128] In the other article, 'Unmassgebliche Vorschläge zu einem umfassenden Austauschplan zwecks Rettung der deutschen Kultur', Walter Guggenheimer wrote cynically of the difficulties facing intellectuals in contemporary Germany. Suggesting that there would be a brain-drain abroad, he felt that this would be balanced by the return of former émigrés ('Remigranten'), but advised that they should be prepared for the worst, leave their families abroad, and ensure that they received 'Care-packages'.[129]

Fellow Germans also retaliated, most notably Erich Kuby, who was himself to be the next editor of *Der Ruf*. He had accused Andersch and Richter of nationalism in an article in the *Süddeutsche Zeitung*, to which Richter responded in *Der Ruf*.[130] Referring to Kuby by his pseudonym of Alexander Parlach, Richter rejected his suggestion that denazification would be assisted by the 'denationalisation' of certain chauvinistic journals. Richter argued that denazification would be better served by a reduction in bureaucracy, and that in any case the term Kuby had used was inappropriate: 'Denationalisierung scheint mir das Gegenteil von Sozialisierung zu sein.'[131] A similar accusation of being 'verkappte Militaristen' had already been refuted by Richter in February 1947. He

---

126 Hans-Werner-Richter-Archiv, 72/86/501, Bl.174.

127 'Stellungnahme A. Anderschs und H. W. Richters zu ihrem Ausscheiden aus der "Ruf"-Redaktion', in Vaillant, *Der Ruf*, p.210.

128 Gerd Klaass, 'Das patriotische Trinkwasser', *Der Ruf*, 1, H.14 (1 March 1947), 8.

129 Walter M. Guggenheimer, 'Unmassgebliche Vorschläge zu einem umfassenden Austauschplan zwecks Rettung der deutschen Kultur', *Der Ruf*, 1, H.14 (1 March 1947), 10-11.

130 Hans Werner Richter, 'Der Bürokraten-Überhang', *Der Ruf*, 1, H.14 (1 March 1947), 7-8.

131 ibid., (p.7).

poked fun at *Der Ruf*'s critics by stating that, when the office was quiet, the journal's staff put on their monocles and played with tin soldiers.[132] He acknowledged that the criticism would not go away — 'und so stehen wir nun da, wir Schreiber des "Ruf", und sind wieder einmal entlarvt'.[133] In an editorial in the same issue, the journal took more seriously the criticism of one of its own previous writers, Ebbinghaus. Writing in the *Neue Zeitung*, Ebbinghaus had warned that *Der Ruf* might encourage 'Beifall von der falschen Seite'. He himself did not agree, however, with the charge, clearly voiced elsewhere, that *Der Ruf* was deliberately using the young in the cause of nationalism. *Der Ruf* in its answer distanced itself from the 'auch-demokratischen' 'Lager der erhobenen Zeigefinger'. It pointed out that it had already made its position clear in the article 'Grundlagen einer deutschen Opposition'. It re-emphasized the journal's stance. Firstly, they were young, internationally-minded socialists; secondly, they were committed to German freedom in the interests of true democracy.[134] In March 1947 Richter's column on 'Die Sprachregelung' again made serious allegations that free journalism was being muzzled: 'der Geist der deutschen Sprachregelung ist [...] nicht ums Leben gekommen. Geheimnisvoll und unsichtbar steht er wie ein Gespenst hinter allen Presseerzeugnissen der Gegenwart'.[135] Richter stated that prohibition of criticism was an attitude characteristic of Nazi times which had not yet been erased — 'gelernt ist gelernt'. This attitude continued, he said, to influence approaches to democracy, socialism and even Christianity. A cartoon showing a man examining copies of *Der Ruf* with a magnifying glass, and a container with the specification 'Lupen 1:1000' accompanied the article. The caption read 'er sucht die nationalen Phrasen'.[136] The comment was simple but clear and underlined the threat to *Der Ruf*.

---

132 Hans Werner Richter, 'Wir verkappten Militaristen', *Der Ruf*, 1, H.13 (15 February 1947), 7-8, (p.7).
133 ibid.
134 (DR), 'Sorgen im Lager der erhobenen Zeigefinger'.
135 Hans Werner Richter, 'Die Sprachregelung', *Der Ruf*, 1, H.15 (15 March 1947), 7-8 (p.7).
136 ibid.

On the departure of Andersch and Richter, the publisher of *Der Ruf*, Curt Vinz, was keen to stress that there had been disagreements between the publishing house and the two editors.[137] They, on the other hand, complained later that they had not been immediately informed by Vinz of the impending withdrawal, and suggested that some arrangement may have been made with the authorities that the journal should continue in a different form.[138] They also quoted an unnamed source as saying that American officers of the CIC had considered removing only Richter, and that they had 'proof' that he was an SED agent. Richter later suggested that the ban may have been the result of 'einer russischen Intervention'.[139] In their own defence, Andersch and Richter pointed to the decision by other journalists, among them Guggenheimer and Heist, to leave the journal in protest.[140] In the issue of 15 April 1947, there was a small announcement to the effect that Richter and Andersch had left the journal.

The action against *Der Ruf* provoked great controversy and, although it continued under a different editorship, *Der Ruf* is still associated primarily with Andersch and Richter. In October 1946 it appeared to embrace the theory of the 'Nullpunkt' in its encouragement to youth: 'Die junge Generation kann ganz von vorn [...] beginnen [...]. Sie braucht nicht umzubauen. [...] Sie kann neu bauen.'[141] This was typical of its approach and a sign of its determination to encourage the Germans to think constructively. This approach, however, inevitably raised questions about the journal's political reliability. Promotion of German self-confidence was perceived widely as being nationalistic. For Thomas Mann, the journal offered 'Frische, Tapferkeit', 'Intelligenz' and the advantages of the editorial staff's experience of 'Außenluft'.[142] Heinz Friedrich later argued that the journal had been characterized by 'einer [...] geradezu selbstmörderischen

---

137 See Vaillant, *Der Ruf*, p.107.

138 'Stellungnahme A. Anderschs und H. W. Richters', p.210.

139 Richter, 'Beim Wiederlesen des ›Ruf‹', p.7.

140 'Stellungnahme A. Anderschs und H. W. Richters', p.211.

141 (DR), 'Deutschland — Brücke zwischen Ost und West', (p.2).

142 'Thomas Mann über den "Ruf"', *Der Ruf*, 1, H.15 (15 March 1947), 3.

Offenheit'.[143] Whatever the reasons behind its suppression, it is perhaps best to leave the last word to Richter himself, who wrote later that 1946 and 1947 were 'die Jahre der großen Hoffnungen und der vielleicht ebenso großen Illusionen'.[144] Although this described the times, it could equally well refer to *Der Ruf*.

Conclusions

Of all the journals of the time, *Der Ruf* is the best-known, particularly in Germany. There, it is revered to this day as heroic in its opposition to foreign occupation. Purely German and committed to progress 'aus der Welt der schönen Täuschungen in die Welt der nüchternen Realität', *Der Ruf* sought to represent what it saw to be the legitimate aspirations of the German people within a democratic system.[145] Paradoxically, *Der Ruf* first appeared as part of the American political re-education programme, only to be subsequently suppressed by the Americans — all in the short space of two years.

Having gained their licence to print on the grounds of their political reliability, Andersch and Richter lost that licence for failing to meet the same criteria. Both socialists, they sought to find a 'Middle Way' in a united Europe. The Americans, however, accused *Der Ruf* of nihilism, the Russians objected to anti-communism, and fellow Germans identified it as nationalistic.[146] Although its suppression can be followed logically from its anti-occupation politics, some mystery remains as to which objecting party played the decisive role. Conveying a strong sense of Germany as a community, the journal absolutely rejected the theory of collective guilt, it rejected the re-education programme as something imposed and therefore of less impact than self-imposed re-education, and it condemned denazification procedures on similar grounds. Richter himself said 'Ich habe diese Radikalität im "Ruf" gefördert als Reaktion auf die kritiklose Zeit der

---

143 Friedrich, 'Deutschland im Jahre Null'.

144 Richter, 'Beim Wiederlesen des ›Ruf‹', p.7.

145 Hans Werner Richter, quoted by Peter Wapnewski, 'König Artus, Lehrer der Autorität', in *Hans Werner Richter und die Gruppe 47*, ed. by Hans A. Neunzig (München: Nymphenburger Verlagshandlung, 1979), pp.25-32 (p.32).

146 Hans Schwab-Felisch, 'Einleitung', in Schwab-Felisch, p.16.

Diktatur'.[147] It is particularly unfortunate that this, the most encouraging of German reactions to the Nazi legacy, was judged to be a threat to German progress and democracy. One American commentator believed that 'the language they used is the only one apt to divert the young generation, for which the magazine is written, from dangerous demagogues'.[148] In all that it did, *Der Ruf* crusaded on behalf of the German people and particularly the young. It cannot be categorized as a journal of the East or of the West, but of a new Germany.

---

[147] Hans Werner Richter, 'Wie entstand und was war die Gruppe 47? - Der Ruf. Sein Entstehen und Untergang', in *Hans Werner Richter*, ed. by Neunzig, pp.43-75, (p.82).
[148] Hans-Werner-Richter-Archiv, 72/86/501, Bl.174.

CHAPTER SIX
FRANKFURTER HEFTE

The *Frankfurter Hefte* first appeared in April 1946 under licence from the American authorities. The two founding editors, Eugen Kogon and Walter Dirks, had both been active in Catholic left-wing politics in their youth, and in Catholic journalism. Concerned at the moral and spiritual crisis in Germany, they sought to establish a forum based on Christian ethics, thereby reasserting some form of religious leadership in the discussion of contemporary issues.

Eugen Kogon had worked as a journalist from 1927 until 1934, mainly for the Catholic journal, *Schönere Zukunft*. Arrested on numerous occasions by the Nazis, he had finally been sent to Buchenwald in 1939, where he remained until its liberation by American troops on 11 April 1945.[1] On his release, he was commissioned by the Allies to write a report on the concentration camps. This report, expanded into a book which appeared in December 1945, was entitled *Der SS-Staat: Das System der deutschen Konzentrationslager* and became the standard and authoritative reference work on the Nazi system of terror.[2] Before the *Frankfurter Hefte* appeared, then, Kogon was already a post-war commentator of some stature.

Walter Dirks had been a student of theology and an assistant to Romano Guardini, the Catholic theologian and religious philosopher. Until 1934 he had worked with the left-wing Catholic newspaper *Rhein-Mainische Volkszeitung*, subsequently liquidated for its anti-Nazi stance, as well as working for several periodicals. He also attracted attention in 1930 as a defence witness at the trial of Georg Grosz, an event that symbolized the opposition of the authorities and left-wing thinkers and artists, and fuelled efforts against 'Kulturbolschewismus'.[3]

---

1 Hubert Habicht, 'Vorwort des Herausgebers', in *Eugen Kogon - ein politischer Publizist in Hessen: Essays, Aufsätze und Reden zwischen 1946 und 1982*, ed. by Hubert Habicht (Frankfurt a. M.: Insel, 1982), pp.7-13 (p.7); see also Brelie-Lewien, *Katholische Zeitschriften*, p.236.

2 Eugen Kogon's *Der SS-Staat: Das System der deutschen Konzentrationslager* was published in 1946 by the Verlag der Frankfurter Hefte in conjunction with other publishing houses.

3 IfZ, OMGUS/ISD, 5/247-2/19.

Consistently under surveillance, he was taken into 'protective custody' in 1933. In 1935 he started to work on the *Feuilleton* section of the *Frankfurter Zeitung*, and continued there until 1943, when he was finally banned from writing altogether.[4] His name figured in the PWD's 'White List' of people regarded as being 'politically clean'.[5]

Both editors had thus been regarded by the Third Reich as in varying degrees hostile. They shared a common commitment to Christianity, and also a common political stance, and together had been involved in 1945 in the founding of the CDU in Hessen.[6] They hoped that the party might successfully combine Christianity and socialist ideals. Dirks described the party as one of 'umwegigen Sozialismus', embodying a tendency to socialist thinking, but in an alternative way.[7] Disillusionment with the CDU swiftly followed. Already in 1944, Dirks had discussed the possibility of a future political-cultural journal with Clemens Münster, before developing the idea further with Kogon on their first meeting in summer 1945.[8] The hopes and aspirations formerly invested in the CDU were to resurface and characterize their work with *Frankfurter Hefte*.

Kogon and Dirks were active in other areas of the contemporary debate. Kogon, highly respected for his campaigning spirit in spite of his physical weakness, a result of his time in Buchenwald, was much in demand as a lecturer, although later, his book made him unpopular in certain circles. He was also active in the support of organisations for the victims of National Socialism, for example the NVV.[9] Dirks's other interests included working with the Südwestfunk from 1948, and with the Frankfurt School in the fifties, when he edited with Adorno the

---

[4] See Walter Dirks, 'Vorwort', in *Walter Dirks: Gesammelte Schriften*, ed. by Fritz Boll and others, 8 vols (Zürich: Ammann, 1991), I: *Republik als Aufgabe: Publizistik 1921-1933* (1991), pp.5-10 (p.6); and Fritz Boll, 'Vorwort', in Walter Dirks, *War ich ein linker Spinner?: Republikanische Texte - von Weimar bis Bonn* (München: Kösel-Verlag, 1983), pp.9-10 (p.9).

[5] IfZ, OMGUS/ISD, 5/247-2/19.

[6] Ulrich Bröckling, 'Einleitung', in *Walter Dirks: Gesammelte Schriften*, IV: *Sozialismus oder Restauration: Politische Publizistik* (1987), pp.11-32 (p.14).

[7] ibid.

[8] See Walter Dirks, 'Vorwort', in *Walter Dirks: Gesammelte Schriften*, IV, pp.5-10 (pp.6 and 10).

[9] Altmann, *Hauptsache Frieden*, p.194.

Frankfurter Beiträge zur Sozialforschung. The two were among the very few former journalists of the Weimar period who attempted to introduce new ideas, rather than reintroduce old ones.

Clemens Münster was a third founding member of *Frankfurter Hefte.* A physicist, he was brought by the Americans to the West from the Zeiss-Werk in Jena.[10] Less prominent initially, Münster became joint editor from January 1948. He too was involved in other media projects, taking charge of culture and education programmes with Bavarian radio in June 1949.[11] Others to join the editorial staff were Alfred Andersch (of *Der Ruf*), Rüdiger Proske, Walter Maria Guggenheimer, Walter Weymann-Weyhe, Eduard Schröder, and Karl Wilhelm Böttcher. Regular contributors included Ida Görres, a writer influenced, like Kogon and Dirks, by her involvement with the Catholic youth movement.

Frankfurter Hefte was intended to explore the boundaries between Christianity, socialism, humanism, and democracy. A figure of around 50,000 is given for its circulation until early 1948. It then rose to a peak of 75,000 in mid-1948, before dropping again to 40,000 at the end of that year. The journal continued until 1985, when it merged with *Neue Gesellschaft* to form *Frankfurter Hefte/ Neue Gesellschaft.*

The first issue

In the first issue of *Frankfurter Hefte*, in April 1946, Walter Dirks paid tribute to Karl Muth, editor of the Catholic journal *Hochland* which had been suppressed during the Third Reich. Muth's journal had been aimed at a 'Wiederbegegnung von Kirche und Kultur', and Dirks emphasized the relevance of this to his own task, stressing that such co-operation was urgently needed now, a generation later.[12] In the editorial, 'Ob man ein Programm machen darf?', the difficulties of

---

10 Martin Stankowski, *Linkskatholizismus nach 1945* (Cologne: Pahl-Rugenstein, [1974(/)]0, p.70.

11 See Clemens Münster, 'Christliche Rundfunkarbeit', *Frankfurter Hefte*, 4 (1949), H.8, 678-86.

12 Walter Dirks, 'Die Wahrheit und die Welt: Karl Muth zum Gedächtnis', *Frankfurter Hefte*, 1 (1946), H.1, 9-10.

developing any journalistic programme were outlined: on the one hand, the catastrophe of the Third Reich had not destroyed Germany totally; on the other, there was no 'tabula rasa' from which to begin anew.[13] The editors announced that they sought philosophically-minded readers prepared to face the difficulties of the necessary revitalization of German thought.[14] While they confirmed the influence of religious thought on the journal, they nonetheless drew attention to the importance of realism in dealing with the secular world as partners: 'Das klärende und nährende Wort, das hier zu lesen sein wird, soll vom christlichen Gewissen bestimmt sein; die Welt aber, auf die es sich bezieht, ist nicht etwa "das Religiöse", sondern die ganze, vielschichtige, reiche, arme Wirklichkeit.'[15]

The first issue embarked upon a series of major articles. The first, 'Nürnberg und die Geschichte', declared that the trials at Nürnberg heralded the start of a new world order. No longer would aggression against foreigners be synonymous with national progress: 'Der "Aggressor" wird Verbrecher, es ist zu Ende mit der Rechtfertigung durch den Erfolg.'[16] The second, Dirks's central political essay, 'Die Zweite Republik', became the foundation of the journal's political agenda. The evocation of a new republic, rejecting Weimar, but learning from it, introduced a unique and vital debate about potential structures of democracy in Germany.[17] This opening issue also brought the last chapter of Kogon's *Der SS-Staat*. Consistently mentioned in every summary of the journal and repeatedly quoted in other works, this chapter, 'Gericht und Gewissen', was a profound and model treatise on the question of the Germans' attitudes to their past. Maintaining that the population at large could not have been aware of the detail of the concentration camp system, Kogon nonetheless insisted that all had heard of, or known someone who had been interned, and indeed that they themselves had feared it. Meanwhile, large sections of the community — lawyers,

[13] 'Ob man ein Programm machen darf?', *Frankfurter Hefte*, 1 (1946), H.1, 10-11.
[14] ibid.
[15] 'An unsere Leser!', *Frankfurter Hefte*, 1 (1946), H.1, 1-2 (p.2).
[16] 'Nürnberg und die Geschichte', *Frankfurter Hefte*, 1 (1946), H.1, 3-5 (p.5).
[17] Walter Dirks, 'Die Zweite Republik: Zum Ziel und zum Weg der deutschen Demokratie', *Frankfurter Hefte*, 1 (1946), H.1, 12-24.

businessmen, security police — were in possession of information which necessarily indicated the intricacy and scale of the undertaking. Lamenting the unwillingness of Germans to discuss the matter, Kogon, as a victim himself, appealed to them to ask questions — 'so leidenschaftslos wie diese Sache es zuläßt', and challenged them to explore their consciences. Resentment of the Allies was common as a kind of cathartic response, but it symbolized the failure to accept this task, and Kogon condemned it as small-mindedness. The only Christian response, he said, was to accept the judgement of others as a sign from God. What they had done, and why, had to be questioned, so that they might ensure it never happened again.[18]

In a more obviously religious vein, there was an article on Saint Theresa of Lisieux and an extract from the writings of Cardinal Newman. The issue ended with the section, 'Glosse', shorter commentaries, book reviews and brief biographies of the contributors. With this, the format of the publication was established, shorter pieces surrounding a central core of several important essays. In all these contributions, the socialist and Catholic stance of the journal was clearly evident.

Guilt and repentance

As befits a journal based on the religious ethic, guilt was a prominent theme. *Frankfurter Hefte* was prompt to address the question of national guilt and the Christian conscience. It professed the Catholic approach to sin and repentance. It was not enough to regret, to apologize, to repent. There had to be some effort to make restitution. *Frankfurter Hefte* was one of the few journals to consider the victims of Nazism. In the 1946 article 'Christen und Juden', Kogon asked 'wie können wir die Schuld gutmachen, die wir dem jüdischen Volk gegenüber auf uns geladen haben?'.[19] The implicit answer was that prayer and humility were required, yet instead of the churches being full of people praying for forgiveness,

---

[18] Eugen Kogon, 'Gericht und Gewissen', *Frankfurter Hefte*, 1 (1946), H.1, 25-37 (p.31).

[19] EK, 'Christen und Juden', *Frankfurter Hefte*, 1 (1946), H.6, 6-8 (p.6).

and instead of patience in the face of condemnation by others, Kogon found indifference, and even some residue of anti-Semitism. The latter at least had to be rooted out. Kogon admitted that the history of the Christian Church's attitude to Judaism was not always exemplary, although he pointed out that this had not extended to pogroms. As to the self-imposed curse, 'His blood be upon us and our children' (Pontius Pilate in Saint Matthew's Gospel), Kogon dismissed it, emphasizing that this did not excuse evil-doers, such as Cain, Judas and Hitler.[20] Referring to an American-Jewish writer's list of Christian efforts to save Jews, ranging from the Vatican to ordinary individuals, Kogon hoped that these reminders might inspire 'echtes Christentum und echte Menschlichkeit'.[21] This was what the response to the past, to the Jews — the inner response — should be. In a later article, Karl Thieme investigated the causes of anti-Semitism, including the Christian accusation that Jews were not true believers. He called for the re-formulation of the prayer for Jews, suggesting the words be changed from praying 'für die treulosen Juden' to 'wir beten auch für die Juden, die dem Glauben noch kein Vertrauen schenken'.[22] Dirks reminded readers of the common ground between Christianity and Judaism. The ten commandments and the message of neighbourly love represented a significant body of common teaching, causing Dirks to emphasize the 'echte religiöse Gemeinsamkeit zwischen Christen und Juden'.[23]

Frankfurter Hefte's approach to guilt was complex. On the one hand, its emphasis on facing up to reality communicated a sense of common responsibility. There had been Christian failure and sin, carrying with it the implication of almost universal responsibility. Everyone had to embark on 'innere Verarbeitung der Schuld', and the journal encouraged this, not only as part of the Christian ethic, but as truly patriotic action.[24] On the other hand, political error did not constitute guilt. In his famous article 'Das Recht auf den politischen Irrtum', Kogon argued

---

20 ibid.

21 ibid., (p.8).

22 Karl Thieme, 'Die Christen, die Juden und das Heil', *Frankfurter Hefte*, 4 (1949), H.2, 113-25, (pp.124-25).

23 WD, 'Noch einmal: Christen und Juden', *Frankfurter Hefte*, 1 (1946), H.7, 583-84 (p.583).

24 Walter Dirks, 'Vaterland', *Frankfurter Hefte*, 3 (1948), H.2, 112-23, (p.117).

that *Mitläufer* had been merely followers of those who had made the original political error, and ought therefore not to be in the dock. What did constitute guilt was to have perpetrated or participated in criminal activities or in negligence.[25] He advocated that justice be based on the decision that '*es ist nicht Schuld, sich politisch geirrt zu haben*'.[26] The journal distinguished therefore between sin and legal guilt, as defined by political action. This stance was unusual in these days of complaints about denazification. It allowed for the building of a new democracy, while condemning the evil of the Third Reich and encouraging all to repent their past and seek to do something constructive for the future as part of this repentance.

As it rejected the universality of political guilt, it is unsurprising that the journal rejected the theory of collective guilt, and its practical application, denazification. Kogon described the policy as 'ein Fiasko':

> Der Anklage-"Schock", daß sie alle mitschuldig seien, sollte die Deutschen zur Erkenntnis der wahren Ursachen ihrer Niederlage bringen. Man kann heute, fast ein Jahr nach Verkündigung der These, nur sagen, daß sie ihren Zweck verfehlt hat. Das spricht nicht so gegen das deutsche Volk als gegen das angewandte pädagogische Mittel, da ja der praktische Wert eines politischen Instruments allemal von der Erreichung des gemeinten Zieles abhängt. Die "Schock"-Politik hat nicht die Kräfte des deutschen Gewissens geweckt, sondern die Kräfte der Abwehr gegen die Beschuldigung, für die nationalsozialistischen Schandtaten in Bausch und Bogen mitverantwortlich zu sein.[27]

Both Kogon and Dirks argued that denazification had failed in its aims. Rather than continue with this 'fiasco', Germany's purge should be self-imposed. The Germans should pass judgement on themselves, while recognizing that God was the ultimate judge.[28] Denazification had to leave room for those who were ready to face the consequences of their error.[29] Most importantly, it should not inhibit any new start. To this end, the most effective denazification programme would

---

[25] Eugen Kogon, 'Das Recht auf den politischen Irrtum', *Frankfurter Hefte*, 2 (1947), H.7, 641-55 (p.649).

[26] ibid., (Kogon's emphasis).

[27] Kogon, 'Gericht und Gewissen', (p.28).

[28] 'Ob man ein Programm machen darf?', (p.11).

[29] Kogon, 'Das Recht auf den politischen Irrtum', (p.651).

involve the proof that democracy was better: realisation of this would represent constructive progress and true liberation — 'nur wirkliche *Demokratie* ist positive Befreiung'.[30] The process had to be fair and clean. The legal framework in the American Zone, by which responsibility for denazification was handed over to the Germans, should be extended to the other zones.[31] Indeed, general responsibility for Germany's progress must be increasingly allocated to the Germans. Kogon regretted in 1947 that even in the American Zone, where the Western form of democracy was being implemented, the occupation powers were still issuing orders.[32]

Frankfurter Hefte had much to overcome in rebutting some of the prevailing attitudes. Kogon criticized the trend among Germans to demand justice for the population and to argue that Germany under the Allies was no better than under the Nazis.[33] He urged them to recognize both guilt *and* responsibility.[34] With regard to Poland, he and Dirks jointly addressed the German-Polish question as one of 'Verhängnis und Hoffnung'.[35] Dirks urged a realistic response to the terrible acts being committed there. Germans had to expect revenge and ought to recognize that the events were part of a chain that they themselves had started. Kogon acknowledged the nostalgic connotations of the German East, but argued that the Germans must reconcile themselves to the loss of territory to Poland. Poland itself had already lost extensive territory to the Soviet Union, which was demanding yet more.[36] Bearing in mind the injustice wrought by Germany, there was some justice in the outcome.[37] Together, they asked readers to examine the options, and pleaded for co-operation between the two neighbouring peoples.

---

30 ibid., (p.655) (Kogon's emphasis).

31 EK, 'Die allmähliche Revolution', *Frankfurter Hefte*, 1 (1946), H.7, 667-70 (p.669).

32 EK, 'Beobachtungen und Bemerkungen', *Frankfurter Hefte*, 2 (1947), H.4, 333-35 (p.333).

33 Eugen Kogon, 'Der Kampf um Gerechtigkeit', *Frankfurter Hefte*, 2 (1947), H.4, 373-83 (pp.373-74).

34 ibid., (p.373).

35 Walter Dirks und Eugen Kogon, 'Verhängnis und Hoffnung im Osten: Das Deutsch-Polnische Problem', *Frankfurter Hefte*, 2 (1947), H.5, 470-87.

36 ibid., (p.482).

37 ibid.

This was all the more urgent as, in Kogon's words, 'Polen und Deutsche sind für die Gegner nur Bauern auf dem Schachbrett, das sich morgen in ein Schlachtfeld verwandeln würde.'[38]

Dirks argued that the pursuit and recognition of the truth was the path to real freedom for Germans.[39] Distancing himself from the population in general, he expressed incredulity at its attitude and enjoined the reader to consider the generosity of spirit shown to Germans by others:

halten sie es für selbstverständlich, daß auf unserer Seite ein paar Millionen Menschen unter der Begleitmusik des verlogensten Welterlösungspathos verbrannt und vergast worden sind, und daß ein Jahr nach dem Ende des Krieges, in dem dieses System mühsam genug niedergezwungen worden ist, auf der anderen Seite nur zarte Rücksicht, lautere Ehrlichkeit, Uneigennützigkeit und tatkräftige Hilfsbereitschaft herrschen?[40]

The kind of person who complained about his bread ration did not display the requisite self-knowledge necessary for a positive German future. The place for this development of self-knowledge was the conscience. While journalism could make a contribution, the onus lay with the individual to establish the nature and extent of his or her guilt.[41] Stressing the importance of acknowledgement of guilt where appropriate, Dirks encouraged a straightforward acceptance: 'Ja, dies ist meine Schuld.' The admission Dirks called for, a kind of 'mea culpa' without sinking into neurosis or depression, signified participation in constructive Christian progress. Similarly, group admission of guilt was positive, but he dismissed the identification of guilt in others and pointed out the inconsistency of agreeing with the theory of collective guilt while excepting one's own group. Even anti-fascists were not excused. They were guilty of not campaigning enough through the early part of the century and had to realize that, precisely because of their perspicuity, their duty was all the more considerable.[42] In Dirks's view, the problem lay in the failure *before* National Socialism to achieve a social and political solution which

---

38 ibid., (p.484).
39 Walter Dirks, 'Der Weg zur Freiheit', *Frankfurter Hefte*, 1 (1946), H.4, 50-60.
40 ibid., (pp.50-51).
41 ibid., (p.52).
42 ibid., (pp.54 and 56).

would have prevented National Socialism.[43] He urged the rethinking of the concept of collective guilt. Guilt had to be clearly defined and localised, so that it might be addressed where appropriate, not shrugged off, or avoided, or misallocated. In arguing that '*der Begriff der Kollektivschuld muß ent-mythisiert werden*', Dirks underlined that it had proved a dangerous notion.[44] He emphasized the individual search, distinguishing between 'Selbsterkenntnis' and 'Bekenntnis'. Self-awareness was the vital building-block for the nation's future: 'Wenn Deutschland sich selbst erkennt, so wird es nicht nur frei werden, zunächst geistig und dann und deshalb auch politisch frei.' Christians had, however, to guard against concentration on their private life and contribute to ideas on public life.[45] In the same issue, Clemens Münster recommended Wilhelm Röpke's *Die Deutsche Frage* as a contribution to 'Selbsterkenntnis', since it represented 'ein Spiegel des deutschen Wesens und der deutschen Geschichte'. Röpke's stress on causality, however, proved too extreme for Münster, who disputed the notion of historical fatality.[46] Just because things had occurred in a certain chain of events did not mean that the original situation necessarily had to lead to the last. Not for Münster 'Post hoc ergo propter hoc'.

The Christian Church

Whether the Churches, as opposed to the individual, had examined their 'collective' consciences was also addressed by *Frankfurter Hefte*. If the Christian community had failed, then the Churches were not free from blame. Their past and present roles too had to be critically assessed. In general, it was regretted that Christian resistance to the National Socialist regime and the Holocaust had been restricted to isolated incidents. Not enough had been done to avert the horrors. Dirks praised the Evangelical Church for its public admission of guilt, but urged it

---

43 ibid., (p.57).
44 ibid., (p.52) (Dirks's emphasis).
45 ibid., (pp.59-60).
46 Clemens Münster, 'Wilhelm Röpke, Die Deutsche Frage', *Frankfurter Hefte*, 1 (1946), H.4, 92-96 (pp.92 and 95).

to apply the consequences of this at parish level. By contrast, Catholics had failed to broach the question sufficiently.[47] Dirks maintained that the Catholic Church had been 'hard of hearing' and had ignored the warning signs during the pre-Hitler years.[48] Judging the Church's stance against National Socialism to have been 'ziemlich wacker', Dirks nonetheless regretted that it had aligned itself with reactionary elements.

The most critical approach to the Catholic Church came not from the editors (although they instigated it), but from another lay Catholic, and one of the few female contributors, Ida Friederike Görres. Her letter, accusing the clergy of mediocrity, caused uproar and precipitated a written episcopal response. She claimed that the priests were guilty of hypocrisy, were lacking in humility and charity, and she argued that the charge of 'Klerikofaschismus' was not altogether unjustified.[49] In their introduction to her letter, the editors underlined the ecumenical basis to their debate — they sought to engage all their readers, not only Catholic and Protestant, but also 'die andersgläubigen, die religiös gleichgültigen, und die Heiden'.[50] This involvement of the wider community in an analysis of the Catholic Church as an institution was typical of the self-analysis advocated by the journal. The public response was immense, mixed, but, the editors claimed, mostly positive. The fact that Christians of both denominations had responded was welcomed as proof of Christian commitment.[51] Despite inevitable criticism from some members of the clergy, the editors restated their conviction that they had a duty to address publicly questions about the Catholic Church. They also condemned as 'Ghetto-Christen' those who feared that such criticism could be used by enemies.[52] Görres herself responded to the debate she

---

[47] Dirks, 'Der Weg zur Freiheit', (p.53).
[48] ibid., (p.57).
[49] Ida Friederike Görres, 'Brief über die Kirche', *Frankfurter Hefte*, 1 (1946), H.8, 715-33 (pp.722-27).
[50] Kogon, Dirks, Münster, 'Vorbemerkung der Schriftleitung', *Frankfurter Hefte*, 1 (1946), H.8, 715.
[51] Dirks, Kogon, Münster, 'Das Gespräch über die Kirche', *Frankfurter Hefte*, 2 (1947), H.3, 275-79 (p.275).
[52] ibid., (p.276).

had provoked by endorsing the editors' campaign for open and constructive discussion.[53] Analysis, she argued, should not be limited to seminaries or the Church hierarchy. She re-emphasized that her letter had been written out of love for the Church. Interestingly, it has been suggested that the editors may have received a blessing from the Pope.[54]

The EKD (Evangelische Kirche in Deutschland) was also challenged in the journal. In November 1947, Otto Fleischer's article 'Gabe und Aufgabe des Protestantismus' rejected previous scholarly work which had identified Luther and Protestantism as the great anti-authoritarian and individualistic movement.[55] This work had argued, erroneously in Fleischer's view, that Luther's concern had been to liberate men from all authority beyond their own consciences. Fleischer countered that Luther and the Protestant movement had stood not for the freedom of the individual against all authority, but rather for the full recognition of the word of God made flesh, with the Holy Scriptures as testament to this.[56] In other words, Luther had been campaigning for authority — for the authority of the word of God, something he had perceived as suppressed in the Catholic Church and sidelined by secular institutions. His protest had in no way given carte blanche to the individual conscience. This misunderstanding had lasted four centuries, and the position needed to be clarified. Fleischer called for a new Reformation, in which worship would be extended from being primarily personal to publicly recognized in the community.[57] He added that only affirmation of God's existence would exclude the temptation to form ideologies where men decided their own formulae of what was good and what was evil. Such purely human definitions of good and evil could lead to other people, who were not of the same persuasion, who did not conform, being despised, hated, or ultimately 'ausgerottet'. The 'wahre

---

53 Ida Friederike Görres, 'Das Gespräch über die Kirche', *Frankfurter Hefte*, 2 (1947), H.3, 279-84.

54 Donald Nicholl, 'A wandering scholar', *The Tablet*, 8 January 1994, 6-8 (p.6).

55 Otto Heinrich Fleischer, 'Gabe und Aufgabe des Protestantismus', *Frankfurter Hefte*, 2 (1947), H.11, 1118-30.

56 ibid., (pp.1118-19).

57 ibid., (pp.1119-20).

evangelische Kirche' should be devoted to communicating the word of God, and responsibility for this applied to all — 'Die Kirche, das sind wir.'[58] Fleischer wanted in particular to see a clear commitment from the Protestant Church to their congregations at this time of re-orientation. He regretted that the Protestant churches were not open to the public more frequently, as Catholic churches were, and bemoaned the impression that 'der Gott des Protestantismus habe [...] nur sonntags vormittags seine Sprechstunden'. The argument that, as the Protestant Church did not hold the Host in it, it did not need open churches, was dismissed by Fleischer, who claimed that some saw in this the domination of clericalism over the actual ministry of the Church.[59] Fleischer's assessment of the main tasks for the Protestant laity was significantly familiar:

die Sorge um *den Behördencharakter* dieser Pastorenkirche; die Sorge um einen neu auflebenden *innerprotestantischen Konfessionalismus*; die Sorge um *die soziale Situation der Kirche im Zusammenhang mit der Frage nach Sozialismus und Arbeiterschaft*; schließlich die viel besprochene Frage nach *einem neuen Verhältnis zwischen der katholischen Kirche und den evangelischen Kirchen.*[60]

These four principles resembled very closely the concerns communicated by *Frankfurter Hefte* itself and reveal a similarity of approach between the two communities — a crucial underpinning of the journal's ecumenical interest. On Fleischer's discussion of new relations between the two Christian Churches, however, the editors intervened. Fleischer argued that, just as the needs of the time had forced the two Christian Churches closer together, so the sober acceptance that the two were not one, but two separate and opposing institutions, was now even more important.[61] In a footnote, the editors sought to temper Fleischer's outright dismissal of any chance of ecumenical union. They argued that division was the '"Pfahl im Fleische" der Christenheit' and urged that Christian unity was to be hoped and prayed for.[62] The editors' description of Fleischer's

[58] ibid., (pp.1121-22).
[59] ibid., (pp.1122-23).
[60] ibid., (pp.1122) (Fleischer's emphasis).
[61] ibid., (pp.1129).
[62] ibid.

approach as looking towards 'jener Erneuerung [...], die am "katholischen Luther" anknüpft', was in contrast to another article's '"bekennende" Weise'.[63] This article by Werner Koch looked back to the traditions established in crisis by the 'Bekennende Kirche' (the evangelical movement established in opposition to National Socialism) and contrasted them with the 'Irrlehre der "Deutschen Christen"' (the members of the Reich Church).[64] Koch took the line of Karl Barth, who warned in 1945 that restoration of sixteenth-century Lutheran or Calvinist teachings ran the risk of encouraging reactionary forces within the Church, and even German nationalism.[65] As with so many issues, the question was one of '*Reformation oder Restauration*', and, according to Koch, the Protestant Church was already in the process of a second Reformation.[66]

Space, then, was given by *Frankfurter Hefte* to discussion and criticism of both Christian Churches — not just to a re-appraisal of Catholicism, but to the debate within the Evangelical Church over Protestant reform. In one article, both were criticized simultaneously for their politics, the problem being laid at the door of their political advisors. The Catholic Church had no proper advisory body, and the EKD had advisors who were too often drawn from nationalist circles.[67] In a separate article, Adolf Arndt criticized the EKD for giving in to the American authorities on the subject of denazification.[68] Elsewhere, the Christian Church as a whole was judged 'mitschuldig' for the fact that the Christian view of the world was no longer valid for many people. Both the 'Bild-Erstarrungen' of Catholicism and the 'Bild-Verneinungen' of Protestantism were deemed equally responsible for this.[69] Most of the material dealing with Christianity, however, concerned general

---

63 'Nachwort der Schriftleitung', *Frankfurter Hefte*, 2 (1947), H.6, 567.

64 Werner Koch, 'Die Evangelische Kirche und die zweite Reformation', *Frankfurter Hefte*, 2 (1947), H.6, 557-67 (p.559).

65 ibid., (p.563).

66 ibid., (p.564) (Koch's emphasis).

67 EK, 'Kirchliche Kundgebungen von politischer Bedeutung', *Frankfurter Hefte*, 2 (1947), H.7, 633-38 (p.638).

68 Adolf Arndt, 'Die Evangelische Kirche in Deutschland und das Befreiungsgesetz', *Frankfurter Hefte*, 1 (1946), H.5, 35-46.

69 Romano Guardini, 'Abschied von der Tübinger Kunstausstellung', *Frankfurter Hefte*, 2 (1947), H.7, 701-05 (p.705).

Christian morality and the recovery of values; the most important of these, charity, became a leitmotif in the journal. However, the religious debate was often highly intellectual. There is clear evidence, for instance, of the influence of dialectical theology.[70] Repeated world conflicts spoke eloquently of the sinfulness of human beings before the ultimate judgement of God, and the resultant eschatological debate, with its concentration on the "Four Last Things" — Death, Judgement, Hell and Heaven, reflected this preoccupation. Dialectical, or crisis, theology came to represent the theological struggle to come to terms with what had happened in Europe. Notable proponents Karl Barth, Romano Guardini and Friedrich Gogarten were acknowledged by Dirks as influential on his own thinking.[71]

There were several articles on abortion. Here, it was presented not just as a matter of Catholic teaching, but as a more broadly Christian issue. Dirks's essay on Paragraph 218 asked those debating it to understand those men and women who had decided to preserve human life at all cost. His attitude to the pro-abortion stance was: 'man braucht nur in den Fußstapfen der SS-Ärzte zu bleiben.'[72]

The religious tenor of the journal permeated even subjects less obviously religious. A review of an art exhibition argued that it offered the opportunity to experience among other things, 'was religiöse, sagen wir genauer, christliche Wirklichkeit sei'.[73] A review of Hemingway's *For Whom the Bell Tolls*, on the Spanish Civil War, raised the question of how a people so Christian, so Catholic, could end up in a state of 'Mißverständnis des Glaubens'.[74] The reader was frequently faced with uncomfortable moral dilemmas. Görres described a hypothetical situation in which the operation of a 'murder switch', which would

---

[70] See for example, Romano Guardini, 'Der Tag des Herrn in der Heilsgeschichte', *Frankfurter Hefte*, 3 (1948), H.1, 38-48, (p.46).

[71] Walter Dirks, 'Marxismus in christlicher Sicht', *Frankfurter Hefte*, 2 (1947), H.2, 125-43.

[72] Walter Dirks, 'Ein Wort an die Arbeiterschaft in Sachen § 218', *Frankfurter Hefte*, 1 (1946), H.9, 792-94 (p.794).

[73] Guardini, 'Abschied von der Tübinger Kunstausstellung', (p.704).

[74] Ida Friederike Görres, 'Zwei Bücher: ein Vergleich', *Frankfurter Hefte*, 2 (1947), H.8, 856-63 (p.863).

dispose of a chosen enemy, would have absolutely no repercussions for the user.[75] The opportunity to remove an offender in a clean, clinical and distant way with no trace of either victim or perpetrator would prove seductive, she argued. The only barrier to operating the switch was 'Wissen um den Willen Gottes'. Görres reminded the reader of the Lord's Prayer, 'Führe uns nicht in Versuchung!'[76] Referring to the scriptural message that hatred which wills someone's death is in itself murder, Görres alluded to the 'inneren Entscheidungen, die in einem Volke vorsichgegangen sind, ehe Dachau, Buchenwald und gar Auschwitz möglich wurden'.[77] Extrapolating from this, she showed how it could lead to the elimination of whole classes or peoples, and how the motives could even become economic.

While the religious interests of the editors were clear (in articles on, for example, the task of German Catholicism, contributions from Jesuits, on Jesuits, etc.), nevertheless the insistence that these had to be accompanied by secular interests was apparent, Dirks even going as far (for a Catholic) as to point up the common ground between Christianity and Marxism.[78]

Political history

With politics, just as with religion, *Frankfurter Hefte* looked to the past as well as to the future. Kogon described the relationship of the German people to the National Socialist state as 'nicht begeistert, aber gehorsam'. They had pursued their own well-being and that of their families, allotting responsibility for the overall development of the country to the National Socialist government.[79] Kogon's assessment of the cause of the problem and the task ahead was this: 'Der

---

[75] Ida Friederike Görres, 'Der Mordknopf', *Frankfurter Hefte*, 1 (1946), H.2, 90-92.
[76] ibid., (p.91).
[77] ibid., (p.92).
[78] See, for example, Dirks, 'Marxismus in christlicher Sicht'; Walter Dirks, 'Die geistige Aufgabe des deutschen Katholizismus', *Frankfurter Hefte*, 1 (1946), H.2, 38-52; and Oswald von Nell-Breuning, S.J., 'Kapitalismus und Sozialismus in katholischer Sicht', *Frankfurter Hefte*, 2 (1947), H. 7, 665-81.
[79] Eugen Kogon, 'Das deutsche Volk und der Nationalsozialismus', *Frankfurter Hefte*, 1 (1946), H.2, 62-70 (p.62).

politische Fehler hat tiefe Wurzeln im deutschen Nationalcharakter. Jetzt ist die Zeit gekommen, ihn zu erkennen, und anzufangen, ihn allmählich auszumerzen.'[80] The fact that German resistance was not taken seriously abroad was lamented as partly the result of disunity among its representatives — 'Es ist ein tragisches Verhängnis der besten und mutigsten Deutschen, daß sie offenbar nicht einig handeln können.'[81] Kogon agreed with Friedrich Wilhelm Foerster, rejected the theory of two Germanies and stated that 'Deutschland ist der Pakt des Teufels mit den Engeln'.[82] The task now was to extricate the good from the bad.[83] Kogon regretted that, for the third time within three generations, the German people had gone to war. 1870, 1914 and 1939 had identified the German people as the 'marchers of history'.[84] Referring to the German 'uniformed collective', Kogon argued that it was charaterized by a relative unawareness of responsibility for their country's path: 'Das Kraftbewußtsein, das die Uniform verlieh, hielt die politische Vernunft in Bann.'[85] Any sense of political awareness had vanished into the few remaining 'Gelehrtenzimmer'.[86] The fact that, over time, this had intensified had meant that Germany and National Socialism had become inseparable.[87] In 'Die Zweite Republik', Dirks described German fascism as an alliance of three factions: 'die großen Kapitalisten und Monopolisten', 'die alte Adels- und Militärkaste' and 'die Massenbewegung des verzweifelnden Mittelstandes'.[88] This threefold collaboration, it was later argued, was exposed by the Nürnberg trials: 'Daß [...] dieses deutsche System [...] "Faschismus" war, ein Komplott von Wirtschaftsführern, Generalen und Mittelstandsführern, ist in Nürnberg offenbar geworden.'[89] The Weimar Republic, also a product of three groupings — 'ein

---

[80] Kogon, 'Der Kampf um Gerechtigkeit', (p.382).

[81] Alice Platen-Hallermund, 'Der deutsche Widerstand', *Frankfurter Hefte*, 3 (1948), H.3, 280-82 (p.282).

[82] Kogon, 'Der Kampf um Gerechtigkeit', (pp.382-83).

[83] ibid.

[84] Kogon, 'Das deutsche Volk und der Nationalsozialismus', (p.70).

[85] ibid., (p.63).

[86] ibid., (p.68).

[87] ibid., (p.69).

[88] Dirks, 'Die Zweite Republik', (p.12).

[89] Walter Dirks, 'Ein falsches Europa', *Frankfurter Hefte*, 3 (1948), H.8, 698-711.

Bündnis der Arbeiter-Mehrheit, der Links-Bürger und der Katholiken', was similarly a disastrous failure.[90] But in that case, all three groups had failed to take their coalition seriously. Dirks considered this failure of the middle ground particularly disappointing in view of the efforts of 'einige Politiker, der Jugend, der Zeitungen und Zeitschriften um den Frankfurter Carolus-Verlag und seine "Rhein-Mainische Volkszeitung" und anderer Kreise verwandten Geistes' — areas in which Dirks and Kogon had themselves been involved.[91] Once a democratic system was instituted, any coalition that might be created should be valued as a sign of willingness to cooperate for the common good. There was repeated rejection in *Frankfurter Hefte* of anything being *re*-constructed, with the dismissal of 'jenes verräterische Wort "Wiederaufbau"'.[92] The Weimar Republic, in particular, should not be reconstructed.

The journal gave prominence to such resistance to National Socialism as had been shown. Günther Weisenborn emphasized that the level of anti-Nazi activity would astound many.[93] Using Gestapo records of arrests, and maintaining that opposition must have been even higher than these official documents indicated, Weisenborn concluded that 60,000 to 80,000 people had resisted Hitler, adding, 'das ist eine Armee'.[94] In one of the fullest lists of anti-Nazi groupings published at the time, Weisenborn emphasized that, while the '20-Juli-Gruppe' was the best-known, other groups had existed in all branches of German society. He gave as examples the socialist group 'Neubeginnen', and the 'Europäische Union', each of which had thousands of members. He stressed too the 'Saefkow-Gruppe', which had attempted to co-ordinate resistance efforts. Weisenborn defended the whole resistance effort, pointing out that the 'death co-efficient' had been higher than in any other resistance movement, and that it was therefore of great historical

---

90 Dirks, 'Die Zweite Republik', (p.13).
91 ibid., (p.15).
92 Walter Dirks, 'Mut zum Abschied', *Frankfurter Hefte*, 2 (1947), H.8, 819-28.
93 Günther Weisenborn, 'Es gab einen deutschen Widerstand', *Frankfurter Hefte*, 2 (1947), H.6, 531-32 (p.531).
94 ibid.

importance.[95] On the second anniversary of 20 July 1944, Kogon wrote of the failure of German culture to resist politics.[96] He praised the insights of Ernst Robert Curtius, who in 1932 had pointed out how the Classical Age had failed to 'form' the German nation, in contra-distinction to France, which the classical culture of Racine's time had pervaded. German humanism had been historicized, according to Curtius, and 'Kulturhass' had become a characteristic of German development.[97] Kogon condemned National Socialism, the only revolution since the 'Bauernkriege', as the 'Organisation des Robotertums in einem nationaldrapierten Zuchthaus'.[98] To ensure that the deaths of the men and women of the 20 July had not died in vain, a revolution was needed now, a political and social revolution, without bloodshed or repression, one of justice, where men and women showed that they had 'ein Herz für den andern', a revolution by 'Menschen, Sozialisten, Europäer — also Deutsche'. While the National Socialist revolution had represented the climax of the 'Tragödie der Trennung von Geist und Politik in Deutschland', this would be 'die Revolution der Wiederbegegnung von Geist und Politik in Deutschland'.[99] The journal commemorated one victim by publishing the letter written by Father Alfred Delp immediately before his execution.[100] He had stated that he was being executed because he was a Jesuit. Nothing had been proven against him; the court was 'eine Funktion des Vernichtungswillens'.[101]

Analysis of recent history included historical revision, and one example of this was Kogon's review of Friedrich Meinecke's *Die deutsche Katastrophe*. Here, he drew particular attention to the distinction between 'homo sapiens' and 'homo faber', and Meinecke's preference for the former. Christianity would make

---

95 ibid.

96 Eugen Kogon, 'Die deutsche Revolution: Gedanken zum zweiten Jahrestag des 20. Juli 1944', *Frankfurter Hefte*, 1 (1946), H.4, 17-26.

97 ibid., (pp.22-23).

98 ibid., (p.24).

99 ibid., (pp.24 and 26).

100 'Der Abschiedsbrief von Pater Delp', *Frankfurter Hefte*, 1 (1946), H.4, 27.

101 ibid.

the two 'brothers', thereby dispensing with the sociological choice.[102] Overall, while praising much of the content of the book, Kogon severely criticized Meinecke's explanation of Hitler's rise on the basis of coincidence.[103] With these reservations, Kogon recommended the text particularly to the older generation.[104] The army's importance in early-twentieth-century Germany was explored in an article by Ignaz Pollmüller. Pollmüller pointed up the role of the *Reichswehr* in the systematic breakdown of the Weimar Republic and in the tenuous alliance of Prussian militarism with the new nationalism. The remnants of the Kaiser's army opposed the Weimar parliament because it did not promise to restore German greatness.[105] By 1924, 'der alte Geist' had resurfaced, as the feudal military gained increasing power under General von Seeckt.[106] Seeckt was portrayed as the prime opponent of Weimar and as the ultimate militarist, with his 'classic formulation' — 'Das Heer ist der Staat.'[107] While radical militarists had been linked to Hitler's putsch, Pollmüller accused the Reichswehr of having stood by, waiting to assess the fate of the National Socialist movement, and then joining with it in pursuit of its own aim — the militarisation of Germany.[108] He referred to the romanticisation of the soldier, the growth in literature about the First World War, and the odium cast on Remarque and Renn, when they refused to participate in the literary alignment of army and people.[109]

The political future

As for the future, *Frankfurter Hefte* saw a new form of republic — Dirks's 'Zweite Republik', forged by two main groups — 'die Arbeiter und die

---

[102] EK, 'Beginn der Geschichtsrevision', *Frankfurter Hefte*, 1 (1946), H.8, 776-79, (p.777).
[103] ibid.
[104] ibid., (p.776).
[105] I. H. Pollmüller, 'Die Reichswehr in der Republik', *Frankfurter Hefte*, 1 (1946), H.9, 833-43 (p.836).
[106] ibid., (p.839).
[107] ibid., (p.835).
[108] ibid., (p.842).
[109] ibid., (p.840).

Christen'.[110] The input of Christians to the political scene was not only desirable, it was essential: 'ohne sie käme die "Linke" nicht durch.'[111] *Frankfurter Hefte*'s combination of socialism and Christianity was seen as a practical as well as a theoretical solution to Germany's problems: 'Sozialismus aus christlicher Verantwortung ist kein leeres Schlagwort [...] aber auch kein täuschendes Lockmittel.'[112] Karl Heinrich Knappstein argued that there were practical political and economic merits in a system based on both, which he outlined as 'Sozialisierung', 'Planwirtschaft', and 'Einordnung der Arbeitnehmerschaft'.[113] Readers were reminded of the link between Christianity and humane action by quotations from Kierkegaard and St. Augustine. St. Augustine's message was that believers had a responsibility to work together with non-believers for peace, because 'auch jene Gemeinschaft von Menschen, die nicht aus dem Glauben leben, strebt nach Frieden auf Erden'.[114] Dirks responded to an article in the SED publication *Neues Deutschland*, which had described Christian socialism, as represented by among others, the *Frankfurter Hefte*, as 'kleinbürgerlicher Sozialismus'. Dirks and Knappstein were described in the same article as 'Jesuiten in Frankfurt'. Dirks rejected these epithets, and dismissed the article as lacking in intellectual rigour because it failed to define the term Christian socialism.[115] The words of the Lord's Prayer were used as a source for learning and guidance. Forgiveness should be practised by both Germans and Allies, and the word 'our' as applied to daily bread remembered even in these days of hunger.[116] Especially now, the needs of others should not be ignored, wrote one priest.[117]

---

110 Dirks, 'Die Zweite Republik', (p.18).
111 ibid., (p.21).
112 K. H. Knappstein, 'Die Stunde der Sozialreform', *Frankfurter Hefte*, 1 (1946), H.3, 1-3 (p.3).
113 ibid.
114 *Frankfurter Hefte*, 1 (1946), H.5, 83.
115 WD, 'Beobachtungen und Bemerkungen', *Frankfurter Hefte*, 2 (1947), H.4, 333-35 (p.334).
116 EK, 'Das erlösende Wort', *Frankfurter Hefte*, 1 (1946), H.5, 84; and 'H. L.', 'Die vierte Bitte', *Frankfurter Hefte*, 1 (1946), H.4, 8-10.
117 ibid.

To achieve the necessary co-operation between workers and Christians, the political parties would have to be flexible. In particular, the SPD would have to ensure that it no longer stood in opposition to Christianity. It would have to prove itself 'gläubiger, jünger, unbefangener, lebendiger, vor allem aber weniger doktrinär-marxistisch und mehr lebendiger-sozialistisch [...], entschiedener und flexibler zugleich'.[118] However, this was the party, in the view of the journal, which faced, above all, 'eine große historische Aufgabe und Verantwortung'.[119] The KPD, by contrast, was more problematic. It might form part of a coalition if refined to its tradition of courageous socialism, and cleansed of its terrorist elements, but it would have to prove that it did not support dictatorship. It too would have to reject its fundamental opposition to Christianity and religion.[120] The CDU, in its attempt to unify all Christians within a political party, should gather together only those Christians who understood the contemporary political 'mission' of Christianity. It would have to liberate 'die evangelischen Christen aus jeder Verstrickung in den Nationalismus, aus jeder Bindung an den Geist des alten obrigkeitlich-militärischen Deutschlands'.[121] In general, political parties were warned against dwelling on the past — they should not 'in allzu starrer Bindung an ihre Vergangenheit die neuen Verantwortungen verfehlen'.[122] A dogmatic Marxist approach, therefore, could not be accepted. What was to be sought was a party which was 'lebendiger-sozialistisch', and the SPD represented the best chance of achieving this. Also unacceptable was any party with a slim majority monopolising the political scene, as for instance in Frankfurt.[123] Co-operation between the SPD and the CDU, in a 'Vernunft-Ehe', was the best option.[124]

As far as the overall political structure of the country was concerned, the journal nominally supported federalism. After the concept had been rejected by a

---

[118] Dirks, 'Die Zweite Republik', (p.22).
[119] ibid.
[120] ibid.
[121] ibid., (p.23).
[122] 'Ob man ein Programm machen darf?', (p.11).
[123] WD, 'Geist der Koalition', *Frankfurter Hefte*, 1 (1946), H.7, 577-78.
[124] WD, 'Die Partner', *Frankfurter Hefte*, 1 (1946), H.9, 787-89 (p.788).

group of representatives of the KPD, the SPD, the CDU and the LDP in April 1946, Kogon argued that 'die Realpolitik erfordert den Föderalismus, weil der Unitarismus den Separatismus im Gefolge hat'.[125] The journal agreed with Ulrich Noack that variety within a nation did not induce particularism, but in fact promoted nationhood. Centralisation of course was rejected outright. In December 1947, Dirks outlined the conditions necessary for an independent German state.[126] The first was the division of responsibilities between the Allies and the Germans. This would foster true German democracy and, gradually, responsible fulfilment of authority. The second was the aforementioned pact between the SPD and the CDU. This did not rule out opposition between the two parties within a parliamentary system, but invited them to co-operate in creating a healthy political system, including the pursuit of political consensus on electoral reform.

Within this political discussion, the definition of socialism was crucial. It was not only one of their founding blocks, but moreover was where lay both the common ground and the tension with Christianity. Dirks alluded to past 'Christliche Sozialisten' to highlight the overlap of ideals between Christianity and socialism. The journal's essentially religious standpoint inevitably clashed with the atheism associated with socialism. It could not be overlooked that socialism had, for one hundred years, been predominantly atheistic, materialistic, and Marxist.[127] The journal regretted that the two parties that currently espoused socialism, betrayed this same approach.[128] The failure of the political parties to meet the need for a centre-left Christian-based programme was of particular disappointment. Even if this were impossible, however, socialism should not be dismissed if presented in its humanistic form, where human values were upheld. Although the movement in this case would not be Christian, socialists and

---

125 EK, 'Berliner Zentralismus oder Frankfurter Bundesregierung?', *Frankfurter Hefte*, 1 (1946), H.1, 5-7 (p.6).

126 WD, 'Die Stunde der großen Reform', *Frankfurter Hefte*, 2 (1947), H.12, 1169-72.

127 Walter Dirks, 'Das Wort Sozialismus', *Frankfurter Hefte*, 1 (1946), H.7, 628-43 (p.636).

128 ibid.

Christians could co-operate on this humanistic basis. Clearly, then, a Christian rather than a humanist basis was preferable, but *Frankfurter Hefte* would settle for a compromise.

The editors were keen to underline that philosophically, the confines of socialism extended beyond Marxism. Dirks argued that the spectrum extended as far as conservative anti-capitalism inspired by 'christlichem Antrieb'.[129] Rejecting totalitarian communism, Kogon called for free socialism.[130] A barrier to unquestioning acceptance of socialist politics had been created by past errors, 'die im Namen des Sozialismus vertreten worden sind'.[131] Historical analysis which attached materialistic, atheistic colours to socialism was similarly rejected by the Catholic Church. As the Church's assessment of contemporary socialism was based on the movement's statements, the Church could not go as far as a 'schlichten Bejahung dieser Bewegung', but Dirks wrote, this was no different a stance to 'wir einzelnen Christen selbst'. For the Christian, then, there could be no uncritical adoption of socialism.[132] This did not mean, however, that the term could not be used in conjunction with other conditioning influences, and Dirks concluded that the political outlook best suited to the realization of peace and democracy in Germany was 'Sozialismus aus christlicher Verantwortung'.[133]

The journal's readiness to accommodate was criticized by the theologian, Karl Thieme, in a discussion with Dirks. Thieme opened by indicating a common Catholicism, and their shared immediate post-war wishes to see an 'Arbeiter-Partei' which might unite Christians and non-Christians. He regretted that Christian parties had emerged in Europe. Political programmes should not be developed from the Christian faith.[134] There ought to be a revision, he wrote, of what he perceived to be 'historistisch' in *Frankfurter Hefte*. The journal was less

---

129 ibid.

130 Eugen Kogon, 'Der Weg zu einem Sozialismus der Freiheit in Deutschland', *Frankfurter Hefte*, 2 (1947), H.9, 877-96.

131 Dirks, 'Das Wort Sozialismus', (p.640).

132 ibid.

133 ibid., (p.639).

134 'Ja und Nein: Zur Politik der "Frankfurter Hefte"', *Frankfurter Hefte*, 2 (1947), H.4, 384-402 (p.384).

likely to judge contemporary matters by the 'philosophia perennis'.[135] He argued: 'Die Aufgabe wäre, scheint mir, diesen "christlichen Sozialismus" zu konkretisieren, ein Tagesprogramm im Lichte der Enzykliken aufzustellen, nicht aber, den säkularen Sozialismus unter Mitübernahme nicht unerheblicher Irrtümer Christen mundgerecht zu machen, weil nun einmal das "Gefälle" dahin führe.'[136] Dirks agreed with Thieme's concern about Christian political parties. He emphasized *Frankfurter Hefte*'s concept of the relationship as one in which, 'die Christen *als* Christen [...] und die Arbeiter *als* Arbeiter [...] in der politischen Arbeit Hand in Hand arbeiten sollen'. The two were 'Geschichtsmächte'.[137] As to the compatibility of the two, Dirks reminded Thieme of the common drive for 'Entproletarisierung der Proletarier'.[138] The editors of *Frankfurter Hefte* identified with Thieme on the judgement of totalitarian Marxism:

In der Beurteilung des *totalitären* Marxismus aber sind wir uns von Herzen einig, und wir verstehen darunter nicht nur den vollzogenen politischen Totalitarismus der Bolschewisten und Kommunisten, sondern auch den drohenden Totalitarismus des bürokratischen Staatssozialismus, aber auch jeden theoretischen Marxismus, der sich selber als geschlossene und totale Weltdeutung versteht.[139]

Their main disagreement was, however, on economic grounds. Thieme supported a free market economy, while *Frankfurter Hefte* proposed a 'Planwirtschaft'.[140] This was not, as Dirks put it, 'total geplante Wirtschaft'.[141] On the contrary, it would be an economy where planning, as part of a responsible democratic system, would apply only to certain areas. It was not to be a free market economy, but the product of the 'Bündnis der Arbeiter und Christen'. This planning had to be carefully specified in order to clearly distinguish it from economic dictatorship. As Dirks explained, 'Plan kann Zwang sein und Plan kann Bürokratie sein: wir sind *gegen* die Bürokratie und *gegen* den Zwang. Plan kann Kooperation sein: wir sind

---

135 ibid., (pp.390-91).
136 ibid., (p.392).
137 ibid., (pp.393-94).
138 ibid., (p.395).
139 ibid.
140 ibid., (p.384).
141 'Ja und Nein', (p.396).

für die Kooperation.'[142] Dirks expressed disappointment that they had been misunderstood by such a reader, and surprise that anyone could have taken from the journal that they supported 'bürokratischen Zwangswirtschaft'.[143] Planning did not have to mean either state or bureaucratic dominance — 'man kann auch durch Rahmengesetzgebung, durch Steuer-, durch Geld-, Devisen-, Kredit- und Investitions-Politik planmäßig lenken und steuern und sich dabei auch des Preis- und Markt-Mechanismus bedienen.'[144] Later, Kogon specified that state ownership should apply to certain areas of public transport, postal services, energy supply, large banking institutions, and agriculture.[145] He urged economic revitalization through the free movement of trade between the zones, under German authority, and the involvement of Germany on equal terms in international trade.[146] Economic unity had to be achieved.

Frankfurter Hefte had a distinctive concept of democracy, Kogon claimed. While modern forms of democracy were mostly characterized either by individualism or by collectivism, Kogon described the democracy *Frankfurter Hefte* envisaged as 'die *lebendige politische Solidarität der Staatsbürger*'.[147] To support this democratic ideal, he repeated their support for federalism as the best form of political infra-structure — '*zentral wird nur geregelt, was alle zusammen in gleicher Weise angeht.*'[148] True socialism depended on it: 'Echter, fruchtbarer Sozialismus, welcher der Gerechtigkeit entspricht [...], kann ohne Föderalismus gar nicht entstehen.'[149]

Federal democracy, political co-operation, responsible economic planning, socialism informed by Christianity, *Frankfurter Hefte* saw these to be the best political formulae for a united Germany within a united Europe.

---

142 ibid., (p.398).
143 ibid., (p.395).
144 ibid., (p.396).
145 Kogon, 'Der Weg zu einem Sozialismus der Freiheit', (p.889).
146 EK, 'München: Versuch eines Starts', *Frankfurter Hefte*, 2 (1947), H.7, 625-27 (p.626).
147 Eugen Kogon, 'Demokratie und Föderalismus', *Frankfurter Hefte*, 1 (1946), H.6, 66-78 (p.74) (Kogon's emphasis).
148 ibid., (p.76) (Kogon's emphasis).
149 ibid., (pp.76-77).

The wider political sphere

To establish new European solidarity, Clemens Münster saw another essential. The Germans would have to forego nationalism and sovereignty.[150] Any campaign for full German sovereignty would compromise immediate plans for the new Germany. The Germans' task was 'nicht einer endgültig verlorenen Tradition nachzutrauern, sondern eine neue Tradition deutschen Weltbürgertums und europäischen Deutschseins zu begründen'.[151] His vision for the future, for this 'europäisches Deutschsein', was essentially a Third Way with Europe between East and West, and involved a uniquely German task — 'Vermittlung zwischen Ost und West'.[152] Arnold Toynbee supported the journal's Third Way rhetoric: 'Vielleicht liegt die Rettung, wie so oft, auf einem Mittelweg.'[153] Toynbee continued by supporting *Frankfurter Hefte*'s emphasis on Christian values:

> jenseits der politischen und wirtschaftlichen Elemente gibt es noch einen anderen Weg. [...] Noch kann uns unser Stichwort durch die Botschaft des Christentums und der anderen höheren Religionen gegeben werden, und die rettenden Worte und Taten können aus einer Gegend kommen, aus der wir sie nicht erwarten.[154]

Walter Weymann-Weyhe's words were stronger — 'Begegnung zwischen Ost und West' could only be fulfilled in the religious sphere.[155] Europe was seen, certainly by Kogon, not just as a political grouping, but almost as a path of righteousness: 'Die Demokratie, die wir einzurichten haben, kann nur föderalistisch und sozialistisch und damit, obschon unsere eigene Sache, der höchste Beitrag zum Neubau Europas sein: *die wahre deutsche Wiedergutmachung*.'[156] Kogon argued that a United States of Europe was essential for the good of the whole continent.[157] The journal saw in this 'eine *Konföderation der europäischen*

---

150 CM, 'Abbau der nationalen Souveränität', *Frankfurter Hefte*, 1 (1946), H.5, 1-3 (p.2)

151 ibid., (p.3).

152 ibid., (p.2).

153 Arnold J. Toynbee, 'Dieser Augenblick in der Geschichte', *Frankfurter Hefte*, 3 (1948), H.1, 29-37 (p.37).

154 ibid.

155 WW, 'Dostojewskij und der Westen', *Frankfurter Hefte*, 3 (1948), H.9, 865-68 (p.867).

156 Kogon, 'Demokratie und Föderalismus', (p.78) (Kogon's emphasis).

157 ibid.

Völker'.[158] It announced that a new Europe was already emerging — 'Europa ist auf dem Marsch, kein Zweifel'.[159]

The idea of a European community was not blindly accepted; *Frankfurter Hefte* treated it with some wariness, warning of the dangers of constructing 'ein falsches Europa'. Business interests and 'criminal idealism' threatened to inspire dangerous selfishness. It warned against overweening Americanization. Dirks expressed anxiety that the European Recovery Programme might mean an influx of foreign practices: 'Man hat sich gegen diese Gefahr zu wappnen. Sie wird der europäischen Politik zu schaffen machen. Wer sie bagatellisiert, macht seine Augen kurzsichtig.'[160] Concern about the vulnerability of Europe vis-à-vis US influence was summed up in the image of 'der amerikanische Elefant im europäischen Porzellanladen'.[161] Despite such misgivings, the United States was identified as the power to whom the Germans were most indebted.[162] Moreover, this was balanced by despairing references to the belligerent campaign conducted by the Soviet Union, the SED and the KPD against Western Europe, and the Marshall plan.[163] A particular risk was identified in neo-fascism. The re-emergence of right-wing politics seemed to threaten the whole continent. General de Gaulle, although the best option available, might, Dirks suggested, suppress French left-wing thought and create a dictatorship of the Right, but he represented. Right-wing Europe presented a threat to 'die schmal gewordene Mitte der Sozialisten und Katholiken'.[164] Despite this, Dirks had no clear solution. He referred to a 'Dritte Kraft' (undoubtedly their own socialist-Christian grouping), but stated that this stood little chance of succeeding in any bid to gain power peacefully. Dirks's article, 'Ein falsches Europa?', is eloquent testimony to the widespread anxiety about the stability of democracy, the fear that it would become

---

158 Dirks, 'Die Zweite Republik', (p.17) (Dirks's emphasis).
159 Dirks, 'Ein falsches Europa?', (p.698).
160 ibid., (p.700).
161 ibid.
162 Dirks, 'Die Zweite Republik', (p.17).
163 Dirks, 'Ein falsches Europa?', (p.700).
164 ibid., (p.701).

corrupt or fail again. Dirks referred to its Achilles heel — 'die demokratische Freiheit, undemokratisch zu sein'.[165] The choice facing France between communism and Gaullism symbolized for Walter Dirks the wider global question: 'Für den Kommunismus optieren, das heißt gegen den Marshallplan und gegen die Flugzeuge der Amerikaner optieren. Kann man das? Man kann es, aber es bedeutet den Krieg der Weltmächte. Also kann man das nicht.'[166] France was in general presented as an important ally. One of the journal's series of portraits featured Jacques Maritain. This Christian dialectician and 'Freund der Deutschen' advocated a Franco-German axis in a new Europe: 'während des Krieges schon hat er erklärt, daß die friedliche Zusammmenarbeit zwischen dem neuen Frankreich und einem vom Nationalismus gereinigten Deutschland das Zentralproblem Europas sei.'[167] There was in some respects, qualification of the European home. In a 1948 article, 'Vaterland', Dirks wrote: '"Europa" erscheint zu oft geradezu als das, was uns einengt, stört und hindert: es ist nicht einfach, angesichts der englischen und französischen Demontageliste europäisch zu empfinden.'[168] 'Die größere Heimat der europäischen Menschen' was not a certainty, Dirks warned, but a hope.[169]

Although *Frankfurter Hefte* remained largely independent, it was more in sympathy with the West than with the East. This was accentuated by its despair at the political manipulation evident in Eastern Zone socialism. Nevertheless, it warned against anti-Soviet prejudice, appealing for 'keine vorgefaßten, unkritischen Meinungen'.[170] Kogon argued cogently for a balanced and considered view. He disputed the equation of Bolshevism with warmongering — 'kein vernünftiger Mensch kann im Ernst behaupten, die Kommunisten der

---

165 ibid.
166 ibid., (p.702).
167 EK, 'Jacques Maritain — Frankreichs Botschafter beim Vatikan', *Frankfurter Hefte*, 1 (1946), H.3, 77-78.
168 Dirks, 'Vaterland', (p.123).
169 ibid.
170 EK, 'Zuschriften und Antworten: Recht oder Unrecht — mein Vaterland', *Frankfurter Hefte*, 1 (1946), H.5, 78-83 (p.80).

verschiedenen Nationen und Staaten seien Kriegshetzer.'[171] Displaying a pragmatic middle line, Kogon argued that the Soviet Union was only one power among others, and that its foreign policy was comparable to that of other states. The global priority was to reject the claim that war would be necessary or unavoidable. *If* there were a war, the roots would be found in three systems — 'beim Bolschewismus, beim Kapitalismus und bei der Dynamik der demokratischen Freiheit'.[172] The addition of this last reveals Kogon's deeper perspective. He was conveying here the vulnerability of all political systems — including the much-vaunted democracy, and the truth that the roots of historical conflict are multifactorial. This wisdom in political theory gives some clue as to the reasons for the journal's impact. Clearly, Kogon's dismissal of the simplistic tendency to equate Bolshevism with aggression is further evidence of its objectivity. His advocacy of openness towards the Russians was accompanied by the plea for caution and realism in considering the future: 'was in zehn Jahren sein wird, wissen wir so wenig, wie es die Propheten eines fatalistischen Pessimismus oder die Spekulanten wissen.'[173] In contrast to the predictions of these messengers, the word of God alone was reliable, and represented the ultimate goal. God's message, that men should live together in peace, should not be interfered with by man.[174]

Events in the Soviet Zone were, however, frequently criticized. Kogon objected to the formation of the SED as a decision 'von oben'.[175] Pointing out that communists were a minority within Germany, he was cynical about the activities of German communists in the Soviet Zone.[176] He claimed that they were profiting from the victory of the Red Army and the power of the Soviet Union, and were merely promoting their own interests by creating the SED. Kogon could not condone the exploitation both of political vulnerability and of the divided state of

---

171 ibid., (p.81).
172 ibid.
173 ibid., (p.82).
174 ibid.
175 EK, 'Die Einheitspartei', *Frankfurter Hefte*, 1 (1946), H.3, 8-10 (p.9).
176 ibid., (p.8).

the German nation: 'Die Führer der Einheitspartei haben genau erfaßt, was es für den Fortschritt ihrer Sache bedeuten würde, wenn ein straff zentralistisches Einheitsdeutschland geschaffen und Berlin zum Sitz der Zentralregierung gemacht würde. [...] Sie präsentieren gegenwärtig ihre Klassenkampfinteressen geschickt als nationale Forderung.'[177] Praising the principle of unified and neutral trades unions, he argued that a centralized political regime in Berlin would be dangerous.[178] He concluded that the consequences of the fusion in Berlin of the SPD and the KPD would depend on the 'Einsicht, Klugheit und Energie' of the 'beiden großen künftigen Koalitionsparteien Deutschlands', the SPD (as a whole) and the CDU.[179] He urged the German people to play their full role — to use their democratic rights and keep these parties informed of public opinion.[180] Later, Dirks described the treatment of Jakob Kaiser and the CDU as tantamount to 'Gleichschaltung'. The Russian authorities and the political elite in the Eastern Zone were inextricably linked in the developments, according to Dirks, who referred to them in the same breath as 'SMA-SED'.[181] Using the administration of Thüringen as an example, Kogon pointed out that the SED, that 'allerantifaschistischeste Partei', would lose no less than a third of its members if the same denazification process as in the western zones was applied in the Soviet Zone.[182] Whether the Moscow conference could resolve these discrepancies in the implementation of occupation rule, he seriously doubted.[183]

The political situation in the West was also seen as unsatisfactory. German political representatives working with the authorities in the American Zone were described by Dirks in 1946 as insufficiently interested in the public.[184] Arguing that the discussions about the Länder constitutions should be regarded as the

---

177 ibid., (p.9).
178 ibid., (p.10).
179 ibid.
180 ibid.
181 WD, 'Einheit und Freiheit', *Frankfurter Hefte*, 3 (1948), H.3, 193-96 (p.193).
182 EK, 'Beobachtungen und Bemerkungen', *Frankfurter Hefte*, 2 (1947), H.4, 333-35 (p.333).
183 ibid.
184 WD, 'Die neuen Verfassungen', *Frankfurter Hefte*, 1 (1946), H.4, 3-5 (p.3).

blueprints for the future German state, Dirks criticized as undemocratic the exclusion of the German public from such important developments.[185] *Frankfurter Hefte* also displayed a critical stance with regard to OMGUS. Kogon expressed understanding for those who complained about Allied rule, and criticized in particular the internment camp system. There was no re-education, as he saw it, only 'politische Verschlimmerung'.[186] Alfred Andersch praised the 'fair play' attitude which had characterized prisoner-of-war camps in America. They had encouraged free speech, and had sent home an elite to rebuild as 'Schöpfer eines neuen deutschen Staates!'. He regretted that this 'Getty-spirit' of co-operation, freedom of opinion, and German unity, were not possible now.[187]

On balance, however, critical comment was mitigated by positive remarks. There was praise of the Länderchefs in Munich, particularly in their campaign for a German body to deal with the question of prisoners-of-war, and in their appeal to exiles to return to Germany, 'als berufene *Mittler zwischen Deutschland und der übrigen Welt* eine historische Aufgabe zu erfüllen'.[188] Kogon, on the subject of internment camps, compared the numbers of deaths in Darmstadt, one of eleven in the US Zone, with those of Buchenwald. Within four months in Darmstadt, forty-three prisoners had died of chronic illnesses, and three had committed suicide, whereas 'im Konzentrationslager Buchenwald starben von 1937 bis 1945 jährlich im statistischen Durchschnitt jedesmal innerhalb von 9 Monaten 7000 Mann. In Auschwitz-...'[189] Here, Kogon deliberately broke off. He again urged balance, when he asked his readers to consider whether they would have sent Polish children condensed milk and care-packages, and whether, if the Ku-Klux-Klan had overrun America, and caused, and then lost a world war, the Germans would have acted any differently from the Allies.[190]

---

185 ibid., (pp.3-4).
186 Kogon, 'Der Kampf um Gerechtigkeit', (p.377).
187 Alfred Andersch, 'Getty oder Die Umerziehung in der Retorte', *Frankfurter Hefte*, 2 (1947), H.11, 1089-96 (p.1094-96).
188 EK, 'München: Versuch eines Starts', (p.626).
189 Kogon, 'Der Kampf um Gerechtigkeit', (p.377).
190 ibid., (p.379).

In the evolution of the new state, the basic rights of the population had to be established, and Dirks proposed as models, the statements on the rights of man contained in the American constitution, and the values of the French revolution. He underlined the central importance of freedom of the press and freedom of speech.[191] The free press was a particular interest. The journal quoted the view that history was ultimately a question of the victory of good over evil, and that the press was the means to fight this battle.[192] There was some disappointment with the German press. Churchill's suggestion that France and Germany should take over joint responsibility for designing a new Europe, received little coverage.[193] The journal alleged that the ills of contemporary life were presented more clearly in the foreign press.[194] The very question of British prisoner-of-war camps in Germany had been the subject of a major public debate in Britain following investigation by British journalists. Kogon believed that Germany should aspire to this: 'eines Tages muß es eine öffentliche Meinung als wachsame Instanz des nationalen Gewissens auch in Deutschland geben.'[195] An article by Dirks and Kogon addressed the role of writers in society. They argued that writers who addressed contemporary issues played a historical role and described their task as 'aufklären'.[196] There were limitations — 'Wir haben nur unsere Feder. Kein Wunder, daß unserem Beruf mancherlei Zweifel entgegengebracht werden', but society needed 'den Mann, der sich einmischt'.[197] The editors described their own contribution: 'Wir haben weder die Autorität, zu lehren oder zu befehlen, noch die Macht, zu entscheiden; wir argumentieren, wir räsonieren, wir klären eben auf.'[198] Measured against the void from which it had emerged, the contemporary German

---

[191] WD, 'Die neuen Verfassungen', (p.4).
[192] 'Eine Geschichtsphilosophie', *Frankfurter Hefte*, 1 (1946), H.2, 88.
[193] Kogon, 'Der Kampf um Gerechtigkeit', (p.383).
[194] Andersch, 'Getty oder Die Umerziehung in der Retorte', (p.1096).
[195] EK, 'Öffentliche Meinung als Kontrollinstanz', *Frankfurter Hefte*, 1 (1946), H.5, 10-11 (p.11).
[196] Walter Dirks und Eugen Kogon, 'Die Rolle der Publizisten', *Frankfurter Hefte*, 2 (1947), H.12, 1185-99, (WD) (p.1187).
[197] ibid., (p.1185).
[198] ibid., (p.1187).

press, in Kogon's view, was something of which they could almost be proud. Nevertheless, when compared to the press of 1932 '("Vossische", "DAZ", "Frankfurter Zeitung", "Berliner Tageblatt" usw. usw.!)', it was shown up as 'Armutszeugnis'.[199] Kogon acknowledged press licensing as an essential measure, and criticized those who rejected it. He simultaneously condemned, however, the opinion that it should continue, as, by definition, it limited free speech.[200] The problem with the daily press, Kogon said, was the lack of experienced and well-qualified editors and journalists. The development of public opinion was truly to be found among the journals, particularly 'in jenen wenigen Zeitschriften [...], die sich im Chor der mehr als 1200 zugelassenen (464 allein in der US-Zone) durch eine weniger laute als eindringliche und überzeugende Stimme Gehör zu schaffen vermochten'.[201] Especially at the time of the 1948 economic reform, which would alter the situation of the press in any case, Kogon called for control of the press to be in German hands. There should be an end to enforced licensing, and to the monopoly of licence holders, and a legal framework for the press.[202] Interestingly, a year later the Soviet press was described as an instrument of 'politische Gleichschaltung'.[203]

Literature

The space devoted by *Frankfurter Hefte* to literature was limited, perhaps in response to its readers' wishes. A questionnaire accompanying the April 1947 issue invited their opinions. 'Literatur und Dichtung' accounted for 4.4% of requests, well below other categories such as 'Religion, Kirche und Christianität' (17.4%), and 'Politik und Zeitgeschichte' (14.9%). As in other journals, the literary selection reflected the journal's interests, in *Frankfurter Hefte*'s case,

---

199 Eugen Kogon, 'Vom Elend unserer Presse', *Frankfurter Hefte*, 3 (1948), H.7, 614-24, (p.619).
200 ibid., (p.616).
201 ibid., (pp.619-20).
202 ibid., (pp.623-24).
203 Alfred Joachim Fischer, 'Die Presse der Sowjetunion', *Frankfurter Hefte*, 4 (1949), H.4, 348-53 (p.348).

Christianity. Hölderlin was viewed as a 'christliche Gestalt der Neuzeit'.[204] A piece on Hermann Hesse started with a quotation from *Glasperlenspiel* which ensured that the Christian message was prominent: 'Die Verzweiflung schickt uns Gott nicht, um uns zu töten, er schickt sie uns, um neues Leben in uns zu erwecken.'[205] Similarly, a quotation from Franz Werfel's aphorisms, 'Theologumena', indicated 'die eisige Banalität des Materialismus' — a Christian message here also.[206] There was a review of the debate about Nietzsche's Christian ethics and atheism, and even where Goethe was mentioned, the emphasis was on the Christian associations of his thinking, particularly the concepts of creation and renewal.[207]

Apart from these, there was little emphasis on pre-1930s German literature. One of the few to publish Nazi writers' names, it dismissed them quickly: 'Laßt die Werke selber sprechen.'[208] The debate about the relative merits of inner and outer emigration was subdued, although individual writers were discussed. On Ernst Jünger, it showed open-mindedness.[209] The journal was more provocative on the subject of Gerhart Hauptmann. Münster's irreverent presentation in one of the early issues is striking.[210] He began by claiming that if the office of poet laureate had existed in Germany, Hauptmann would have held it in the Kaiserreich, in the republic, and perhaps in the Nazi state — 'obschon seine Dramen und Epen umstritten, seine Gedichte schlecht und seine Romane fragwürdig sind'.[211] Münster explained Hauptmann's importance, despite the dubious political standing of his work:

---

204 Wilhelm Kütemeyer, 'Hölderlin als christliche Gestalt der Neuzeit', *Frankfurter Hefte*, 1 (1946), H.9, 799-810.

205 Eduard Schröder, 'Hermann Hesse', *Frankfurter Hefte*, 3 (1948), H.9, 841-45 (p.841).

206 Franz Werfel, 'Aus den "Theologumena"', *Frankfurter Hefte*, 2 (1947), H.7, 706.

207 WW, 'Nietzsche-Bücher', *Frankfurter Hefte*, 3 (1948), H.2, 187-91; and Ernst Michel, 'Zurück zu Goethe?', *Frankfurter Hefte*, 4 (1949), H.8, 667-78.

208 Hans-Peter Berglar-Schröer, 'Kleines Deutsches Lyrikum 1947', *Frankfurter Hefte*, 2 (1947), H.11, 1131-40, (p.1139).

209 Gottfried Stein, 'Ernst Jünger', *Frankfurter Hefte*, 3 (1948), H.5, 443-454 (p.454).

210 CM, 'Gerhart Hauptmann', *Frankfurter Hefte*, 1 (1946), H.5, 73-75.

211 ibid., (p.73).

Der eigentliche Grund aber sowohl der Popularität und des Ruhmes, wie der Ablehnung und des Ärgernisses scheint der zu sein, daß Gerhart Hauptmann bestimmende Züge des deutschen Charakters und des deutschen Schicksals in seinem Leben und in seinem Werk in einer geradezu beängstigenden Deutlichkeit zeigt.[212]

The exile novel *Stalingrad* by Theodor Plievier was reviewed by Hans-Peter Berglar-Schröer as a text which depicted *all* human characters. In the context of war, Plievier was held to have produced an experimental novel, one where there was no hero, and where all were victims. The effect on the German reader, Berglar-Schröer implied, was considerable: 'so haben wir das Empfinden, daß es nicht nur die Sechste Armee ist, die da ihren bitteren Todesgang geht, sondern in ihr das ganze deutsche Volk, ja die ganze Welt, die klaftertief im Irrtum gefangen liegt.'[213] Dirks identified this novel, together with Elisabeth Langgässer's *Das unauslösliche Siegel*, Anna Seghers's *Das siebte Kreuz* and, 'vielleicht', Gertrud von Le Fort's *Kranz der Engel* as the forerunners of the post-war novel.[214] All draw on the experience of the recent past, whether of war, of exile, or of persecution.

The tragedy of the Third Reich in personal terms was recalled by the publication of Albrecht Haushofer's 'Moabiter Sonette'.[215] Haushofer, who had been arrested after the resistance effort of 20 July 1944, and executed the following April, had named his sonnets after Moabit, the Berlin jail. The last of the six sonnets, 'Schuld', compared his culpability in the eyes of the court with what he felt was his real guilt — 'ich mußte früher mein Pflicht erkennen, / ich mußte schärfer Unheil Unheil nennen'.[216] The sonnet ended 'ich hab' gewarnt — nicht hart genug und klar! / und heute weiß ich, was ich schuldig war...'. This powerful confession of guilt by omission, coming, as it did, from such a victim, underlined the message of the journal that no-one was exempt from examining his conscience.

---

212 ibid., (p.75).

213 Hans-Peter Berglar-Schröer, 'Memento Stalingrad', *Frankfurter Hefte*, 3 (1948), H.4, 375-76 (p.376).

214 Walter Dirks, 'Elisabeth Langgässer', *Frankfurter Hefte*, 3 (1948), H.12, 1127-30 (p.1127).

215 Albrecht Haushofer, 'Moabiter Sonette', *Frankfurter Hefte*, 1 (1946), H.4, 83-85.

216 ibid., (p.85).

A further series of sonnets by Maria Jochum, entitled 'Vor einem Jahr', were devoted to the human despair, and beseeching of God coincident with the end of the war.[217]

Dirks commented on the preponderance of the sonnet form in current literature, explaining that only lyric poetry could communicate with all sections of the population after such events. He described many of the lyric poems of the time as 'echt, stark und gültig'.[218] By contrast, the prose writer had a more difficult task. Dirks asked how could they expect a writer 'des universalen goethischen Typus' to emerge at such a time?[219] His overview of the literary situation was somewhat bleak — 'wir haben keine universalen Dichter. Wir haben keinen großen Dramatiker. Wir haben eine Reihe von beachtlichen Romanautoren, aber weder heute noch früher einen großen Romancier, ihrer aller Thematik ist beschränkt.'[220] Berglar-Schröer was later to lament the standard of much of the new lyric poetry, although Langgässer was again praised as being one of the few most notable.[221]

The style of emerging writers was considered to be especially important. In a moving tribute to Wolfgang Borchert, Alfred Andersch claimed his post-war existential angst to be so eloquent that it defied emulation. Andersch particularly praised Borchert's language: 'wie frisch ist seine Sprache, wie blühend, wie neugeboren.'[222] He compared him to Büchner especially with reference to *Draußen vor der Tür*, where Beckmann searches for the old man who calls himself God. Introducing three prose extracts, Andersch focused on what was for him Borchert's vital contribution — he did not accuse, but rather asked questions: 'dieser Dichter weiß, daß niemand anzuklagen ist. Nur eines bleibt: fragen. Borcherts Werk ist eine einzige Frage, unwiederholbar und sprachmächtig gestellt,

---

217 Maria Jochum, 'Vor einem Jahr', *Frankfurter Hefte*, 1 (1946), H.2, 86-87.
218 WD, 'Dichter', *Frankfurter Hefte*, 1 (1946), H.5, 5-6 (p.5).
219 ibid.
220 ibid.
221 Berglar-Schröer, 'Kleines Deutsches Lyrikum 1947'.
222 Alfred Andersch, 'Das Gras und der alte Mann', *Frankfurter Hefte*, 3 (1948), H.10, 927-29 (p.929).

darin liegt sein geistiger Wert.'[223] Style and language were also emphasized in Andersch's assessment of the poet Günter Eich. Commenting on a selection from a new edition shortly before its publication, he commemorated Eich's 'mystisches Verhältnis zur Sprache'.[224]

A report by Friedrich Minssen of the first meeting of the Gruppe 47 emphasized the experimental nature of their writing.[225] Their attempt at a new language was deemed appropriate — 'unserem bedrohten und illusionslosen Zeitalter angemessen'. Their readings were described as characterized by 'Wahrheitsliebe'.[226] The writers not only opened themselves up to mutual criticism, but even demanded it. This was hailed as a fresh new approach. Minssen described the uniquely contemporary character of this critical requirement: 'Sie hat vor allem den Sinn für die existentiellen Bezüge zwischen dem Geist und dem Leben [...] in den jungen Schriftstellern wachzuhalten.' He claimed their efforts as proof that there were young writers freeing literature from the 'selbstgenügsamen, ästhetisierenden Einsamkeit' of the past.[227] As to how this new literature was received, the journal urged balance and tolerance. This was particularly notable with Andersch's own story, 'Anfang und Ende'. Discouraging rejection of this as nihilistic, *Frankfurter Hefte* published a statement reminding readers that fifty years previously, the accusation might have been 'subversive', and twenty years previously — 'entartet'.[228]

Where more controversial issues were involved, the journal was restrained. It published Ulrich Sonnemann's New York attack on Thomas Mann. Included in the same issue was an extract from a letter by Mann, which concluded by asking the reader if Sonnemann was justified. The editors, however, judged that no final

---

223 ibid.

224 Alfred Andersch, 'Freundschaftlicher Streit mit einem Dichter', *Frankfurter Hefte*, 4 (1949), H.2, 150-54.

225 Friedrich Minssen, 'Notizen von einem Treffen junger Schriftsteller', *Frankfurter Hefte*, 3 (1948), H.2, 110-11.

226 ibid., (p.110).

227 ibid., (p.111).

228 'Mitteilungen', *Frankfurter Hefte*, 4 (1949), H.8, 894.

verdict could be given, since it was too early for people to be objective.[229] The journal had earlier addressed the topic, Minssen regretting that Mann had not returned to Germany, and Kogon suggesting that he should be more careful in his accusations.[230] Later, *Frankfurter Hefte* published an extract from Mann's letter in *Aufbau* — pointedly without comment, in an effort to present the full range of opinions.[231]

Foreign literature published or reviewed, included the French poets Aragon and Cassou, in particular their prisoner poetry from recent conflicts, and a review of Alfred Kazin's book on the American novel, which highlighted the predominant names and trends of this genre in the twentieth century.[232] On Russian art and literature, Andersch imputed a certain parallel between its approved Socialist Realism and the Third Reich's prescriptions of artistic creativity.[233]

Frankfurter Hefte was even more political when dealing with the theatre or with radio. Kogon in particular was adamant that theatre had a central role to play in the recovery:

Eine Nation, die das hinter sich hat, was die deutsche hinter sich hat, braucht große und wahre Kunst. Auf Tingeltangel, Krampf, Hysterie, Panoptikum, Perückenschau und Operetten-Flachlandschaften soll sie verzichten, — auf einiges davon für immer, auf anderes vorerst. Auch das Theater muß *neues* Theater werden, gewandeltes Theater.[234]

He expressed disappointment that the performance of Zuckmayer's *Des Teufels General* had not left the audience shocked and ashamed at their recent 'mitverschuldetes Verhängnis'.[235] The possibility that the sabotage featured

---

229 Ulrich Sonnemann, 'Thomas Mann oder Maß und Anspruch', *Frankfurter Hefte*, 3 (1948), H. 7, 625-40 (p.625).

230 Friedrich Minssen, 'Thomas Mann', *Frankfurter Hefte*, 2 (1947), H.9, 953-57; and Kogon, 'Die deutsche Revolution', (p.22).

231 'Beobachtungen und Bemerkungen', *Frankfurter Hefte*, 3 (1948), H.9, 788-90 (p.790).

232 See John L. Brown, 'Dichter des Widerstandes', *Frankfurter Hefte*, 1 (1946), H.1, 83-88; and Eduard Schröder, 'Literatur und Gesellschaft in USA', *Frankfurter Hefte*, 1 (1946), H.4, 79-82.

233 RA, 'Vom Sinn der Malerei', *Frankfurter Hefte*, 3 (1948), H.2, 183.

234 EK, 'Theater der Gegenwart (und Zukunft?)', *Frankfurter Hefte*, 1 (1946), H.3, 91-92 (p.92).

235 EK, '"Des Teufels General"', *Frankfurter Hefte*, 3 (1948), H.2, 183-85 (p.184).

therein would be taken by people to mitigate in some way their own guilt, Kogon viewed with alarm.[236] Kurt Wortig lamented the Nazis' suffocation of the free evolution of theatre, and in particular the ending of the experimental theatre of Expressionism.[237] He encouraged the development of 'politisches Theater' or 'Zeitstück'.[238] While Berlin and some Soviet theatres led the field, there was a comparative dearth in the western zones.[239] He encouraged readers to support the growth and development of theatre by more active attendance.[240] Berglar-Schröer regretted that contemporary drama — German and foreign — was dominated by pieces which were 'keineswegs echte Dramen und nur sehr selten Dichtungen'.[241] 'Die Zeit ist [...] nicht günstig für das Drama', he wrote.[242] Audiences were tired, and every word of their language had been devalued. Dramatists themselves were similarly affected.[243] In addition to financial worries, there was an attitude after two world wars that theatre was somewhere to be distracted and entertained, rather than a 'Bildungsstätte'.[244]

Dirks appeared to understand this when he described the duties and responsibilities of the new German radio: 'er wird vielmehr zwar nicht nur ernst, gründlich, nährend, bildend, erziehend sein, sondern auch munter, spritzig, elegant, ironisch, kämpferisch, mutig, kühn und scharf, je nach Stoff und Anlaß und Stunde.'[245] It should promote Dirks's aims of the establishment of a 'Second Republic' in being 'weder neutral, noch parteiisch', and should encourage the listener to achieve breadth of mind. Music should include jazz, which he praised as morally and politically superior to 'Singsang- und Operettenkitsch'![246] Above all,

---

236 ibid., (p.185).
237 Kurt Wortig, 'Das Theater der Zeit', *Frankfurter Hefte*, 1 (1946), H.8, 734-44 (p.737).
238 ibid., (p.740).
239 ibid., (pp.739 and 743).
240 ibid., (p.744).
241 Hans-Peter Berglar-Schröer, 'Vom grossen und vom kleinen Welttheater', *Frankfurter Hefte*, 3 (1948), H.2, 137-45 (p.143).
242 ibid., (p.145).
243 ibid.
244 Hans-Peter Berglar-Schröer, 'Theaterruinen', *Frankfurter Hefte*, 4 (1949), H.4, 291-93 (p.292).
245 WD, 'Der ideale Sender', *Frankfurter Hefte*, 1 (1946), H.4, 13-15 (p.14).
246 ibid., (pp.13-14); and WD, 'Jazz', *Frankfurter Hefte*, 3 (1948), H.9, 790-91 (p.791).

what had been offered under Goebbels was to be rejected — 'Verschmiertes, Verklimpertes, Routiniertes, Witzloses und Gleichgültiges', along with 'den zackigen Militärmarsch'.[247]

The readers

The question of youth was rather underplayed when compared with other publications of the time. Dirks argued that the problems of the young generation were actually those of the old generation.[248] Nevertheless, in the debate on university education, it identified intervention by the military governments as a threat, and forwarded themes which it considered to be essential areas of teaching (to Germans by Germans) — the reasons for German historical failure, 'Sozialismus in neuer Sicht', and above all, 'das Human-Sein'.[249]

In contrast to the young generation, the place of women in the new society received more attention in *Frankfurter Hefte* than in the other journals. Maria Jochum's article 'Frauenfrage 1946', appealed for women to be the central pivot of the new society — 'so und nicht anders wollen die Frauen ihre Rolle in der Politik verstanden wissen, als Instanz des Gewissens, als unbestechliche Hüterinnen und Wahrerinnen wirklicher Menschlichkeit.'[250] Jochum used Goethe's *Iphigenie* as an example to German womanhood, arguing that her intervention had repealed the dominance of fear and hate, and led through generosity of spirit to a potential new solution.[251] She commended the position of English women — singled out as having particularly loud voices within organisations! She herself pleaded for quietude in the emerging order:

Wir haben für immer genug vom heroischen Aufbruch; wenn wir die Gesichter der jungen Generation ansehen, die bei dem letzten Aufbruch unter die Räder gekommen ist, blutet uns das Herz. Wir wollen nicht mehr zittern müssen vor neuen Wahnideen, wir wollen ruhig leben.[252]

---

247 WD, 'Der ideale Sender', (p.14).

248 WD, 'Nicht die Jugend, die Erwachsenen!', *Frankfurter Hefte*, 1 (1946), H.3, 4-6 (p.6).

249 CM, 'Die Universität 1946', *Frankfurter Hefte*, 1 (1946), H.1, 7-9 (p.8).

250 Maria Jochum, 'Frauenfrage 1946', *Frankfurter Hefte*, 1 (1946), H.3, 24-31 (p.31).

251 ibid.

252 ibid., (p.30).

Editha Klipstein found models in German women — writers Annette Kolb, Frieda Duensing, and Regina Ullmann. All these women had been 'stolze Kinder', ready to fight as if 'in Jugendfeuer'.[253] The journal supported the feminist approach. In editorial notes at the end of the March 1948 issue, it admitted that it frequently wrote 'Männer' when 'Frauen' were included.[254] It explained its 'deep-lying' error by the assumption that 'die Männer = das politische Geschlecht'. While one reason for this, it suggested, might be that, since 1918 and Expressionism, the word 'Mensch' was not as easily used, it wondered whether this might be 'ein nationalsozialistisches Erbteil?'.[255]

At all times the journal sought dialogue with its readers, whether men or women, Christians or atheists. In the later years, following the economic crisis of 1948, it strove to, and encouraged its readers to continue in the task they both shared. In the editorial introduction to the July 1948 issue, the journal, referring to the frequently heard comment that *Frankfurter Hefte* would survive 'Tag „X"' (economic reform), acknowledged its readership's confidence: 'Natürlich wissen wir, daß unsere Leser die FH nicht bloß für "nützlich und angenehm", sondern für notwendig halten.'[256] It announced a reduction in the price as part of the journal's contribution to its shared responsibility and exhorted readers to share the cost, reminding them that their shared task was more important than any financial concerns. The new order was one of division, and in the light of this demanding and precarious intellectual situation, both editors and the publishing house expressed their urgent desire to continue their work.

'Losing the peace'

By 1948, political developments had advanced at such a pace that they had achieved their own momentum. Economic reform brought added impetus to

---

[253] Editha Klipstein, 'Erinnerung an Bücher von Frauen', *Frankfurter Hefte*, 1 (1946), H.3, 93-94.
[254] 'Mitteilungen', *Frankfurter Hefte*, 3 (1948), H.3, 286-88 (p.288).
[255] ibid.
[256] Die Herausgeber und der Verlag, 'An unsere Leser', *Frankfurter Hefte*, 3 (1948), H.7, 585.

Frankfurter Hefte's pronouncements. The issue of July 1948 was especially significant. It contained articles by each of the three editors, all voicing deep anxiety about the situation. Kogon explored actual political events; Dirks wrote of the socialist-Christian partnership (his preoccupation since the beginning); and Münster re-emphasized Christian values.

In his article 'Der entscheidende Schritt', Kogon described the dangers as he saw them. 'Decisive' moves were being made to draw western Germany into opposition to the East, close alignment with the West, and even remilitarisation: 'Ein Bundesstaat auf zwei Dritteln des deutschen Bodens und mit drei Vierteln seiner Bewohner könnte den Sinn einer atlantisch-westeuropäischen Mark gegen den Osten haben. Binnen zweier Jahre müßte sie mit Gütern vollgestopft sein; *aber auch mit Soldaten.*'[257] His acute anxiety about the prospect of reintroducing arms so soon after the war is almost palpable. Not just remilitarisation, but European division was anathema: '*Weder Deutschlands noch Europas Grenzen liegen an der Elbe.*'[258] The creation of a 'Bundeseinheit Europas' would extend far beyond the Eastern Zone, and he understood why the Soviet Union regarded Western Europe with distrust.[259] Kogon went on to contest the so-called *logic* of the self-acclaimed 'Verteidiger des Abendlandes'. To be persuaded by one part of the world into believing there was only one solution was wrong. The American 'Politik des Wohlstandes und der starken Hand', was indeed the most persuasive argument, but he regretted that these ideas had not been implemented immediately in 1945. He lamented the progress of Germany since the war. There should have been similar political developments in all zones, leading to all-German bodies deciding economic matters for all of Germany, and following this, a pause for these to take effect, and for economic, social and cultural life to emerge. The re-education programme did not help — 'was für eine hohle, unglaubwürdige

---

257 EK, 'Der entscheidende Schritt', *Frankfurter Hefte*, 3 (1948), H.7, 586-91, (p.586) (Kogon's emphasis).
258 ibid.
259 ibid., (pp.586-87) (Kogon's emphasis).

Propagandahülle mußte da die "Umerziehungspolitik" werden!'[260] In the wake of the London agreement, which called for Germans to have the freedom to form democratic government, Kogon urged that 'das dauernde Hin und Her von Entgegenkommen, Befehlen, Verhandlungen, Willkürmaßnahmen, wohlwollenden Erklärungen, Verfügungen, Bitten und gegenseitigen Vorwürfen oder einseitigen Verstimmungen muß ein Ende haben, sonst gelingt nicht, was jetzt angestrebt wird'.[261] Partnership was vital, and he encouraged fellow Germans to regard the controversial Ruhr statute as the prelude to wider European co-operation. At least the raw materials of industry would be able to move from one centre to another within Europe. Kogon again pressed for co-operation when acknowledging the resurgence of nationalist sentiment. Provided democrats were sufficiently strong in their convictions, this was the best way to achieve balanced politics. The ultimate reason for co-operation was overwhelming: 'wir sind *ein* Volk.'[262]

In his article, Dirks wrote of the crisis of the 'Mitte' in Germany. The CSU had lost voters, particularly in Bavaria to the Bayernpartei. Unless the CDU found a truly Christian way of dealing with contemporary problems, it would disintegrate. As for the SPD, Dirks claimed that its advantage over the CDU in 1945 and 1946 no longer applied. In addition, especially after the recent events in Prague, a pact with the KPD was impossible.[263] The SPD had other problems. Kurt Schumacher was too dominant and was in poor health. More fundamentally, the party had no clear political agenda. Furthermore, if the American-supported economic recovery were rapid, and the crisis of the monetary reform short-lived, then the SPD would again find itself in the left wing of bourgeois democracy, as in the 1920s and 1930s. As such, it would share in the historical blame which would accrue to the new democracy — 'die soziale Republik zum dritten Mal und die Stunde des Sozialismus zum zweiten Mal zu verfehlen'.[264] *Frankfurter Hefte* had

---

260 ibid.
261 ibid., (p.589).
262 ibid., (p.590) (Kogon's emphasis).
263 WD, 'Die Krise der Mitte', *Frankfurter Hefte*, 3 (1948), H.7, 591-96 (p.593).
264 ibid., (p.594).

hoped that the workers and Christians together would steer Europe to a new future, but the CDU and the SPD had failed in their peacetime pact. In particular, the crisis of the SPD was symptomatic of the European scene — 'die Krise der SPD ist *eine Krise des europäischen Sozialismus.*'[265] Nationalism in France, and communism on the other hand in Italy, would not help Germany to maintain a middle ground position. It could find itself characterized by 'europäischer Biederkeit, kapitalistischem Geld und amerikanischen Panzern'. Dirks feared that '*die "Dritte Kraft" und damit die lebendige Demokratie selbst in die hoffnungslose Minderheit gerät*'.[266]

Münster, in his article, argued that the overview had been lost, and that the forces of disorder threatened to reign over those of order. He claimed that Allied mistakes in Germany had allowed Germans to forget their mistakes, both before and during the war, to such an extent that people no longer admitted responsibility. Referring, as did Kogon, to the resurgence of nationalism and anti-Semitism, he accused the Germans of making demands as if their country were a reliable partner and an unthreatening neighbour.[267] Münster began and finished the article with Pope Pius XII's words: 'Die große Stunde des christlichen Gewissens hat geschlagen.'

In early 1949, *Frankfurter Hefte* admitted that there was no chance of a government for all of Germany.[268] It had moved with the times, and was now discussing the practical implementation of policies for the future of a divided Germany. One concern was the formation of a democratic police force; decentralization had produced a situation where there were essentially different forces in the different zones.[269] This was part of an increasing emphasis on the 'Weg der innerdeutschen Entwicklung'.[270] This piece provoked a response from

---

[265] ibid., (p.595) (Dirks's emphasis).

[266] ibid., (p.594).

[267] CM, 'Der Aufruf des Gewissens', *Frankfurter Hefte*, 3 (1948), H.7, 596-600 (pp.596-97).

[268] Eugen Kogon, 'Man braucht Deutschland... Auch deutsche Soldaten?', *Frankfurter Hefte*, 4 (1949), H.1, 18-33 (p.19).

[269] Karl W. Böttcher und Rudolf Schäfer, 'Die Polizei in Deutschland', *Frankfurter Hefte*, 4 (1949), H.2, 132-49 (p.132-33).

[270] EK, 'Offene Fragen', Böttcher und Schäfer, 'Die Polizei in Deutschland', (p.149).

Konrad Adenauer, who denied promoting 'eine starke Polizeimacht'.[271] Karl Wilhelm Böttcher analysed the activities of former Nazis.[272] Interestingly, this also precipitated a rebuttal by a member of the Parlamentarischer Rat, Gerhard Kroll, who suggested that this information should go to the relevant authorities, and that the *Frankfurter Hefte* might be acting illegally in publicizing individual case-histories.[273] Alfred Andersch reported that Nazi feeling had not been rooted out by denazification; on the contrary, there were still 'wahre Pestherde nazistischen Geistes'.[274] Münster underlined the influence of the occupation powers:

> ihre Ansätze einer politischen Erziehung im Sinne der Demokratie und des Weltbürgertums sind im großen und ganzen vorerst unfruchtbar geblieben. (Das besagt nicht, daß das deutsche Volk so schlecht sei, wie der Nationalsozialismus war; aber es besagt, daß es bis jetzt politisch anscheinend nicht besser und nicht klüger geworden ist, als es zu der Zeit war, da Hitler über uns kam).[275]

Münster asked the crucial question of what they would do when occupation came to an end.[276] There were already marked differences between East and West Germans: 'Das politisch-wirtschaftliche Gefüge, der Aufbau und die Wirksamkeit des Verwaltungsapparates, die Auffassungen von Demokratie und die körperlich-seelische Verfassung der Bevölkerung sind im Osten und im Westen Deutschlands bereits bedenklich verschieden.'[277] One of the most essential tasks, along with the designing of a 'Bundesverfassung', was 'die sorgfältige, umfassende Vorbereitung des Zusammenschlusses der Ostzone mit den Westzonen, mag ihr Zeitpunkt auch ungewiß sein'.[278] In April, Kogon too advised that the drafting of a provisional German constitution should not hinder the future resolution of the German Question.[279] He listed certain aspects of German life which he would wish

---

271 'Mitteilungen', *Frankfurter Hefte*, 4 (1949), H.3, 278.
272 Karl Wilhelm Böttcher, 'Menschen unter falschem Namen', *Frankfurter Hefte*, 4 (1949), H.6, 492-511.
273 ibid.
274 RA, 'Merkwürdige Vorkommnisse', *Frankfurter Hefte*, 4 (1949), H.2, 103-05 (p.105).
275 CM, 'Probealarm: Räumung', *Frankfurter Hefte*, 4 (1949), H.2, 99-101 (p.99).
276 ibid., (p.100).
277 ibid.
278 ibid.
279 EK, 'Das zureichende Minimum', *Frankfurter Hefte*, 4 (1949), H.4, 283-84 (p.283).

to see changed — 'das Beamtengesetz, die Verwaltungsreform, die Bodenreform, das Pressegesetz' among others, and tried to dissuade the Western powers and their military governors from hindering developments.[280] As the year progressed, *Frankfurter Hefte* became almost a diary of parliamentary events. In July, it encouraged its readers to vote.[281] This might close the gap that had emerged between politics and reality — 'Kriegsversehrten, Heimkehrer, Vertriebenen, Kleinrentner, Kleinverdiener, Arbeitslosen'.[282] The nature of any coalition would also be decided. While the SPD-CDU coalition was now as good as dead, it had served a purpose — it had represented German interests as they faced military occupation.[283] Now, as the two were about to divide into government and opposition, there had to be a revitalized sense of a 'Grundpakt', informed by conscience, Dirks wrote. Without this, 'haben wir wenig Aussicht, den in Bonn wiederaufgenommenen weimarer Versuch diesmal zu einem guten Ende zu führen'.[284] In September, the results were published, together with the comment that they had confirmed the fears of those advocates of a majority system.[285] An article by Kogon and Dirks on the new republic called for three political levels to be established — party, coalition, and state.[286] Dirks underlined the importance of economic co-operation by restating the journal's frequent formula of the 'Sozialen Volksstaates'.[287] The European dimension was inevitably once more central — foreign policy had to be European policy.[288]

From 1948 onwards, the journal repeatedly stated that the German question involved the whole of Europe. It pressed for maximum communication between East and West.[289] Tracing the idea of a European community, Rudolf

---

280 ibid., (p.284).
281 WD, 'Ende der alten Koalitionen', *Frankfurter Hefte*, 4 (1949), H.7, 545-47.
282 ibid., (p.545).
283 ibid., (pp.545-46).
284 ibid., (p.547).
285 WD, 'Die ersten Entscheidungen', *Frankfurter Hefte*, 4 (1949), H.9, 721-22 (p.721).
286 Eugen Kogon und Walter Dirks, 'Der Beginn — Unsere letzte Gelegenheit', *Frankfurter Hefte*, 4 (1949), H.9, 738-49 (p.744).
287 ibid., (p.748).
288 ibid., (p.747).
289 See, for example, EK, 'Krieg und "Frieden"', *Frankfurter Hefte*, 3 (1948), H.9, 777-80.

Schäfer referred among others, to Kant, who in his 1795 essay, *Vom ewigen Frieden*, had argued 'Das Völkerrecht soll auf einem Föderalismus freier Staaten gegründet sein'.[290] This reinforced *Frankfurter Hefte*'s pursuit of a peaceful federalist Europe. Schäfer argued that there was no option: 'Was innerhalb der Weltorganisation der *Vereinten Nationen* nunmehr fehlt, sind die *Vereinigten Staaten von Europa*. Daß sie eine Notwendigkeit sind, kann kaum jemand, der die geschichtliche Entwicklung im Auge hat, bezweifeln.'[291] Writing in conjunction with Schäfer, Kogon again commended Churchill's strategy for Franco-German co-operation to be at the centre of European plans, but recalled the anti-Soviet line that Churchill had then taken with his Western Europeanism. Kogon saw the whole idea of Europe as connected to Christian thought. He referred to the proceedings of a Catholic conference on Europe ('Christliche Sozialphilosophie und Föderalismus'), which had recommended 'eine Bewegung aus christlichem Geiste und auf demokratischer Grundlage zur Unterstützung und Förderung der Idee einer europäischen Föderation, die ihren Platz im Rahmen einer Weltkonföderation finden soll'.[292] Walter Dirks saw Europe as already a political entity: 'Europa [...] ist nicht ein Verein von Nationalstaaten, sondern ein einheitliches politisches Feld.'[293] Accordingly, Schumacher, Bevin, Blum and Saragat should work together as colleagues in a European socialist movement.[294] According to Dirks, Europe could not become Bolshevistic, but neither should it be anti-Bolshevistic.[295] In a later article, Münster qualified this essentially middle position: 'ein [...] Verzicht auf totale Einseitigkeit bei uns heißt [...] nicht, neutral sein.'[296] Although a majority of Germans would favour following 'einer mittleren

---

290 RS, EK, RP, 'Die Vereinigten Staaten von Europa: Idee und beginnende Wirklichkeit', *Frankfurter Hefte*, 3 (1948), H.1, 72-77, RS (p.73).
291 ibid., (p.74) (Schäfer's emphasis).
292 EK, ibid., (pp.74-75).
293 WD, 'Europa und die Sozialisten', *Frankfurter Hefte*, 3 (1948), H.10, 876-79 (p.878).
294 ibid.
295 Walter Dirks, 'Der Nationalismus der SED', *Frankfurter Hefte*, 3 (1948), H.11, 1001-12 (p.1001).
296 CM, 'Illusionäre Neutralität', *Frankfurter Hefte*, 4 (1949), H.5, 375-76 (p.376).

Linie', he argued that pursuing this was impracticable.[297] The neutrality sought by the Nauheimer Kreis and Ulrich Noack, might even intensify the conflict.[298] The Germans should not be trying to construct 'ein neutralisiertes Wolkenkuckucksheim auf einem brodelnden Vulkan'.[299] Although there were some positive ideas in the Nauheim plans, Germany should be thinking of constructively working for European solutions.[300]

The futility of the Cold War was repeatedly stressed, especially in the face of the human despair which existed — this time of misery, Dirks wrote, when a man lost his job because he had been a Nazi, when refugees had no decent place to live, when many had to cope with the legacy of Auschwitz. Dirks reminded *Frankfurter Hefte*'s reader of 'Gottes absolutes Ja zu jedem einzelnen Menschen'.[301] Referring to these tribulations, Dirks concluded, 'Das Elend der Menschen verführt viele zum Nihilismus. Es ist in Wahrheit ein doppelter Ruf: zur brüderlichen Hilfe und zu tieferem Vertrauen.'[302] Kogon used the horrific symbols of Lidice and Oradour-sur-Glane alongside that of the suicide note to him of a former National Socialist official, pleading that he had not been without conscience or humanity. In this powerful argument for 'Politik der Versöhnung', he asserted that people needed each other for the horrors to be overcome.[303] Against this background, the journal reported the American allegation that the Russians had accused them of spoiling the harvest in the Eastern Zone, through removing literature on weather-forecasting from German libraries![304] On the Russians' explanation for the Berlin blockade as a protective measure, the journal posed the

---

297 CM, 'Probealarm: Räumung', (p.100).
298 CM, 'Illusionäre Neutralität', (p.375).
299 ibid., (p.376).
300 ibid.
301 Walter Dirks, 'Das Elend der Menschen und die Vatergüte Gottes', *Frankfurter Hefte*, 3 (1948), H.4, 305-17 (pp.305 and 313).
302 ibid., (p.317).
303 Eugen Kogon, 'Politik der Versöhnung', *Frankfurter Hefte*, 3 (1948), H.4, 317-24.
304 'Beobachtungen und Bemerkungen', *Frankfurter Hefte*, 3 (1948), H.10, 887-88 (p.888).

question of whether the will of those supposedly being protected was unimportant.[305]

In a speech at the Sorbonne in 1949, Kogon pleaded that 'Deutschland muß normalisiert werden'.[306] He judged the Allies' attempt to provoke 'Besinnung' in the German people as a whole, and 'Bekenntnis' among the leading sections of the people, to have failed.[307] However, the young generation had survived the trauma of recent years. They mistrusted political parties, but they recognized the value of Europe.[308] In a separate article, he praised the progress made in the process towards European unification, represented by the creation of the European council and the European parliament, as a victory of the political 'avant-garde' of Europe.[309]

At the end of 1949, the two editors reflected on the current situation. German social democracy hesitated because, since 1914, it had remained attached to the nineteenth century.[310] The Bundesrepublik could not be accepted as a full partner by the Western states. Western Allies' policy on Germany, in their view, had been 'Reflex-Politik' in response to Russian moves, and the Russian 'response' of creating the 'Ostzonenstaat' was comparable.[311] In an issue of *Frankfurter Hefte* in early 1950, Walter Dirks mourned the passing of Europe's chance. They had, he stated dramatically, lost the peace.

Comment

Frankfurter Hefte's aim, above all, was to re-establish the fundamental human values lost during the Third Reich. It could itself claim to have extended charity to all quarters in its journalistic practice. It strove consistently to be a truthful and

---

[305] ibid., (p.887).
[306] Eugen Kogon, 'Deutschland von heute', *Frankfurter Hefte*, 4 (1949), H.7, 569-82 (p.569).
[307] ibid., (p.570).
[308] ibid., (p.576).
[309] EK, 'Der Internationale Rat der Europäischen Bewegung: Die deutsche Teilnahme', *Frankfurter Hefte*, 4 (1949), H.3, 185-87 (p.185).
[310] Walter Dirks, 'Die Sozialdemokratie und der deutsche Nationalstaat', *Frankfurter Hefte*, 4 (1949), H.12, 1019-28 (p.1028).
[311] EK, 'Deutschland in zwei Staaten', *Frankfurter Hefte*, 4 (1949), H.11, 897-99 (p.897).

balanced commentator, advocating co-operation between both East and West, evangelicals and Catholics, Marxists and even fascists, in the interests of a true democracy.

Although speaking from a Catholic viewpoint, its call for co-operation with all Churches was reinforced by a Papal instruction in 1949, since described as a turning-point in the official approach of the Catholic Church to ecumenism. *Frankfurter Hefte* explicitly sought reconciliation with the Jews. Kogon's question 'wie können wir die Schuld gutmachen, die wir dem jüdischen Volk gegenüber auf uns geladen haben?' bears repetition, and Dirks's reminder that both Christians and Jews shared the Ten Commandments and the message of neighbourly love underlined the religious ethic of the journal. The true path should also leave room for non-believers.

Frankfurter Hefte has been described as a Christian-Marxist journal.[312] It was certainly Christian, but not uncritically so. The conduct of both Christian Churches came in for criticism. In addition to the highly controversial article by Ida Görres, Dirks and Kogon themselves criticized the Catholic Church when dealing with the later question of excommunication of communists. They accepted that those who spread the materialistic and anti-Christian messages of communism should be excommunicated, but added the caveat — only if this had been willingly done. Not only that, they reminded their readers that the Church also condemned capitalism as anti-Christian. Arguing for honesty and balance, the tone of criticism became sharper: 'manche Unterdrücker von Menschenrechten sind katholische Exzellenzen.'[313] In 1949, the journal, recalling its tribute to Karl Muth in its very first issue, published an article on Catholic journalism by the then editor of *Hochland*, Franz Josef Schöningh. His reminder that all should be involved, Christians, Jews and non-believers, fitted *Frankfurter Hefte*'s own desire not to be exclusively Christian. Dirks stressed that Christian journalists and politicians had a

---

[312] Bark and Gress, p.160.

[313] WD/EK, 'Die Exkommunizierung katholischer Kommunisten', *Frankfurter Hefte*, 4 (1949), H.8, 647-48 (p.648).

duty to find a way, but this way had to be 'ein *gemeinsamer* Weg [...], den alle gehen können, die Christen und die Heiden'.[314] The essence of the journal was captured by his words, '*Der Weg ist profan. Der Weg ist für alle gemeinsam. Wir wissen den Weg nicht. Das ist es.* Darum muß es Zeitschriften geben, die nicht katholische Zeitschriften sind, sondern Zeitschriften von Katholiken gemacht, Zeitschriften von Christen gemacht.'[315] Clearly influenced by Christian interests, nevertheless, as Dirks put it: 'So geben wir, die wir viel Religiöses drucken und vieles auf religiöse Weise sagen, insgesamt doch nicht eine religiöse Zeitschrift heraus; denn der Weg ist profan. So sind die "Frankfurter Hefte", die katholisch verantwortet werden, doch keine "katholische Zeitschrift".'[316] Dirks's own words are *Frankfurter Hefte*'s best defence against any dismissal as narrowly Catholic or Christian: 'So können wir nichts anderes sein als etwas Bescheidenes: eine Zeitschrift, von Christen gemacht, die hilft, gemeinsam mit anderen den Weg zu suchen und — wir hoffen es — zu finden. Das ist es, was den Typus dieser Zeitschrift begründet.'[317]

The label of Marxist is also best answered by Dirks in two major debates. In the first, 'Marxismus in christlicher Sicht', he drew attention to the fact that Marxism was closer to Christianity than were 'die relativistischen, libertinistischen und idealistischen, also ungehorsamen Mächte der Neuzeit'.[318] In response to the mainly Marxist criticism which greeted this, Dirks wrote a second essay, 'Christen und Marxisten über Christentum und Marxismus', in which he explained further.[319] The closeness could be defined in terms of Marxism's own passionate commitment, '*die Wahrheit tun zu wollen* und absolut zu gehorchen'. To the Christian accusation of naiveté, he argued that it was not Marxism itself that was

---

[314] Walter Dirks, 'Zeitschrift, von Christen gemacht', *Frankfurter Hefte*, 4 (1949), H.1, 59-63 (p.62).

[315] ibid., (p.62-3) (Dirks's italics).

[316] ibid., (p.63).

[317] ibid.

[318] ibid., (p.81).

[319] Walter Dirks, 'Christen und Marxisten über Christentum und Marxismus', *Frankfurter Hefte*, 3 (1948), H.1, 78-83 (p.78).

dangerous, but the animosity and fear that excluded understanding.[320] It was integrity and the pursuit of truth that created the link between Christianity and Marxism. Marxism, however, had to allow more room for faith in God.[321] The journal rejected a dogmatic Marxist approach, and publicly regretted the Marxist tendencies of those contemporary parties that espoused socialism. *Frankfurter Hefte*'s description, then, as 'Christian-Marxist' runs the danger of seriously underestimating the scope of discussion of both of these entities, and its independence in dealing with them.

Perhaps a Christian-socialist epithet would be more apposite since it describes the journal's ideal of co-operation between the two groups — Christians and workers. Indeed, it promoted this in the political pact between the SPD and the CDU. However, the journal undertook a rigorous scrutiny of socialism together with its historical connotations. Its conclusion was that any acceptance must be heavily qualified. In its political and economic overview, it envisioned not a 'sozialistischen', but a 'sozialen' 'Volksstaat', and perhaps conforms better to its description as proving 'die sozialreformerische Tendenz'.[322] Moreover, Christians' approval had to be conditional, Dirks reminding that this depended on the contemporary formulation of socialism. The editors themselves rejected the term 'christlichen Sozialismus'. At the time, they thought it suggested promotion of an exclusive type of socialism.[323] Dirks later confirmed his rejection of the label:

immer wieder wird [...] unser politisches Konzept »christlicher Sozialismus« genannt. Dieser Ausdruck führt in die Irre. Der Versuch, die moralische, politische soziale und ökonomische Vision zu verwirklichen, die wir in bewußter Solidarität mit der Arbeiterbewegung des 19. und 20. Jahrhunderts »Sozialismus« nennen, ist nicht ein christliches Unternehmen, sondern ein weltliches.[324]

To simply describe it as socialist is again to understate.

---

320 ibid., (p.81).
321 ibid., (p.80).
322 Erdmann, *Das Ende*, p.148.
323 WD, 'Noch einmal', (p.584).
324 Dirks, 'Vorwort', in *Walter Dirks: Gesammelte Schriften*, I, (p.7).

Could the journal be more aptly described as Christian-centrist? Dirks and Kogon's own political drive was informed by disappointment at the failure of the middle ground in the Weimar Republic.[325] Now they sought its successful establishment in the new Germany. Perhaps this time, the coalition would succeed. Their middle ground view of the 'Third Way' was not narrowly directed to Germany alone. Its aspirations were that the 'dritten Kraft' could achieve centre politics on a European basis. To embrace Europe fitted its Christian ideals. Seeing the essence of democracy threatened again made it more urgent. Within such a stable system, the worst extremes such as resurgent Nazism or totalitarian communism would, it hoped, be negligible. To say *Frankfurter Hefte* was Christian-centrist is perhaps acceptable.

Some might say that it was actually Christian-Western. Certainly, as Europe became Western Europe, the journal found itself aligned, whether it wanted to be or not, with the West. Despite its anti-materialism, it recognized the fact that economic stability brought with it political stability. By 1949, the contents are markedly more evocative of a West German identity. Nevertheless, the journal rejected the destructive overemphasis on materialism it saw in the West. Adenauer's claim that the establishment of the West German state was the first happy day for the German people was denied. *Frankfurter Hefte* did not see this as something to celebrate, but rather an 'Ausgangsstellung'.[326] The editors' mournful perception of developments in western Germany as 'restoration' heralded the approach they were to take to Adenauer's Germany. This restoration had begun immediately after the war with the communists and the Social Democrats. Walter Dirks wrote that history must judge the 'second' failure of the workers-Christians-social-democrats coalition.[327] Dirks was ready himself to accept some blame, and left it to history to judge also the efforts of the *Frankfurter Hefte*. It was forced into alignment, but regarded this as a failure,

---

325 Dirks, 'Die Zweite Republik', (pp.13-15).
326 WD, 'Bundesrepublik Deutschland', *Frankfurter Hefte*, 4 (1949), H.6, 457-59 (p.457).
327 Dirks, 'Vorwort', *Walter Dirks: Gesammelte Schriften*, IV, (p.8).

implicating the editors among others. The journal was certainly more pro-Western than pro-Eastern, but to say that it was Western is not to say enough.

Throughout these years, *Frankfurter Hefte* never abandoned its Christian approach. Kogon demonstrated this when invoking the power of prayer in the healing process of history: 'Gott ist der Herr der Geschichte und jeder betende Mensch von größerem Einfluß zum Heil als jeder noch so gescheite, aber ungläubige Staatsmann.'[328] Albert Görres similarly asserted that 'der Christ kennt Gott als Herrn der Geschichte'.[329] The message was a powerful one: God, when acknowledged as eternal truth and presence represented a more stable repository of trust than any transient political order.

It was the true test, and value of the journal that its unquestioned basis of faith was not permitted to alienate the non-Christian reader. On the contrary, despite statements of faith, contributions from Jesuits and explorations of Christian theology, the non-Christian reader was consistently and clearly addressed. It is unsurprising that there was enduring demand for the journal. It rose above the immediate political situation, desperate as it was, to challenge the ordinary German reader as to the ultimate in human moral behaviour. It cannot be categorized as a journal of the West, but more a journal of Christianity and the German middle ground.

Conclusions

Frankfurter Hefte first appeared in April 1946 and survives in an amalgamated form to this day. Under its editors, Eugen Kogon, Walter Dirks, and Clemens Münster, all committed Catholics, its aim was to reassert Christian guidelines in post-war Germany. It recognized an overlap between Marxism and Christianity, resulting in its frequent labelling as Christian-Marxist. This is unfair. It was more socialist than Marxist, more centrist than socialist, and as 'humanist' as Christian. It sought to be a balanced and objective commentator accommodating all

---

[328] Eugen Kogon, 'Das Jahr der Entscheidungen', *Frankfurter Hefte*, 3 (1948), H.1, 16-28 (p.22).

viewpoints. It consistently advocated the authentic idea of freedom within democracy for all. Limits to that freedom which would be imposed by totalitarianism in the East or excessive materialism in the West were condemned. Ahead of its time, it saw Europe as the future, France as Germany's main partner within it, and the ultimate victory of a western zone form of economic stability. *Frankfurter Hefte* could not be regarded as a journal of the East or of the West, but as surpassing these constraints in the interests of more constant human values.

[329] Albert Görres, 'Der Christ und die Welt', *Frankfurter Hefte*, 1 (1946), H.4, 40.

CHAPTER SEVEN
THE COMMON GROUND

Andersch and Richter, Becher and Gysi, Kogon and Dirks, Kantorowicz, Lasky — almost more than the titles of the journals, the names of their editors ring out. German and Catholic, German and Jewish, American and Jewish, German and atheist; imprisoned in Buchenwald, imprisoned in Dachau, imprisoned in America; exiled in France, America, Russia — such a constellation of writers from such a variety of backgrounds very much represents a 'Republic of Letters'. Almost more importantly, these men had a similar political background, which could loosely be described as left of centre. They shared a desire for socialism, and their convictions persisted. Such political trustworthiness after the Third Reich ensured the award of a licence to publish.

Their political sympathies not only inspired their journalistic activity, but illustrated the diversity of the intellectual elite in Germany at the time. Melvin Lasky's dramatic debut at the Berlin Writers' Congress in 1947, and his subsequent success as editor, have gained him a place on the international cultural scene. Alfred Andersch and Hans Werner Richter became important figures in the cultural history of West Germany. Their association with Gruppe 47 and their own writings have created lasting reputations and have stimulated great interest in *Der Ruf.* Walter Dirks and Eugen Kogon represented with distinction the intellectual side of Christianity, specifically Catholicism, producing thoughtful and intelligent guidelines for social reconstruction. Alfred Kantorowicz was a more mysterious character, for questions about the integrity of his political sympathies remain unanswered. He had returned to Germany in 1945 as a freedom fighter — part of that 'other Germany' which could with validity make proposals for the country's future. His early communism, his time in exile, and his contribution to the cultural scene of the GDR contrasted with his eventual flight to the West. Johannes R. Becher and Klaus Gysi are much easier to place. They personified the intellectual drive which bolstered the emergence of a monolithic state in Eastern Germany.

Several of these men participated in the first Writers' Congress to take place after the war, in Berlin in 1947. Their task was identified by Gunter Groll: 'Wir sollen die Verbindenden, nicht die Trennenden sein. Die Mitte Europas. Die Brücke. Wir brauchen Brücken, von West nach Ost und von Ost nach West. Das allein sind die Brücken in die Zukunft.'[1] In Groll's epilogue, published by *Ost und West*, he concurred with the sentiment that the congress represented the first German parliament — one of intellectuals. Klaus Gysi, in his opening address, chose to issue a warning against inner emigration as a cover for opportunists.[2] Lasky gave his controversial address attacking the lack of literary freedom in Stalinist Russia. But despite heated exchanges the congress symbolized the hope that Germany would remain a single cultural unit. By the second Writers' Congress in May 1948 in Frankfurt, the mood had changed. Kantorowicz sent last minute excuses, causing speculation as to the reasons for his non-attendance. In 1950 another writers' conference revealed the gulf between East and West Germans. The first Congress for Cultural Freedom, attended by Lasky and Kogon, was vituperatively dismissed by Becher as a 'Spitzel- und Kriegsbrandstifter-Kongreß'.[3]

Initial aims, however, were very similar or at least did not seem incompatible. The editors hoped to see a peaceful Germany characterized variously by: independence (Richter and Andersch); democracy (Lasky); Christian renewal (Dirks and Kogon); a role as mediator (Kantorowicz); and united efforts towards reconstruction (Becher and Gysi). Their journals revealed much common ground in their ideals: humanism and socialism (*Aufbau*); humanism and democracy (*Ost und West*); democratic humanism on an international basis (*Der Monat*); socialism and democracy (*Der Ruf*); Christianity and socialism (*Frankfurter Hefte*). All five journals shared the particular anxieties of their time, and sought to steer their readership towards solutions. The earliest of the journals had to deal more

---

1 'Wir gehören zusammen', (p.90).

2 See press cuttings, AKN, 65.

3 Johannes R. Becher, *Publizistik III 1946-1951* (Berlin: Aufbau-Verlag, 1979), p.355.

particularly than the others with the thorniest of all questions facing the German people, that of collective guilt. To the frequent rejoinder that the German people knew nothing of politics, Becher in *Aufbau*, the first journal to appear, was blunt — 'wer sich als unpolitisch erklärt, erklärt damit: "Ich will mit meinem Volk nichts zu tun haben"'. With this, he appeared uncompromisingly to accept the theory of collective guilt. By the following year he had changed his approach and replaced the early *mea culpa* with frank rejection of the whole premise. This rejection was echoed by the newly appeared *Frankfurter Hefte*. Whether this was in part due to the religious background of its editors (Catholicism refusing to condemn the sinner, but instead the sin), or for other reasons, Dirks and Kogon implacably resisted the notion of collective guilt, Kogon notably defending the right to political error. Of all five journals, the most obstinate in its rejection of national guilt was *Der Ruf*, in which Richter and Mannzen attributed the blame to generals, party officials and top industrialists. The population at large, it protested, was not directly guilty of crimes committed in its name. By 1947 *Ost und West* was commenting on the widespread denial of collective guilt. Scheer, cautioning against taking the 'Ich habe nichts davon gewußt' approach, accepted the necessity for the 'cleansing' of the population. While there was general agreement that Nazism must be rooted out, the journals uniformly condemned the Allied denazification process. Writing for *Der Monat* in 1949, Dolf Sternberger called the Allied policy a grave mistake. Rather than categorizing the population ('die Menschen, die Schuldigen, die Belasteten, die Mitläufer, die "Betroffenen" insgesamt und in ihrer Masse'), it would be better to recognize that the German people could not be forced to be denazified. This could only be achieved by each individual, through 'Reue'.[4]

Although the theory of collective guilt was explored, Jews, political prisoners, and other victims of the Third Reich were rarely mentioned. Even *Frankfurter Hefte*, which espoused Catholic religious values, failed to expound the Catholic practice of expiating guilt by making reparation to the victims. What is even more striking is that the German people themselves were, in many instances,

---

[4] Dolf Sternberger, 'Die Deutsche Frage', *Der Monat*, 1 (1948/9), H.8/9, 16-21 (p.19).

presented as the victims. The defence of the German people against the charge of collective guilt and the condemnation of denazification made these journals vulnerable to accusations of nationalism. *Der Ruf* was particularly vulnerable in this respect for it campaigned vigorously for Germany's returning soldiers, for her political prisoners, and for her beleaguered youth. *Aufbau*, on the other hand, could not be accused of nationalism, as its allegiance was to an ideological community. In its alignment to Russia and to communist culture it necessarily distanced itself from uniquely German interests. The larger community would absorb and help Germany, and loyalty to it was seen as better than loyalty solely to the national unit. *Ost und West* was nationally-minded only in so far as it promoted a contemporary national way in politics. This was never deemed nationalism, as it was non-aggressive. *Frankfurter Hefte* rejected nationalism as a dangerous emotional influence. Here a simple 'love' of the fatherland was acceptable as a force which could be channelled into peaceful, constructive motivation. *Der Monat*, like *Aufbau*, looked outwards towards the international community, thereby also achieving a certain distance.

Much of the tenor of the early debate was in fact religious — guilt, sin, evil, conscience — all falling mainly within the Christian idiom. Croce, discussing twentieth-century developments in *Der Monat*, wrote of the manifestation of the Antichrist. *Der Monat* elsewhere explored Christianity as a solution to contemporary dilemmas.[5] *Aufbau* appealed to the Christian conscience in its attempt to weld together anti-fascist forces for the rebuilding of the country. Its language also made much use of religious terminology, with references to Germany's 'Auferstehung', and to 'Reformationswerk'. It preferred 'Christentum' to 'Christianität'. *Ost und West* tolerated Christianity, but only in terms of its compromise with humanism, or reconciliation with Marxism ('Ein Christ sagt Ja zu Karl Marx').[6] *Der Ruf*, decidedly non-religious, nevertheless referred to the search

---

[5] See 2 (1949), H.14.

[6] Alexander Miller, 'Ein Christ sagt Ja zu Karl Marx', *Ost und West*, 1 (1947), H.6, 20-28.

for truth and justice as a religious experience, and stated that freedom of religious belief was fundamental to a free society. *Frankfurter Hefte*, decidedly Christian, enlisted the help of God in historical trial and advocated that Christianity should be 'lebendig', that it should inform action. Most striking was the parallel between the efforts of *Aufbau* and *Frankfurter Hefte* to enrol Christians in a partnership with socialists. The perverted value system of the Third Reich clearly had to be rejected, but in a constructive way. Christian values were espoused not just by believers, but by non-believers, aware of their emotional appeal to much of the population. For those who wished for a purely secular morality, humanism, the belief in human potential for good, often provided the philosophy, although there was at times a less formulated appeal for humane thought and action, as for instance in *Ost und West*, where one contributor wrote, 'wir müssen Humanität nicht als ein fernes Ziel, sondern als tägliche Aufgabe betrachten.'[7]

In their attempts to encourage and reinvigorate their readership, there was frequent recourse to Germany's better past. The journals wished to reinstil confidence and faith in the future. This, they hoped, would establish continuity and some sense of stability. With this in mind, the journals harked back in particular to the 'Golden Age' of German literature, and especially to Goethe and Schiller. There was, however, very broad coverage of literature after the poverty of literary expression in the Third Reich. From the early twentieth century, such writers as Franz Kafka, Thomas Mann and Carl Ossietzky featured in all five journals. From the recent past, they published both exile literature — Brecht, Heinrich Mann, Kantorowicz, Feuchtwanger, Seghers, Becher — and inner emigration literature — Günter Weisenborn, Ernst Jünger, and Ricarda Huch. Contemporary German writers featured included former exiles in addition to those publishing for the first time. Foreign literature was also widely published. This tended to be contemporary and included writers such as George Orwell, Arthur Koestler, Dostojewski and Sartre, who had been largely ignored during the Third Reich.

---

[7] J. B. Kozák, 'Die Aufgabe der Universität', in *Ost und West*, 2 (1948), H.8, 33-37 (p.37).

Within this outburst, important literary trends, ultimately leading to separate traditions, are identifiable. The Socialist Realism to be adopted in East Germany was already apparent in works published and praised in both Eastern Zone journals. In *Aufbau*, Becher's poetry of Russian exile and German homecoming combined reverence towards Russia with German socialist celebration. The regular inclusion of several pages of Russian literature held up Russian Socialist Realism as the literary manifestation of a freedom-loving society. The journal's use of past German literature and particularly of exile literature reflected Eastern Zone publishing emphases. The emergent socialist culture in the East laid claim to continue a tradition of humanist writers of the past. In reflecting this, *Aufbau* heralded the GDR's key concept of its cultural inheritance. *Ost und West* relied less on Soviet thought and literature, but also recruited predominantly socialist writers, some of them still in exile, for example Brecht and Heinrich Mann. Heinrich Mann was important enough to figure in the very first article of the first edition, and a compilation of his works commissioned by the East Berlin Academy of Arts was later edited by Kantorowicz. Other writers favoured by Kantorowicz were Heine and Lessing, as well as Thomas Jefferson, and Spanish Civil war writers, a somewhat eclectic set of choices, but on which excluded conservatives or reactionaries.

In the West, *Der Ruf* championed new German literature. For it, past models did not have as much appeal, and Schnurre was categorical in his rejection of old idols, including Goethe. Its support of new young writers resulted in exposure of the Kahlschlag's radical, succinct, poetic style. Among major figures brought into prominence in the journal's short life were the poet Günter Eich and the dramatist Wolfgang Borchert. New poetry by Eich received its first publication here after a thirteen year hiatus. *Der Monat* preferred writers of established international standing. Contemporary foreign writers Orwell, Koestler, Sartre, Gide, took centre stage as part of the re-education of the German people. For *Frankfurter Hefte*, literature was almost a sideline, and coverage of it rather bland, allowing consideration of Eastern Zone writers and even Nazi writers.[8] It was nevertheless made clear that for *Frankfurter Hefte*, literature bore a heavy responsibility. It had to expose the truth, particularly of recent horrors, as Kogon's remarks on Zuckmayer's *Des Teufels General* bear witness.[9]

Unsurprisingly, the particular political nuances of their editors were detectable within the literature they selected for attention. The styles and sympathies of the new order were apparent, as were theories of literary criticism and ideas for the future. The thread of socialist thinking throughout German literary history identified by *Aufbau* allowed not only justification of socialism, but eventually also condemnation of the West for its perpetuation of capitalism. *Ost und West*, like *Aufbau*, viewed Russia as Germany's friend and literary ally. It differed from *Aufbau* in using American literature to expose undemocratic tendencies such as censorship and racism towards blacks. Both presented Western European Existentialism as decadent. *Der Monat* also criticized Sartre; the reason here was his unrealistic picture of a communist cell in *Les Mains Sales*. In *Der Ruf*, the emphasis on French, especially Existentialist, literature underlined its policy of rapprochement within Europe. Common to these two Western journals was the prominence given to Orwell's *Animal Farm* as an effective piece of anti-communist literature. Socialist Realism was a common target; Andersch, writing in *Der Monat*, compared it to literary theory and practice in the Third Reich.

There was, however, a good deal of consensus within the journals' approach to literature. All agreed about the need for socialist, realistic forms in a new literature, and all joined in praising the novels *Stalingrad* by Theodor Plievier and *Das Siebte Kreuz* by Anna Seghers. They all sought to integrate both inner and outer émigrés, with the two Eastern Zone journals the most forthright in their acceptance of the two as equals. All published the debate about Thomas Mann, although their approaches revealed somewhat varying attitudes. In addition, although *Der Ruf* and *Frankfurter Hefte* were in the forefront of new writing,

---

[8] See, for example, Berglar-Schröer, 'Kleines Deutsches Lyrikum 1947'.
[9] EK, '"Des Teufels General"'.

Aufbau also, despite cherishing old models, was distinctly forward-looking in its celebration of new German literature as 'Wiedergutmachung'. All looked to the theatre as a particular forum for education, both *Ost und West* and *Frankfurter Hefte* regretting the demise of German drama and particularly of experimental theatre in 1933.

The uncertainty about the way forward for the country accounts for much of the emphasis in all five journals on 'Middle Way' politics. The widening gap between East and West left Germany in the middle, not just geographically, but politically. It is unsurprising that the old tradition of the 'Third Way' resurfaced. All five differed over the detail of such a way forward. *Der Ruf* saw Germany in a middle position within a united Europe. It should combine the best features from both East and West — socialism in justice and public service, and free market democracy. *Ost und West* best epitomized 'Third Way' thinking. The impracticality of the journal's political standpoint was wholly in tune with 'Third Way' idealism. Rather than trying to develop tangible policies of its own, or at least to align itself with specific current policies, *Ost und West* persisted in its glorified concept of Germany as a magnanimous peacekeeper between Russia and America. It saw for Germany a global vocation, a true 'Sonderweg'. For *Ost und West* itself, Kantorowicz saw a role as 'ambassador' for the 'Third Way'. The result of *Ost und West*'s 'middle' identity is the journal's frequent exclusion from classification with its peers.[10] It is of singular interest that his co-editor, Maximilian Scheer, seemed to distance himself from Kantorowicz in describing the 'Third Way' as 'ein Knusperhäuschen im Niemandsland'.[11] Although perhaps over-idealistic at times (an easy judgement in retrospect), *Ost und West* did seem to have to defend its middle ground position in a 'Zweifrontenkampf'. *Aufbau* also favoured the idea of mediation and strove to promote debate between East and West — a 'Gespräch zwischen West und Ost'.[12] It constantly referred to itself as a

---

[10] See, for example, *Handbuch Deutsche Zeitschriften* (1947).

[11] Scheer, 'Nachwort', (p.91).

[12] See 'Inhalt', 4 (1949), H.11.

campaigner for German cultural unity, and to the Kulturbund as 'Brückenbauer'.[13] It represented the early Soviet Zone impetus for a 'besonderen deutschen Weg zum Sozialismus', but largely saw 'Middle Way' politics as corrupt and weak, a left-over from the Weimar Republic. *Frankfurter Hefte* saw reconciliation and co-operation as rooted not in political strategy, but in Christian faith: 'Die Begegnung zwischen Ost und West kann nur auf der religiösen Ebene ihre Erfüllung finden.'[14] It was wary, however, of the idealism which characterized 'Middle Way' politics. Idealism was something which *Der Monat* also repudiated, but even it sought middle politics in the interests of European social democracy. *Der Monat* has been accused of adopting a 'Middle Way', only to damage the credibility of 'Middle Way' politics with its anti-communism and its criticism of Soviet Russia.[15] For *Der Monat*, however, the 'Third Way' lay not between capitalism and communism, but between capitalism and socialism, the two unacceptable extremes being fascism and communism. It is clear that the position of the 'Middle Way' depends on the viewer's perspective. It is undeniable, however, that in June 1949, *Der Monat* published an eloquent condemnation of 'Third Way' theory:

> Politische Neutralität im Nachkriegsdeutschland wäre eine furchtbare Illusion, und ebenso würden deutsche Politiker, die sich in der Rolle kleiner Machiavellisten zwischen West und Ost sehen, bald entdecken müssen, daß sie damit in eine Sackgasse geraten sind. Zwischen der Freiheit eines demokratischen Europas und der Finsternis des Ostens gibt es keinen Mittelweg.[16]

Also in *Der Monat*, Erik Reger of *Tagesspiegel* seems almost to address Kantorowicz, describing the whole idea of a global role for Germany as 'Vermittler' as irrational and negligent.

Europe, for many, provided the most concrete framework for 'Third Way' ideas. In *Der Monat* Alfred Weber saw a Europe with democratic socialism as the middle ground between two social 'religions', and Silone, the former communist, postulated a political middle ground for Europe in the adoption of socialism. A

---

13 Pfarrer Grossek at meeting of the Präsidialrat, 25.5.48: KA, 15/211.

14 WW, 'Dostojewskij und der Westen', (p.867).

15 Borchers and Vowe, pp.44 and 59.

16 Walter L. Dorn, 'Im neuen Europa', *Der Monat*, 1 (1948/9), H.8/9, 4-7 (p.7).

vision of Europe as the future was held by all five journals. *Der Ruf*'s image was of a socialist Europe, a 'Staatenbund' in which all the young people of Europe, including those from a united Germany, would play a part. *Frankfurter Hefte* also saw the future in Europe and socialism. A federalist socialist Germany would be the best contribution to a reconstructed Europe and would represent true German restitution. It looked forward to tolerance and a sense of belonging in an 'europäisches Deutschsein'. In a whole issue devoted to Europe in January 1949, 'Wege zu einem neuen Europa', *Der Monat* proclaimed this sense of European identity. Walter Maria Guggenheimer, previously of *Der Ruf*, affirmed this new identity — 'der Glaube an ein neues politisches *Wir*: an das *Wir* der Europäer'. Much of the emphasis in the *Der Monat* issue was on economics, and it brought a call for supra-national institutions. This sense of European development as 'übernational' rather than 'zwischennational' was repeated by Kogon in the same issue. An American contributor proposed further help towards military security for the European union, now termed a 'West-Union', stating that this was an essential addition to the existing European Recovery Programme. Still in the same issue, Karl von Schumacher argued that the new Europe should not be built on the charity of others, but he backed some degree of monetary support as immunisation against communism. Predominantly, Europe was envisaged as part of an Atlantic pact.

The question of Europe was more muted in the Eastern Zone journals. *Aufbau* saw European unity as a natural extension of German unity, and, therefore, not a separate issue. It saw Germany as the heart of Europe, repeating Arnold Zweig's assertion that Germans were 'mehr als Europäer'. It also advocated a new European order, which it described as a 'dritte Kraft'. *Ost und West*'s approach was also rather restrained. However, its very first article propounded Kantorowicz's ideal of a unified European culture, and later he supported Heinrich Mann's exhortation to Germans to become European patriots. Within the debate about Europe, the French question was of particular interest. *Frankfurter Hefte* saw France as Germany's partner in a future Europe and published an article from a French contributor reciprocating this idea of a Franco-German axis. *Der Ruf* also saw Germany's relationship with France as crucial and revered French culture as the source of modern Existentialist theory. *Ost und West* urged Franco-German rapprochement, and even *Aufbau* included French spokesmen such as Romain Rolland in its portrayal of a socialist Europe. By doing so, the journals communicated a clear sense of European identity and the expectation of some form of a united socialist Europe.

The definition of 'socialist', however, became increasingly problematical. Andersch wrote in *Der Ruf* of socialism's 'Wegkreuzung', echoed later by Silone in *Der Monat*: 'Sozialismus am Kreuzweg'. It was widely accepted that any redefinition would involve severe problems. A whole debate in *Der Monat* centred on the reconciling (or not) of socialism and democracy, and socialism and communism. Richter in *Der Ruf* clearly demonstrated the confusion: 'Die Kommunisten nennen sich Demokraten, die Sozialisten Christen, die Christen Sozialisten, die Marxisten Humanisten und die Humanisten Marxisten'. *Der Ruf* drew attention to the debate taking place in the international anti-/post-Marxist community, involving Koestler, Silone, Malraux and others. It identified itself with these critics of socialism, referring to them with approval as the 'rebellion of socialists', and commended Westminster and the British Labour Party as good models of workable socialism. In the five journals, the visions of socialism extended from Marxism in *Aufbau* to conservative social(ist) democracy in *Der Monat*, and neither of these two insisted on narrow definitions. While *Der Monat* provided a platform for the most vehement opponents of Marxist ideology (the ex-communists), there was still considerable empathy with the ideals of moderate socialism. Fundamentally, *Der Monat* wished to avoid overweening materialism. It was joined in this by *Frankfurter Hefte*, which with *Der Ruf* emphasized the importance of socialism in the economic sphere. The anti-capitalist consensus on the part of all these writers, at a time of diverging political allegiances, is notable. It contained traces of their earlier common ground. At the heart of the ideological conflict were Kantorowicz of *Ost und West*, Max Schroeder, involved with

Aufbau, and Arthur Koestler, published in both *Der Monat* and *Der Ruf*, — all had been involved in the Berlin Red Block of the thirties.

A possibly even more important conflict arose with regard to what constituted democracy. Both sides, East and West, claimed it as their own and inevitably criticized its form in the opposing bloc. Among Germans, the term created anxieties after the experience of the Weimar Republic. Only *Der Monat* defended Weimar, Boris Schub arguing that it had preserved freedom by its accommodation of opposites, both good and evil. *Frankfurter Hefte* called for a true democracy which would accommodate even right-wing nationalism. It itself tried to observe democratic principles, whether in its journalistic practice or in its ecumenism. In contradistinction, Scheer in *Ost und West* categorically ruled out any idea of working with former Nazis. In *Der Monat*, Willy Brandt urged socialist democracy as the best bulwark against totalitarianism, while Hayek dismissed democratic socialism as the greatest contemporary delusion. All these journals shared an ideal of democracy, although again definitions varied.

What these journals shared above all was their time and place. In the course of the four years, the Cold War advanced around and amidst them. Accordingly, the journals were drawn into that conflict. Absolute values and judgements became more evident. Both *Ost und West* and *Aufbau* objected to capitalist practice in industrial western Germany and to the involvement of former Nazis there. *Ost und West* accused the West of censorship and control, Kantorowicz criticizing particularly the ban on the Kulturbund. Intellectuals on either side of the growing divide were already being accused by their opposites of failing in their duty to their people. Walter Pollatschek, also in *Ost und West*, pointed to the crisis afflicting the West German cultural scene. He claimed that even the German language had become divided. Scheer meanwhile declared the West's emphasis on re-education the greatest hindrance to recovery. Both Eastern Zone journals blamed not only the West German intellectual community, but the West Germans in general for the division. *Frankfurter Hefte* strongly criticized the Eastern Zone, alleging that if Western denazification procedures were applied there the SED would lose at least a third of its members. Eastern politicians were described by *Der Ruf* as fraudsters and spies. It and *Frankfurter Hefte* rejected totalitarian systems outright. *Der Monat* was also highly critical of events in the 'annexed' Eastern Zone, with Lasky seeking to expose the SED as a front for a ruthless secret police and the apparent toleration of other parties as insidious betrayal. Already advocating the containment of communism, it compared the dangerous communist fellow-traveller to the 'Mitläufer' of the Third Reich.

Despite this, the journals established a significant degree of communication between Germans which shows that they were not simply tools in the hands of the Allied powers. *Aufbau* had a particular journalistic interest in *Frankfurter Hefte*. Referring to two of Dirks's articles, *Aufbau* praised their critical approach, but argued that they were not sufficiently anti-Western.[17] It also accused Dirks of accepting the image of a 'bolschewistisches Schreckgespenst'.[18] The two journals differed fundamentally in that *Aufbau*'s main platform, unity, was dismissed by *Frankfurter Hefte* as a seductive slogan. Nevertheless, there was consensus between the two in that they both rejected the neofascism which they saw in the West. *Aufbau* maintained that the East was the bulwark against this.[19] Unlike *Der Monat*, viewed by *Aufbau* as in direct opposition to it within the same city (Berlin), *Frankfurter Hefte* was viewed with approval. Its popularity extended, despite its openly Christian views, to official circles of the Eastern Zone. In 1948 *Aufbau* identified it as 'eine der wichtigsten Zeitschriften der Westzone'.[20] Günter Caspar spoke of discussions between the two, and this accords with *Aufbau*'s efforts to establish German-German dialogue. Its campaign for 'Gespräch' was already evident in the July 1949 issue, 'Gespräch um den Frieden', — not only after 1949, as one commentator has suggested.[21] *Frankfurter Hefte* was not only admired by

---

[17] See 'Ein falsches Europa'; and Alexander Abusch, 'Mahnendes Jubiläum', *Aufbau*, 4 (1948), H.11, 935-39.
[18] ibid., (p.938).
[19] ibid., (p.939).
[20] 'Ein falsches Europa', (p.831).
[21] Colin Smith, 'All quiet on the Eastern Front? East German literature and its Western reception (1945-61)', in *German writers and the Cold War 1945-61*, ed. by Rhys W.

Aufbau. *Der Ruf*, known for its highly critical attitude to much of the German press, also held *Frankfurter Hefte* in respect. *Der Monat* welcomed Eugen Kogon as a contributor, describing him as one of the 'bedeutendsten Meinungsbildner in Westdeutschland'.[22]

Frankfurter Hefte could with some justice then, be described as the journals' journal. *Der Ruf*, on the other hand, could perhaps be called the people's journal. It was steadfast in championing what it perceived to be the most vulnerable sections of the German population: the young; the prisoners-of-war; the 'Zwischengeneration'. It was guilty of standing up, perhaps before due time, for the cause of a mature democratic system in Germany, complete with opposition. Hans Werner Richter had vowed to lead the Germans 'aus der Welt der schönen Täuschungen in die Welt der nüchternen Realität'.[23] To describe *Der Ruf*'s aims as 'illusory', as one recent commentator has done, on the basis of its fourteen issues, is derisory.[24] *Ost und West*, also, it seems, suppressed, was, in its very last edition, still calling for mediation. Whether its aims could more appropriately be described as illusory depends ultimately on the judgement as to whether at any point the 'Middle Way' was achievable and therefore worth pursuing.

Of the five journals, *Der Monat* and *Aufbau* above all have suffered from accusations of bias. *Der Monat*, supposedly the tool of the CIA, was committed to wide debate on an international level and did not present a narrow American view. Its contributors included not Adenauer, but Willy Brandt. It opened up debate rather than narrowing it down to propaganda. Similarly, *Aufbau*, the supposed organ of the Eastern political elite, was judged by the Kulturbund as not fulfilling its political duty. The archival material provides evidence of differences between it and centre of power in East Berlin. There is also some indication that the Russians

---

Williams, Stephen Parker, and Colin Riordan (Manchester: Manchester University Press, 1992), pp.7-26.

22 Kogon, 'Der Nationalismus als Gegner', (p.58).

23 Quoted by Wapnewski, 'König Artus', (p.32).

24 See K. Stuart Parkes, *Writers and Politics in West Germany* (London: Croom Helm, 1986), p.21.

favoured *Ost und West*.[25] In fact, all the journals display an astonishing degree of independence. *Der Ruf*, which above all sought to foster true democratic practice (and to implement it itself), for instance as practised in Westminster, could not be regarded as a pawn of the US authority which suppressed it after fourteen issues. The hostility to *Ost und West* also attests to its independence of thought. Above all, it incriminates German nationals in the struggle of the Cold War. *Frankfurter Hefte* strove throughout for objectivity in its criticism of political activities in both East and West. All displayed resentment of the Allies. *Frankfurter Hefte* referred to the German perception of the Americans as the creators of the 'Fragebogen'. In *Der Monat*, Raymond Aron argued that the occupation powers were partly responsible for the upsurge in German nationalism, and A.J.P. Taylor wrote of the inevitable progression from feelings of victimization to nationalist thinking. Throughout the journals we find the insistence that German re-education should be the domain of Germans. Kantorowicz, in *Ost und West*, stated that the German victory had to be won by Germans. The fact that two of the journals were suppressed is a reminder of the severity of censorship which could be applied. Their attacks on the occupation authorities in these instances are testament to the steadfastness with which they pursued freedom of expression. We can see in retrospect that the 'hardliners' were not as outrageous as their reputations suggest, and that there is sufficient common ground and common motivation within all five journals to dispel as Cold War myth much denigration of them. Their shared exposure to the struggle of the superpowers required these journals to adapt, and they did this while maintaining as many of their original aims as possible. Inevitably, these aims were also the result of the editors' own earlier experience. No one journal could be said to fully represent the official line, whether German or Allied, in either East or West. They refute their simplistic categorization as journals of the East or journals of the West.

These journals provided an inestimable contribution to the immediate post-war scene and cannot just be dismissed as 'the various short-lived utopias played

---

[25] ZPA, W. Pieck, NL 36/750, 102-05.

out in the earliest post-war publications'.[26] Besides bringing to attention writers such as Eich and Huchel, in itself a major achievement, they formulated ideas which remain valid, and are, in some cases, now in practice. The most notable of these is Europe. Although forced ultimately into alignment, they illustrate a wealth of effort aimed at moderation. They had much in common. They shared a similar left of centre background, from which they saw socialism and Europe as the future for Germany. In defence of their people, they rejected collective guilt, and occupation efforts to cleanse them. Informed by in many cases their own persecution during the Third Reich, their editors strove to revive systems which revered human values. Whether the values were those of humanism, co-operation, Christianity, whether establishing a true record of times past, whether tackling the silence, the apathy, the problems of the young or of prisoners-of-war, they are more representative of the German people than of the Allied powers. These journals provide a second tier to the Cold War debate, for they show the struggle as it advanced amongst the Germans themselves.

---

[26] Smith, 'All quiet on the Eastern Front?', (p.24, note 16).

EPILOGUE

In 1992 there was yet another writers' conference in Berlin. It was chaired by Melvin Lasky and was entitled 'A Last Encounter with the Cold War'.[1] The Reichstag and the former 'House of Soviet-German Friendship' provided a symbolic backdrop. Inevitably, that first Writers' Congress in 1947, comes to mind. That conference in which the whole ideological conflict was to resurface and in which Melvin Lasky himself was a major protagonist, could in retrospect be entitled 'A First Encounter with the Cold War'. The intensity of ideological feeling became personified. The fact that it was a writers' conference which came to symbolize division is unsurprising given the role that writers occupied at the time. In default of full and clear political representation, politically committed writers filled the vacuum. This they did significantly through the medium of the political-cultural journals.

The five journals presented here demonstrate this. They show the determination of these writers to fulfil what they perceived to be their political duty. They portray not only German nationals as protagonists in the Cold War, but also German nationals striving to avert Germany's involvement in it. Clearly, they fought their own political corner, but what is most striking about these journals is their common ground. They display a breadth of debate from a broad spectrum of thinkers from which much consensus emerges. The failure to build on these areas of consensus is what is most tragic. Walter Dirks's 'loss of the peace' is haunting.

Today, many of the issues dealt with by the five are again current. The future of the new Germany, the remembrance of resistance, the threat of neo-fascism, the (re-)definition of socialism — all are familiar. The same concerns are

---

1 'A Last Encounter with the Cold War: Lessons of the Past, Problems of the Future', Conference in Berlin, 9-11 October 1992.

voiced about European politics, including Franco-German co-operation, economic stability, membership of the community and, again, fears for its security. Within Germany itself, there is again discussion as to the identity of political culprits, in the re-exploration of the Nazi past and in the debate about the more recent, GDR, past. There is the repeated problem of the political integrity of writers, this time of the former GDR. Eugen Kogon's remark that all political systems are vulnerable seems prophetic.

In 1995, on the fiftieth anniversary of Germany's capitulation, the veteran journalist Marion Gräfin Dönhoff saw fit to urge reconciliation among her fellow Germans — a response to the disagreement as to whether 1945 brought true liberation or not.[2] The significance and consequences of that year continue to be the subject of active debate. It is indisputable that the first post-war years, 1945 until 1949, were particularly rich in political theory. They should not be dismissed, however, as simply the founding years of one or other German republic, as seems likely with the recognition of a post-war order, 1945-1990. This most volatile of periods will continue to be worthy of separate consideration. The breadth of political cultural debate, the renaissance of literature, the intellectual leadership of writers — nowhere are these better displayed than in the political journals of the time. 'Periodicals of opinion' have 'played a great part in the intellectual history of Europe for nearly two hundred years. They have been instruments of propaganda, instruments of effective political action, carriers of culture, arenas in which celebrated and often competent controversialists have performed'.[3]

The five journals chosen here as representative of the time fit this description. They also fully merit Melvin Lasky's description as Cold Warriors. To ignore their wider contribution, however, would be to underestimate their cultural impact. They were resolute in their attempts to repair the cultural damage

---

[2] 'Sollten wir siegen?', *Die Zeit*, 21 April 1995, p.1.

[3] D. W. Brogan on *Encounter*, *Atlantic Monthly* etc., 'Introduction', in *Encounters*, p.xv.

wrought by the Third Reich. They strove to educate and rehabilitate the survivors and to enable them to take their places in the Germany of the future. They tried in their various ways to analyse the reasons for the cataclysm that was Nazism. In their exploration of a wide range of options for their people, in their pursuit of their ideals, in their attempts at conciliation, and in their indications of consensus, these journals reflect and represent the rethinking of Germany.

BIBLIOGRAPHY

PRIMARY SOURCES

Journals

Aufbau: Kulturpolitische Monatsschrift (1945-1958), Berlin (East)

Ost und West: Beiträge zu kulturellen und politischen Fragen der Zeit (1947-1949), Berlin (East) (Athenäum reprint: Königstein, 1979)

Der Monat: Eine internationale Zeitschrift (1948-1971), Berlin (West)

Der Ruf: Unabhängige Blätter der jungen Generation (1946-1984), Munich (Kraus Reprint: Nendeln/Liechtenstein, 1975)

Frankfurter Hefte: Zeitschrift für Kultur und Politik (1946-1984), Frankfurt a.M.

Documents

Zentrales Parteiarchiv (ZPA) former Institut für Marxismus-Leninismus beim ZK der SED (since January 1993 Stiftung Archiv der Parteien und Massenorganisationen der DDR im Bundesarchiv), Berlin:
Agitation, IV 2/9.02/2
Kartei Agitation und Propaganda
Kartei West-Propaganda
Konferenzen und Beratungen der SED, IV 2/1.01/407
W. Pieck, NL 36/750
Erinnerungen, EAO 888/5

Kulturbund-Archiv (since January 1993 also under Stiftung Archiv der Parteien und Massenorganisationen der DDR im Bundesarchiv), Berlin:
907 Präsidialrat Protokolle 1945
908
909
Präsidialrat Protokolle 1945-1948, 10/112
15/211
373/715
97/498
495/844
Aufbau-Verlag, 530/782

Institut für Zeitgeschichte, Munich:
OMGUS, NA, RG 260
OMGUS/POLAD 803-14
Information Control/Services Division, Press Branch
OMGUS/ISD, 5/247-2/19
OMGUS/ICD Opinion Surveys, Dk 110.001
OMGUS, ODI, 7/42-3/1-2 (11.1949-4.1950)
Dc 15.02, No.173
Nachlaß Wilhelm Hoegner, ED 120
Sammlung W. Hammer, ED 106
Sammlung Glaser, ED 202
ED 119/10

Akademie der Künste, (East) Berlin
Teilnachlaß Alfred Kantorowicz (now in Hamburg Staats- und Universitätsbibliothek):
65, 69, 72, 83, 92, 102

Akademie der Künste, (West) Berlin:
Hans-Werner-Richter-Archiv
72/86/501

Interviews

Günter Caspar, 18 September 1992, Berlin
Melvin J. Lasky, 3 May 1993, Berlin
Carsten Wurm, Aufbau-Verlag, September 1992, Berlin

SECONDARY LITERATURE
Published Sources

Altmann, Peter, ed., *Hauptsache Frieden: Kriegsende, Befreiung, Neubeginn: Vom antifaschistischen Konsens zum Grundgesetz 1949* (Frankfurt a. M.: Röderberg, 1985)

Andersch, Alfred, *Deutsche Literatur in der Entscheidung* (Karlsruhe: Verlag Volk und Zeit, 1947)

—*"...einmal wirklich leben". Ein Tagebuch in Briefen an Hedwig Andersch 1943 bis 1975*, ed. by Winfried Stephan (Zurich: Diogenes, 1986)

Arnold, Heinz Ludwig, ed., *Die Gruppe 47: Ein kritischer Grundriß*, *Text und Kritik* Sonderband (Munich: Text und Kritik, 1980)

—ed., *Literaturbetrieb in Deutschland* (Munich: Boorberg, 1971)

Baerns, Barbara, *Ost und West: Eine Zeitschrift zwischen den Fronten*, Studien zur Publizistik, Bremer Reihe, 10 (Münster: 1968)

Balfour, Michael, and J. Mais, *Four-Power-Control in Germany and Austria 1945-1946* (London: OUP, 1956)

Bariéty, Jacques, 'Deux Après-Guerres: Recherches d'Une Politique Culturelle Française en Allemagne après les Déceptions des Années 1920 et 1930', in *Frankreichs Kulturpolitik in Deutschland 1945-1950*, ed. by Franz Knipping and Jacques Le Rider (Tübingen: Attempto, 1987), pp.3-8

Bark, Dennis L., and David R. Gress, *A History of West Germany*, 2 vols (Oxford: Blackwell, 1989), I: *From Shadow to Substance 1945-1963*

Becher, Johannes R., *Publizistik III 1946-1951* (Berlin: Aufbau-Verlag, 1979)

Becker, Winfried, ed., *Die Kapitulation von 1945 und der Neubeginn in Deutschland* (Cologne: Böhlau, 1987)

Bell, Daniel, 'Our New York Days', in, *Melvin J. Lasky: Encounter with a 60th Birthday*, ed. by Helga Hegewisch (*Encounter* Special edition, 1980), pp.3-7

Bender, Hans, 'Reflexionen über Zeitschriften', in *Literaturbetrieb in Deutschland*, ed. by Heinz Ludwig Arnold (Munich: Boorberg, 1971), pp.224-33

Benz, Wolfgang, *Die Bundesrepublik Deutschland Geschichte in drei Bänden*, 3 vols (Frankfurt a. M.: Fischer, 1983) III: *Kultur*

Bidwell, Percy W., 'Emphasis on Culture in the French Zone', *Foreign Affairs*, (October 1948), 78-85

Birkert, Alexandra, *"Das Goldene Tor": Alfred Döblins Nachkriegszeitschrift; Rahmenbedingungen; Zielsetzung; Entwicklung* (Frankfurt a. M.: Buchhändler-Vereinigung, 1989)

Birr, Ewald, *Ost und West: Berlin 1947-1949. Bibliographie einer Zeitschrift* (Munich: Saur, 1993)

Böhme, Kurt W., *Geist und Kultur der deutschen Kriegsgefangenen im Westen*, Zur Geschichte der deutschen Kriegsgefangenen des zweiten Weltkrieges, 14 (Bielefeld: Gieseking, 1968)

Borchers, Hans, and Klaus W. Vowe, *Die zarte Pflanze Demokratie: Amerikanische Re-education in Deutschland im Spiegel ausgewählter politischer und literarischer Zeitschriften (1945-1949)* (Tübingen: Narr, 1979)

Borkovsky, Dieter, 'A Tale from the Underground', in *Melvin J. Lasky: Encounter with a 60th Birthday*, ed. by Helga Hegewisch (*Encounter* Special edition, 1980), pp.31-33

Borsdorf, Ulrich, and Lutz Niethammer, eds, *Zwischen Befreiung und Besatzung: Analysen des US-Geheimdienstes über Positionen und Strukturen deutscher Politik 1945* (Wuppertal: Hammer, 1976)

Börsenblatt für den deutschen Buchhandel (Wiesbaden), 1 (6 Oktober 1945)

Boulby, M., 'Aspects of the Work of the 'Brücken' in Germany', *GLL*, 7 (1953/1954), 3 (April 1954), 206-10

Brandt, Helmut, 'Lizenz und Presse', in *Handbuch der Lizenzen Deutscher Verlage: Zeitungen, Zeitschriften, Buchverlage* (Berlin: de Gruyter, 1947), V-XIV

von der Brelie-Lewien, Doris, *Katholische Zeitschriften in den Westzonen 1945-1949: Ein Beitrag zur politischen Kultur der Nachkriegszeit* (Göttingen: Muster-Schmidt, 1986)

—and Ingrid Laurien, 'Zur politischen Kultur in Nachkriegsdeutschland: Politische-kulturelle Zeitschriften 1945-1949, Ein Forschungsbericht', *PVS 24* (1983), 406-27

Broszat, Martin, ed., *Zäsuren nach 1945: Essays zur Periodisierung der deutschen Nachkriegsgeschichte*, Schriftenreihe der Vierteljahreshefte für Zeitgeschichte, 61 (Munich: Oldenbourg, 1990)

—and Hermann Weber, eds, *SBZ-Handbuch: Staatliche Verwaltungen, Parteien, gesellschaftliche Organisationen und ihre Führungskräfte in der Sowjetischen Besatzungszone Deutschlands 1945-1949 (Im Auftrag des Arbeitsbereiches*

Geschichte und Politik der DDR an der Universität Mannheim und des Instituts für Zeitgeschichte), ed. by (Munich: Oldenbourg, 1990)

Bucher, Peter, ed., *Nachkriegsdeutschland 1945-1949* (Darmstadt: Wissenschaftliche Buchgesellschaft, 1990)

Clay, Lucius D., *Decision in Germany* (London: Heinemann, 1950)

Coleman, Peter, *The Liberal Conspiracy: The Congress for Cultural Freedom and the Struggle for the Mind of Postwar Europe* (New York: Macmillan, 1989)

Deuerlein, Ernst, *Deutsche Geschichte der neuesten Zeit von Bismarcks Entlassung bis zur Gegenwart* (Konstanz: Akademische Verlagsgesellschaft, 1965) III: *Von 1945 bis 1955*

Deutsche Presse 1947: Zeitungen und Zeitschriften von heute (Recklinghausen: 1947)

Deutsche Zeitschriften 1945-1949 (Frankfurt a. M.: Buchhändler-Vereinigung, 1950)

Dirks, Walter, *War ich ein linker Spinner?: Republikanische Texte - von Weimar bis Bonn* (Munich: Kösel-Verlag, 1983)

—*Gesammelte Schriften*, ed. by Fritz Boll and others, 8 vols (Zurich: Ammann, 1991)
I: *Republik als Aufgabe: Publizistik 1921-1933* (1991)
IV: *Sozialismus oder Restauration: Politische Publizistik* (1987)
VIII: *Für eine andere Republik: politische Essays und Kommentare, autobiographische Aufsätze 1969-1987* (1991)

Doderer, Klaus, ed., *Zwischen Trümmern und Wohlstand: Literatur der Jugend 1945-1960* (Weinheim: Beltz, 1988)

Dovifat, Emil, 'Eine erste Pressestatistik', in *Lizenzenhandbuch Deutscher Verlage 1949: Zeitungen, Zeitschriften, Buchverlage* (Berlin: de Gruyter, 1949), pp.XXI-XXV

Drews, Richard, and Alfred Kantorowicz, *Verboten und Verbrannt: deutsche Literatur 12 Jahre unterdrückt* (Berlin: Ullstein-Kindler, 1947)

Eberan, Barbro, *Luther? Friedrich »der Grosse«? Wagner? Nietzsche?...?...? Wer war an Hitler schuld?: Die Debatte um die Schuldfrage 1945-1949* (Munich: Minerva Publikation, 1983)

Eliot, T. S., *Notes Towards the Definition of Culture* (London: Faber and Faber, 1948)

Engelbach, Horst, and Konrad Krauss, 'Der *Kulturbund* und seine Zeitschrift *Aufbau* in der SBZ', in *Zur literarischen Situation 1945-1949*, ed. by Gerhard Hay (Kronberg: Athenäum-Verlag, 1977), pp.169-188

Erdmann, Karl D., *Das Ende des Reiches und die Entstehung der Republik Österreich, der Bundesrepublik Deutschland und der Deutschen Demokratischen Republik*, (Munich: dtv, 1980)

Eschenburg, Theodor, *Jahre der Besatzung 1945-1949 Geschichte der Bundesrepublik Deutschland Band 1* (Stuttgart: Deutsche Verlags-Anstalt, 1983)

Ewald, Hans-Gerd, *Die gescheiterte Republik: Idee und Programm einer "Zweiten Republik" in den Frankfurter Heften (1946-1950)*, Europäische Hochschulschriften, 31 (Frankfurt a. M.: Lang, 1988)

Forster, Leonard, *German Poetry 1944-1948* (Cambridge: Bowes and Bowes, 1950) (first pub. 1949)

Frei, Norbert, *Amerikanische Lizenzpolitik und Deutsche Pressetradition: die Geschichte der Nachkriegszeitung Südost-Kurier*, Schriftenreihe der Vierteljahreshefte für Zeitgeschichte, (Munich: Oldenbourg, 1986)

—'Amerikanische Pressepolitik im Nachkriegsdeutschland', *ZfK* 37 (1987/2), 306-18

Friedmann, W., *The Allied Military Government of Germany* (London: Stevens, 1947)

Friedrich, Heinz, 'Deutschland im Jahre Null: Die Zeitschrift "Der Ruf", nach 25 Jahren wiedergelesen', *Süddeutsche Zeitung*, (Feuilleton), 18/19 December 1971

Gehring, Hansjörg, *Amerikanische Literaturpolitik in Deutschland 1945-1953: Ein Aspekt des Re-education-Programms*, Schriftenreihe der Vierteljahreshefte für Zeitgeschichte, 32 (Stuttgart: Deutsche Verlags-Anstalt, 1976)

Gimbel, John, *The American Occupation of Germany: Politics and the Military 1945-1949* (Stanford: Stanford University Press, 1968)

Glaser, Hermann, *Kulturgeschichte der Bundesrepublik Deutschland* (Munich: Hanser, 1985), I: *Zwischen Kapitulation und Währungsreform, 1945-1948*

—'Kultur und Gesellschaft in der Bundesrepublik: Eine Profilskizze 1945-1990', *Aus Politik und Zeitgeschichte*, 1-2 (1991)

Glick, Nathan, 'In the Bronx, and After...', in *Melvin J. Lasky: Encounter with a 60th Birthday*, ed. by Helga Hegewisch (*Encounter* Special edition, 1980), pp.2-3

Grebing, Helga, 'Demokratie ohne Demokraten?: Politisches Denken, Einstellungen und Mentalitäten in der Nachkriegszeit', in *Wie neu war der Neubeginn?: zum deutschen Kontinuitätsproblem nach 1945: Wissenschaftliche Tagung am 7. und 8. Juli 1989 im Kollegeinhaus Universität Erlangen Nürnberg*, ed. by Everhard Holtmann, Erlanger Forschungen, 50 (Erlangen: Universitätsbibliothek, 1989), pp.6-19

Greuner, Reinhart, *Lizenzpresse, Auftrag und Ende: Der Einfluß der anglo-amerikanischen Besatzungspolitik auf die Wiedererrichtung eines imperialistischen Pressewesens in Westdeutschland* (Berlin: Rütten & Loening, 1962)

Haacke, Wilmont, and Günter Pötter, *Die Politische Zeitschrift*, 2 vols (Stuttgart: K.F. Koehler, 1982), II: *1900-1980*

Habe, Hans, *Im Jahre Null: Ein Beitrag zur Geschichte der deutschen Presse* (Munich: Desch, 1966)

Habicht, Hubert, ed., *Eugen Kogon — ein politischer Publizist in Hessen: Essays, Aufsätze und Reden zwischen 1946 und 1982* (Frankfurt a. M.: Insel, 1982)

Handbuch der Lizenzen Deutscher Verlage: Zeitungen, Zeitschriften, Buchverlage (Berlin: de Gruyter, 1947)

Handbuch Deutsche Presse, ed. by Norwestdeutscher Zeitungsverleger-Verein (Bielefeld: Deutscher Zeitungs-Verlag, 1947)

Hay, Gerhard, ed., *Zur literarischen Situation 1945-1949* (Kronberg: Athenäum-Verlag, 1977)

Hearndon, A., ed., *The British in Germany* (London: Hamilton, 1978)

Heckel, Erna, and others, eds, *Kulturpolitik in der Bundesrepublik von 1949 bis zur Gegenwart* (Cologne: Pahl-Rugenstein, 1987)

Hegewisch, Helga, ed., *Melvin J. Lasky: Encounter with a 60th Birthday* (*Encounter* Special edition, 1980)

Heinschke, Christian, '*Ost und West* oder die Eintracht der Literaten', in *Zur literarischen Situation 1945-1949*, ed. by Gerhard Hay (Kronberg: Athenäum-Verlag, 1977), pp.189-202

Henke, Klaus-Dietmar, *Politische Säuberung unter französischer Besatzung: Die Entnazifizierung in Württemberg-Hohenzollern*, Schriftenreihe der Vierteljahreshefte für Zeitgeschichte, 42 (Stuttgart: Deutsche Verlag-Anstalt, 1981)

Hermand, Jost, Helmut Peitsch, and Klaus R. Scherpe, eds, *Nachkriegsliteratur in Westdeutschland 1945-49: Schreibwesen, Gattungen, Institutionen* (Berlin: Argument-Verlag, 1982)

Heydorn, Heinz-Joachim, ed., *Wache im Niemandsland: Zum 70. Geburtstag von Alfred Kantorowicz* (Cologne: Verlag Wissenschaft und Politik, 1969)

Hoenisch, M., K. Kämpfe, and K.-H. Pütz, *USA und Deutschland: Amerikanische Kulturpolitik 1942-1949, Bibliographie, Materialien, Dokumente* (Berlin: Zentrale Universitätsdrückerei, 1980)

Hurwitz, Harold, *Die Stunde Null der deutschen Presse: Die amerikanische Pressepolitik in Deutschland 1945-1949* (Cologne: Verlag Wissenschaft und Politik, 1972)

—'Die Pressepolitik der Alliierten', in *Deutsche Presse seit 1945*, ed. by Harry Pross (Bern: Scherz, 1965), pp.27-55

—*Die Eintracht der Siegermächte und die Orientierungsnot der Deutschen 1945-1946*, Demokratie und Antikommunismus in Berlin nach 1945, 3 (Cologne: Verlag Wissenschaft und Politik, 1984)

Institut Français de Stuttgart, ed., *Die französische Deutschlandpolitik zwischen 1945 und 1949* (Tübingen: Attempto, 1987)

Institut für Marxismus-Leninismus beim ZK der SED und Kulturbund der DDR, eds, *...einer neuen Zeit Beginn: Erinnerungen an die Anfänge unserer Kulturrevolution 1945-1949* (Berlin: Aufbau-Verlag, 1980)

Jaesrich, Hellmut, 'An American in Berlin', in *Melvin J. Lasky: Encounter with a 60th Birthday*, ed. by Helga Hegewisch (*Encounter* Special edition, 1980), pp.9-12

James, Harold, *A German Identity 1770-1990* (London: Weidenfeld and Nicolson, 1989)

Kantorowicz, Alfred, *Exil in Frankreich: Merkwürdigkeiten und Denkwürdigkeiten* (Bremen: Schünemann, 1971)

—*Deutsches Tagebuch Band 1* (Munich: Kindler, 1959)

—*Deutsches Tagebuch: Zweiter Teil* (Munich: Kindler, 1961; repr. Berlin: Verlag Anpassung und Widerstand, 1979)

—*Spanisches Kriegstagebuch* (Cologne: Verlag Wissenschaft und Politik, 1966; repr. Fischer-Taschenbuch-Verlag, 1982)

—*Vom moralischen Gewinn der Niederlage: Artikel und Ansprachen* (Berlin: Aufbau-Verlag, 1949)

—*Deutschland-Ost und Deutschland-West: Kulturpolitische Einigungsversuche und geistige Spaltung in Deutschland seit 1945*, Sylter Beiträge (Münsterdorf: Hansen and Hansen, 1971)

—'Professor Kantorowicz: Rechenschaft', *Die Zeit: Sonderdruck aus den Ausgaben Nr.36/37/38 vom 5.12.19. September 1957*, 1-6

King, Janet K., *Literarische Zeitschriften 1945-1970* (Stuttgart: Metzler, 1974)

Knipping, Franz, and Jacques Le Rider, eds, *Frankreichs Kulturpolitik in Deutschland 1945-1950* (Tübingen: Attempto, 1987)

Kogon, Eugen, *Die unvollendete Erneuerung: Deutschland im Kräftefeld 1945-1963. Aufsätze aus zwei Jahrzehnten* (Frankfurt a. M.: Europäische Verlagsanstalt, 1964)

Koszyk, Kurt, *Pressepolitik für Deutsche 1945-1949: Geschichte der deutschen Presse 4* (Berlin: Colloquium Verlag, 1986)

—'The Press in the British Zone of Germany', in *The Political Re-education of Germany and her Allies after World War II*, ed. by Nicholas Pronay and Keith Wilson (London: Croom Helm, 1985), pp.107-38

Kraiker, G., ed., *1945 — Die Stunde Null?* (Oldenbourg: Bibliotheks- und Informationssystem, 1986)

Kröll, Friedhelm, *Die Gruppe 47: Soziale Lage und gesellschaftliches Bewußtsein literarischer Intelligenz in der Bundesrepublik* (Stuttgart: Metzler, 1977)

Lasky, Melvin J., *Wortmeldung zu einer Revolution: Der Zusammenbruch der kommunistischen Herrschaft in Ostdeutschland* (Frankfurt a. M.: Ullstein, 1991)

Latour, E. F., and Thilo Vogelsang, *Okkupation und Wiederaufbau: Die Tätigkeit der Militärregierung in der amerikanischen Besatzungszone Deutschlands 1944-1947* (Stuttgart: Deutsche Verlags-Anstalt, 1972)

Laurien, Ingrid, *Politisch-kulturelle Zeitschriften in den Westzonen 1945-1949: Ein Beitrag zur politischen Kultur der Nachkriegszeit* (Frankfurt: Lang, 1991)

Lefebvre, Joël, 'La vie intellectuelle dans la République Démocratique Allemande', *La Pensée*, n.s.50 (September/October 1953), 139-41

Leithäuser, Joachim G., *Journalisten zwischen zwei Welten: Die Nachkriegsjahre der Berliner Presse* (Berlin: Colloquium Verlag, 1960)

Liedtke, Rüdiger, *Die verschenkte Presse: Die Geschichte der Lizenzierung von Zeitungen nach 1945* (Berlin: Verlag für Ausbildung und Studium in der Elefanten Presse, 1982)

Lizenzenhandbuch Deutscher Verlage 1949: Zeitungen, Zeitschriften, Buchverlage (Berlin: de Gruyter, 1949)

Loth, Wilfried, 'Das Ende der Nachkriegsordnung', *Aus Politik und Zeitgeschichte*, 18/91, (26 April 1991), 3-10

Majut, Rudolf, 'The Cultural Periodicals of Post-War Germany' *GLL*, 7 (1953/4), 17-27

Marigold, W. G., 'Some notes on the Cultural Periodicals of Post-war Germany', *GQ*, 29 (1956), 38-42

Meissner, Boris, *Russland, die Westmächte und Deutschland: Die Sowjetische Deutschlandpolitik 1943-1953* (Hamburg: Nölke, 1953)

de Mendelssohn, Peter, *Zeitungsstadt Berlin: Menschen und Mächte in der Geschichte der deutschen Presse* (Berlin: Ullstein, 1959)

Menz, Gerhard, 'Deutschlands Neue Zeitschriften', in *Handbuch Deutsche Presse*, ed. by Norwestdeutscher Zeitungsverleger-Verein (Bielefeld: Deutscher Zeitungs-Verlag, 1947), pp.130-32

Meyn, Hermann, *Massenmedien in der Bundesrepublik Deutschland* (Berlin: Colloquium Verlag, 1966)

Mosberg, Helmuth, *Reeducation: Umerziehung und Lizenzpresse im Nachkriegsdeutschland* (Munich: Universitas, 1991)

Müller, Helmut, *Die Literarische Republik: Westdeutsche Schriftsteller und die Politik* (Basel: Beltz, 1982)

Nettl, John P., *The Eastern Zone and Soviet Policy in Germany* (London: OUP, 1951)

Neunzig, Hans A., ed., *Der Ruf, Unabhängige Blätter der jungen Generation: Eine Auswahl* (Munich: Nymphenburger Verlagshandlung, 1976)

—ed., *Hans Werner Richter und die Gruppe 47* (Munich: Nymphenburger Verlagshandlung, 1979)

Niethammer, Lutz, *Entnazifizierung in Bayern: Säuberung und Rehabilitierung unter amerikanischer Besatzung* (Frankfurt a. M.: Fischer, 1972)

—*Die Mitläuferfabrik: Die Entnazifizierung am Beispiel Bayerns* (Bonn: Dietz, 1982)

Noelle-Neumann, E., Winfried Schulze, and Jürgen Wilke, eds, *Das Fischer Lexikon: Publizistik: Massenkommunikation* (Frankfurt a. M.: Fischer, 1989)

Noll, Dieter, ed., *Aufbau, Berlin 1945-1958: Bibliographie einer Zeitschrift* (Berlin: Aufbau-Verlag, 1978)

Olson, Kenneth E., *The History Makers: The Press of Europe from its Beginnings through 1965* (Baton Rouge: Louisiana State University Press, 1966)

Overesch, Manfred, ed., *Die Gründung der Bundesrepublik Deutschland: Jahre der Entscheidung 1945-1949: Texte und Dokumente* (Hannover: Niedersächsische Landeszentrale für Politische Bildung, 1989)

Parkes, K. Stuart, *Writers and Politics in West Germany* (London: Croom Helm, 1986)

Peitsch, Helmut, *»Deutschlands Gedächtnis an seine dunkelste Zeit«: Zur Funktion der Autobiographik in den Westzonen Deutschlands und den Westsektoren von Berlin 1945 bis 1949* (Berlin: Ed. Sigma Bohn, 1990)

Pike, David, *The Politics of Culture in Soviet-occupied Germany, 1945-1949* (Stanford: Stanford University Press, 1992)

Pilgert, Henry P., *Press, Radio and Film in West Germany 1945-1953* (HICOG Historical Division, 1953)

Plischke, Elmer, and Henry P. Pilgert, *U.S. Information Programs in Berlin* (HICOG: 1953)

Pronay, Nicholas, and Keith Wilson, eds, *The Political Re-education of Germany and her Allies after World War II* (London: Croom Helm, 1985)

Pross, Harry, *Literatur und Politik: Geschichte und Programme der politisch-literarischen Zeitschriften im deutschen Sprachgebiet seit 1870* (Olten: Walter, 1963)

—ed., *Deutsche Presse seit 1945* (Bern: Scherz, 1965)

Raue, Günter, *Im Dienste der Wahrheit: Ein Beitrag zur Pressepolitik der Sowjetischen Besatzungsmacht 1945-1949* (Leipzig: Karl-Marx-Universität, 1966)

Richter, Hans Werner, 'Wie entstand und was war die Gruppe 47? — Der Ruf. Sein Entstehen und Untergang', in *Hans Werner Richter und die Gruppe 47*, ed. by Hans A. Neunzig (Munich: Nymphenburger Verlagshandlung, 1979), pp.43-75

—'Beim Wiedersehen des "Ruf", in *Der Ruf: Eine deutsche Nachkriegszeitschrift*, ed. by Hans Schwab-Felisch (Munich: dtv, 1962), pp.7-9

Riechert, Ernst, with Carola Stern and Peter Dietrich, *Agitation und Propaganda: Das System der publizistischen Massenführung in der Sowjetzone* (Berlin: Vahlen, 1958)

Roloff, Gerhard, *Exil und Exilliteratur in der deutschen Presse 1945-1949: Ein Beitrag zur Rezeptionsgeschichte* (Worms: Georg-Heintz, 1976)

Rudolph, Hermann, 'Die Intellektuelle Front im Kalten Krieg', *Der Tagesspiegel*, (Feuilleton), 9 October 1992, p.15

Rüther, Günther, *"Greif zur Feder, Kumpel": Schriftsteller, Literatur und Politik in der DDR 1949-1990* (Düsseldorf: Droste, 1991)

Scharf, Claus, and Hans-Jürgen Schröder, eds, *Die Deutschlandpolitik Großbritanniens und die Britische Zone 1945-1949* (Wiesbaden: Steiner, 1979)

—*Die Deutschlandpolitik Frankreichs und die Französische Zone 1945-1949* (Wiesbaden: Franz Steiner, 1983)

Schneider, Rolf, 'Unvollkommene Versuche, einen Schriftsteller zu beschreiben', *Sinn und Form*, 24 (1972), H.4, 798-807

Schub, Boris, 'An Incident in Berlin (October, 1947)', in *Melvin J. Lasky: Encounter with a 60th Birthday*, ed. by Helga Hegewisch (*Encounter* Special edition, 1980), pp.26-30

Schwab-Felisch, Hans, ed., *Der Ruf: Eine deutsche Nachkriegszeitschrift* (München: dtv, 1962)

Schwarz, Hans-Peter, *Vom Reich zur Bundesrepublik. Deutschland im Widerstreit der außenpolitischen Konzeptionen in den Jahren der Besatzungsherrschaft 1945-1949*, Reihe Politica, 38 (Neuwied: Luchterhand, 1966)

Smith, Colin, 'All quiet on the Eastern Front? East German literature and its Western reception (1945-61)', in *German writers and the Cold War 1945-61*, ed. by Rhys W. Williams, Stephen Parker, and Colin Riordan (Manchester: Manchester University Press, 1992), pp.7-26

Spender, Stephen, *Journal 1939-1983*, ed. by John Goldsmith (London: Faber and Faber, 1985)

—, Irving Kristol and Melvin J. Lasky, eds, *Encounters: An Anthology from the First Ten Years of Encounter Magazine* (London: Weidenfeld and Nicolson, 1963)

Stomps, V. O., 'Die literarischen und Kunst-Zeitschriften', in *Deutsche Presse seit 1945*, ed. by Harry Pross (Bern: Scherz, 1965), pp.173-210

Stankowski, Martin, *Linkskatholizismus nach 1945* (Cologne: Pahl-Rugenstein, [1974?])

Strack, Manfred, 'Amerikanische Kulturbeziehungen zu (West-)Deutschland 1945-1955', *ZfK* (1987/2), 283-300

Trommler, Frank, and Joseph McVeigh, eds, *America and the Germans: An Assessment of a Three-Hundred-Year History*, 2 vols (Philadelphia: University of Pennsylvania Press, 1983), II: *The Relationship in the Twentieth Century*

Unsere Presse — die scharfste Waffe der Partei: Referate und Diskussionsreden auf der Konferenz des Parteivorstandes der SED v. 9./10.2.1950 in Berlin (Berlin: [n.pub.], 1950)

Vaillant, Jérôme, *Der Ruf: Unabhängige Blätter der jungen Generation (1945-1949): Eine Zeitschrift zwischen Illusion und Anpassung* (Munich: Saur, 1978)

—ed., *La dénazification par les vainqueurs: La politique culturelle des occupants en Allemagne 1945-1949* (Lille: Presses Universitaires de Lille, 1981)

—ed., *Die französische Kulturpolitik in Deutschland 1945-1949: Berichte und Dokumente* (Konstanz: Universitätsverlag, 1984)

Vielberg, Iris and Ingrid Laurien, eds, *Politisch-kulturelle Zeitschriften in den deutschen Besatzungszonen 1945-1949: Eine Sammlung bibliographischer Daten* (Göttingen: [n. pub.], 1986)

Vollnhals, Clemens, ed., *Entnazifizierung: Politische Säuberung und Rehabilitierung in den vier Besatzungszonen 1945-1949* (Munich: dtv, 1991)

Wapnewski, Peter, 'König Artus, Lehrer der Autorität', in *Hans Werner Richter und die Gruppe 47*, ed. by Hans A. Neunzig (Munich: Nymphenburger Verlagshandlung, 1979), pp.25-32

Wehdeking, Volker Christian, *Der Nullpunkt: Über die Konstituierung der deutschen Nachkriegsliteratur 1945-1948 in den amerikanischen Kriegsgefangenenlagern* (Stuttgart: Metzler, 1971)

Weinberg, Gerhard L., 'From Confrontation to Cooperation: Germany and the United States, 1933-1949', in *America and the Germans: An Assessment of a Three-Hundred-Year History*, ed. by Frank Trommler and Joseph McVeigh (Philadelphia: University of Pennsylvania Press, 1983), II: *The Relationship in the Twentieth Century*, pp.45-57

Wende-Hohenberger, Waltraud, ed., *Der erste gesamtdeutsche Schriftstellerkongreß nach dem Zweiten Weltkrieg im Ostsektor Berlins vom 4. bis 8. Oktober 1947* (Frankfurt a. M.: Lang, 1988)

—ed., *Der Frankfurter Schriftstellerkongreß im Jahr 1948* (Frankfurt a. M.: Lang, 1988)

Willis, Roy, *The French in Germany 1945-1949* (Stanford: Stanford University Press, 1962)

Williams, Rhys, Stephen Parker, and Colin Riordan, eds, *German writers and the Cold War 1945-61* (Manchester: Manchester University Press, 1992)

Wintzen, René, 'Le Catholicisme dans son authenticité: Walter Dirks (1901-1991)', *Allemagne d'aujourd'hui*, 60-65 (juillet-septembre 1991)

Wurm, Carsten, *Das Haus in der Französischen Strasse: Eine Verlagsgeschichte in Bildern. Aufbau-Verlag Berlin und Weimar* (Berlin: Aufbau-Verlag, 1990)

Zeller, Bernhard, ed., *Als der Krieg zu Ende war: Literarisch-politische Publizistik 1945-1950. Eine Ausstellung des Deutschen Literaturarchivs* (Stuttgart: Klett, 1973)

Zink, Harold, *The United States in Germany 1944-1955* (Princeton, NJ: van Nostrand, 1957

Unpublished Sources

Kiwus, Karen, 'Die politische Funktion des *Aufbau* in der antifaschistisch-demokratischen Periode der SBZ 1945-1948' (unpublished master's thesis, Freie Universität Berlin, 1970)

Lasky, Melvin, 'Ein Amerikaner in Berlin (im Jahre 0)', unpub. Ms.

Vorfelder, Jochen, 'Der Neuaufbau der Berliner Tagespresse zwischen April und Dezember 1945 durch die alliierten Siegermächte' (unpublished master's thesis, Freie Universität Berlin, 1985)

INDEX

STUDIES IN GERMAN THOUGHT AND HISTORY

1. William A. Pelz, **The Spartakusbund and the German Working Class Movement, 1914-1919**
2. **Bedarf Deutschland Der Colonien? / Does Germany Need Colonies?, Eine politisch-ökonomische Betrachtung von D[r. Theol.] Friedrich Fabri. Dritte Ausgabe**, translated, edited and introduced by E.C.M. Breuning and M.E. Chamberlain
3. Eric von der Luft (ed. & trans.), **Hegel, Hinrichs, and Schleiermacher on Feeling and Reason in Religion: The Texts of Their 1821-22 Debate**
4. Karla Poewe, **Childhood in Germany During World War II: The Story of a Little Girl**
5. Bruno Bauer, **The Trumpet of the Last Judgment Against Hegel, the Atheist and Antichrist: An Ultimatum,** Lawrence Stepelevich (trans.)
6. Fanny Lewald, **Prinz Louis Ferdinand**, Linda Rogols-Siegel (trans.)
7. Rodler F. Morris, **From Weimar Philosemite to Nazi Apologist: The Case of Walter Bloem**
8. Marvin Thomas, **Karl Theodore and the Bavarian Succession (1777-1778)**
9. Peter Petschauer, **The Education of Women in 18th-Century Germany**
10. Eric von der Luft, **Schopenhauer: New Essays in Honor of His 200th Birthday**
11. Arthur Hübscher, **The Philosophy of Schopenhauer in Its Intellectual Context: Thinker Against the Tide**, Joachim T. Baer and David E. Cartwright (trans.)
12. Linda Siegel, **Dora Stock, Portrait Painter of the Korner Circle in Dresden (1785-1815)**
13. Wilhelm Heinrich Riehl, **The Natural History of the German People**, David J. Diephouse (trans.)
14. Jonathan Zophy, **Patriarchal Politics and Christoph Kress (1484-1535) of Nuremberg**

15a. Alexander Jacob (ed. & trans.), **Translation of Edgar Julis Jung's *Die Herrschaft der Minderwertigen/The Rule of the Inferiour*, Volume I**

15b. Alexander Jacob (ed. & trans.), **Translation of Edgar Julis Jung's *Die Herrschaft der Minderwertigen/The Rule of the Inferiour*, Volume II**

16. August K. Wiedmann, **The German Quest for Primal Origins in Art, Culture, and Politics 1900-1933: die "Flucht in Urzustände"**

17. Victor Klemperer, **An Annotated Edition of Victor Klemperer's LTI: Notizbuch eines Philologen,** with notes & commentary by Roderick H. Watt

18. Christopher J. Wickham, **Constructing Heimat in Postwar Germany: Longing and Belonging**

19. Clare Flanagan, **A Study of German Political–Cultural Periodicals from the Years of Allied Occupation, 1945-1949**